Sue Vetick

Bob, Please return at the end of
May so I can pack.
Thank you.

Speech Communication

William D. Brooks
Purdue University

Speech Communication

WM. C. BROWN COMPANY PUBLISHERS
Dubuque, Iowa

To
Susan
Debra
Steven
Randy

Contents

Bring - Newspaper Headline or magizine,

31 - 63
191 - 20

Describe, Person, Place or Thing,
3 minutes.
1. Effective Chose of words, Note card,
2 Listenery visualization, Tues.
Hold interest.
Variety of words.

vii

cliche.

Preface

In most colleges and universities, students are required or encouraged to take a basic speech course to help them develop a skill they will use throughout their lives. Previously, most of these courses were oriented to meeting the student's public speaking needs. Currently, however, the growing trend is toward sharpening the student's awareness of the entire human interaction process and its relationship to speech forms other than platform speaking. As a result, the scope of college speech courses is being modified to assure greater relevance—to focus on human communication behavior across a variety of situations.

Speech Communication presents a view of speech which enables the student to become fully aware of his role as both *initiator* and *recipient* of messages. For too long the study of speech communication has been unnecessarily limited to the sender of messages. In this volume the citizen's auditor-role is given the same careful attention as the speaker-role.

Second, this text treats speech communication broadly rather than narrowly. It is concerned with understandings and skills relating to various types of speech communication. In this respect, among others, the text departs significantly from the traditional public speaking textbook which offers "rules" designed to enhance the student's public speaking ability while neglecting his role as a communicator in situations other than public speaking. It is commonly acknowledged that man's speech communication problems are no longer related exclusively to public speaking—are often within the context of informal, interpersonal communication situations. If the basic course in speech is to be more relevant to man's communication needs, it must be concerned with the application of communication skills beyond the context of public address. *Speech Communication* presents a view of speech that harmonizes and unifies all areas of our discipline.

Finally, this text is based on the premise that speech study is not merely an isolated activity, but that it is on the contrary a study area consisting of an exceptionally valuable body of knowledge dealing with the art and science of human communication. *Speech Communication* is based on the most discerning and perceptive prescriptions growing out of man's experiences in speech communication as verified and supplemented by empirical research. The book is intended to help the student understand the concepts and principles underlying speech communication and apply those understandings to his own speech communication behavior. Thus, the serious student of speech communication should acquire a coherent view of the essential concepts of our discipline and consequently improve his behavioral skills in a wide variety of communication situations. Because the basic course is often the student's only exposure to the problems of speech communication, a basic text should include materials relevant to the most important communication situations of daily life. As such, *Speech Communication* treats interpersonal communication (with its subsequent application to the small group process, the interview, the conference, on-the-job communication, and informal daily dialogue), public address, and societal and cultural communication.

Content treatment in this text is predicated upon the belief that today's college student is, for the most part, receptive to and capable of understanding the basic concepts of communication theory and their application to public address and interpersonal communication.

Through communication man solves his problems—political and personal; through communication man is social; and through communication all men have hope for a fuller and freer existence. This book is written in the belief that no learning can be of greater importance to a person than that which concerns his speech behavior. The quality of our speech behavior has a direct bearing on our satisfactions and accomplishments, our management of conflict, our decision-making behavior, our leadership—our very survival.

Acknowledgments

The writer is indebted to Professor Gustav Friedrich, Purdue University, for his interest and counsel throughout the writing of this book; to Rena Friedrich for her editing and typing of the final draft of the manuscript; to Grace for her sustaining encouragement and for her typing of the first drafts from my handwriting; to the many students, undergraduate and graduate, with whom I have discussed the ideas in this book; and to my colleagues, Professors Larry Barker, Charles Redding, and Charles Stewart who offered suggestions, contributed ideas, and influenced me in the writing of this book.

A special acknowledgment is made to Miss Jo Sprague, Mr. James Booth, and Mr. John Bittner, graduate instructors in speech communication at Purdue University, who are the authors of chapters 11 and 13. Miss Sprague and Mr. Booth wrote chapter 11 on The Audience, while Mr. Bittner wrote chapter 13 on the Responsibilities and Skills of Senders and Receivers in Mass Communication.

W.D.B.

Chapter 1

Introduction: An
Overview of Communication

Man is a communicator, as is any organism, and his survival, as well as the *quality* of his survival, depends upon communication. Primitive man's attempts to make recognizable sounds were undoubtedly motivated by the need to meet the threats of survival that he encountered. He learned to make sounds that were warnings of impending danger —threatening sounds to frighten away intruders—pleasant sounds to establish friendship and rapport. Such communication, observable also in animal behavior, is called *presymbolic communication.*

The presymbolic communication of animals is sometimes amazingly efficient. The signals animals send—through sounds, positions, and movements—can express such definite things as "Get out of my territory!" "Help!" "Build a nest with me," or "Fly straight ahead keeping about twenty degrees right of the sun and then, at one hundred yards, there is a patch of clover bloom." Crickets and grasshoppers have an astonishing variety of songs with accompanying moods that vary from courtship to combat-to-the-death. Mice communicate with high pitched tones—tones in the ultrasonic range, and ants convey various messages by tapping other ants with their antennae. Some species of butterflies change their color in a fraction of a second and give off an odor as a mating signal. The male unicorn fish, within seconds of becoming interested in a female, signals to her by developing a bright blue spot on his back and light blue stripes down his side, to which she responds appropriately if she is ready to mate.

Perhaps the most interesting animal communication is that of monkeys and apes. Since 1960 more than two dozen excellent studies have described communication among the primates. All describe communication systems that are elaborate in their establishment and maintenance of intragroup and intergroup relationships and modes of behavior. For example, the group leader determines the direction of the group's movements for the day, gives the signals for starting and stopping (the early morning howling of the Howler Monkeys gives directions for their movement throughout the entire day—thus they can communicate so as to influence behavior which will occur several hours later),[1] arbitrates disputes in the group, and is responsible for the defense of the group. Elaborate social hierarchies and status positions are defined and maintained.

In human communication, as in animal communication, the object is survival. Regardless of the level of communication used or the sophistication of the communication system, its purpose is to alert organisms to adjust to their environments and live. Whether it is the presymbolic language of animals or the highly abstract and symbolic language of man, the purpose is the same—communication is *existence-related.* Through effective communication one is more likely to achieve integration and to cope successfully with his environment. When one's communication skills and behaviors are unsatisfactory, his influence over his environment decreases, isolation is likely to set in, and pathological behavior and death are the extreme outcomes.

⊥ Implications of Effective Communication Behavior for Man

This text is concerned with human communication behavior. If man's communication behavior is the key to the enhancement of his existence, and if such behavior can be described, studied, and understood, then it follows that it can be taught and should be taught in educational institutions. Why is it important that men acquire behavioral skills in speech communication? The reasons are many, a number of which fall within three categories: political, vocational, and personal.

POLITICAL—There is a direct relationship between a people's quality of communication and their ability to solve problems collectively through governmental organizations. From local school boards to the Congress of the United States of America, governmental units are faced with the task of finding solutions to an ever increasing number of serious problems. Poverty, inflation, population explosion, air and water pollution, depletion and waste of natural resources, nuclear war, denial of human rights, loss of privacy, inadequate housing, unequal educational opportunity—all are problems threatening the survival of man. These problems cannot be solved without effective communication

1. C. R. Carpenter, "The Howlers of Barro Colorado Island," in *Primate Behavior,* ed. I. DeVore (New York: Holt, Rinehart and Winston, Inc., 1965), pp. 250–91.

within governmental units as well as among the general citizenry. Various groups and organizations bombard and saturate the citizenry with communications to "push" their viewpoint and to influence social action in a direction beneficial to them. The ordinary citizen faces the challenge to be sufficiently knowledgeable and skilled in communication, both as sender and as receiver, that he can contribute to the understanding and solution of problems in society. He must be able to identify the demagogue; to resist the appeals to hatred, prejudice, and fear; to see the illogic of faulty discourse; to express himself clearly; and to listen openly and empathically—yet with high critical standards.

Man can solve problems through democratically constituted political agencies, or he can turn to the alternative procedure of force and violence to initiate change. A citizenry skilled in communication is better able to cope with the problems of society by keeping open the channels to orderly change, by evaluating accurately the programs of persuasion of various groups and organizations, and by withstanding the persuasion of confrontation and violence. A free democratic society places great responsibility upon the individual. To be a responsible citizen, one must be able to think clearly, listen critically, evaluate objectively, and to communicate ideas, feelings, and attitudes efficiently. Being an effective citizen consists of much more than simply casting a ballot on election day; it also includes productive living as an individual and as a member of the various groups and organizations necessary to the convenience and welfare of society.

VOCATIONAL—A second set of reasons for improving one's communication behavior relates to vocational success. In recent years, business and industry have placed an increasingly higher value upon their employees' ability to communicate effectively. Many firms have established speech training programs for their employees, and some corporations give speech communication tests to applicants for positions at certain levels.

Business, industrial, and governmental officials are keenly interested in a person's ability to communicate effectively because they recognize the close relationship between this ability and job proficiency. Poor communication can be costly. When orders or instructions are unclear, when information is misinterpreted, or when misunderstood messages anger people (and result in lower morale), production may fall and profits lag. A great many people are dismissed from their jobs not because they lack the necessary job skills, but simply because they cannot get along with other people—superiors, fellow employees, subordinates, and customers or clients. They have *communication problems.* Good speech communication is a necessity when people are to work together effectively.

PERSONAL—Man, as a social being living with others, has a need to communicate. Communication is not something useful only to the political leader; effective communication behavior is needed by every person. Communication is the means through which personality expresses itself in interpersonal relations; consequently, improved communication behavior can benefit the individual personally. There is no question but that communication and personality grow, develop, and become refined together. Man's ability to live in wholesome, meaningful, and mutually profitable relationships with others is related directly to his interpersonal communication skills and behavior.

Defining Speech Communication

The word communication, without a qualifier, is extremely broad in its application. It includes all of the procedures by which one organism affects another. One essential characteristic of communication is that the receiving organism, animal or man, responds. If some environmental disturbance impinges on an organism and the organism does something about it, communication has occurred; but, if the stimulus is ignored by the organism, there has been no communication. The message that gets no response is not a communication.

All behavior—oral verbal, written verbal, tonal, postural, contextual, tactile—is communicative. Moreover, the behavior does not have to be intentional behavior for communication to occur. The term communication is broad enough to include unintentionally sent stimuli which receive responses. The person who allows junk to accumulate in his front yard communicates something to his neighbor whether he knows it or not. Any action or event, intentional or unintentional, can have communicative aspects as soon as it is perceived and responded to by an organism.

When communication is defined broadly as the eliciting of a response, no distinction is made between the communication involved in the interaction of animate or inanimate matter or between animals and humans as regards the purpose of communication; but when we are concerned with the methods, efficiency, and general sophistication of communication, then clear distinctions can be made between animal and human communication.

Although all human communication is communication, not all communication is human communication. Human communication is characterized by its emphasis on the use of symbols, especially verbal symbols, but human beings have access also to the entire range of nonsymbolic communication available to all animals and to inanimate matter. When we speak of speech communication, we are referring to human communication—communication relying primarily on the use of symbols or symbolic behavior.

The major symbols used in speech communication are verbal symbols. At this time we should differentiate verbal communication from vocal communication. The confusion of *verbal* for *vocal* in reference to communication is widespread. A verbal symbol can be either vocal or nonvocal. A vocal sound need not always be symbolic. A scream, for instance, may be vocal and nonverbal, having no meaning. On the other hand, a scream, when interpreted by a passerby in terms of circumstances, may have meaning for the passerby. Another example is the traffic signal. It derives its meaning from the observer's past experience in learning law and order through words. The traffic signal, then, is nonvocal and verbal. The essential attribute of *verbal* is not the existence of sound in acoustic space, but the representation of abstractions of many specific instances by one sign that becomes a symbol. Thus, when a person is engaging in speech communication, he is primarily engaged in using *verbal symbolization that is vocal,* although he also uses nonverbal symbolization. When we use the term speech communication, we are not referring to *all* human communication: we are not referring to music or art, for example. For that reason, this book is entitled *Speech Communication.*

III Communication as a Process

The key concept evident in almost all the definitions considered in the preceding section is that of *process.* Speech communication is a process by which meanings are exchanged—information sent and received.

Although the scientific concept of process is relatively new as compared to man's history, testimony concerning the existence of the phenomenon is quite old. More than two thousand years ago, Heraclitus stated that "a man can never step in the same river twice" (the river has changed and is a "different" river, and the man has changed and is a "different" man). Thomas Wolfe made the same observation in his 1940 novel entitled *You Can't Go Home Again.* And the phenomenon is noted in the words of a popular song which states "the times—they are a-changin.' " Times have always been "a-changin' " because life is a process. Similarly, communication is a process. When we accept the concept of process, we view events and relationships as dynamic, ongoing, ever-changing, continuous. When we label something as a process, we also mean that it does not have *a* beginning, *an* end, a fixed sequence of events. It is not static, at rest. It is moving. The ingredients within a process interact. Everything affects everything else all the time. It means that there are innumerable variables operating and acting upon each other—i.e., interacting. Again, since the classical Greek and Roman times, it has been recognized that there are variables that operate to influence the outcome or success of communication attempts. One variable, identified by Aristotle and others in the public speaking situation, is the audience. Aristotle pointed out that some speeches were given to legislative assemblies, some to the courts, and some for special occasions such as funerals. Each of these communication situations imposed constraints as to the type of speech that could be successful. Of course, there are many variables other than the audience that operate in communication situations. One beneficial result of the behavioral science approach to the study of communication (besides providing a means for verifying the observations of communication principles noted by rhetorical scholars), is that it has motivated a search for total descriptions of communication events and for disparities that make a difference. Despite the fact that man does not yet fully understand the complex process of communication, a rather substantial body of knowledge has been accumulated and a number of important principles of communication have been identified that are useful when applied in communication situations. Let us consider some of the major components in communication.

IV Major Components in Communication

One of the most widely used, and most easily understood, attempts to present schematically the basic pattern of human communication is that developed by Claude Shannon and Warren Weaver.[2] The model was devised originally as a means of describing electronic communication for use in connection with engineering problems. There are, therefore, certain limitations in applying it to human communication. There are limitations in any model, of course, since models are simplistic and always identify certain selected variables while ignoring others. Models are also static (they freeze the process at one point in time as a photograph "freezes" action at one point), so cannot portray changes and interactions. Nevertheless, over the years the Shannon-Weaver has become one of the most commonly used models in discussing the communication which occurs between human beings. The components identified by Shannon and Weaver as being present in any communication situation are: (1) source, (2) transmitter, (3) signal, (4) receiver, (5) destination, and (6) noise (Figure 1).[3]

2. Claude E. Shannon and Warren Weaver, *The Mathematical Theory of Communication* (Urbana: The University of Illinois Press, 1949), p. 5.
3. Ibid. Diagram reproduced by permission.

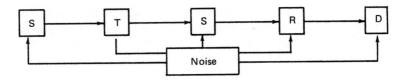

Figure 1

The Shannon=Weaver model may be adapted to speech communication. One adaptation that identifies additional elements in the speech communication process is schematized in Figure 2.

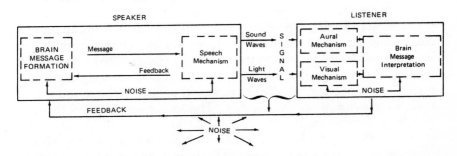

Figure 2

In a general sense, the human brain may be thought of as the *source* of all the messages we send. It is true, however, that this "storehouse of ideas" is being fed constantly by the senses of sight, hearing, smell, taste, and touch. A flower that is seen, a song that is heard, a scent that is smelled, a flavor that is tasted, or a surface that is touched—each of these individually (as well as in any possible combination) or linked with one or more previous experiences arising out of the background of the memory may be the stimulus for a message to be launched along the communication channel. In the simplest sense, a message may be thought of as an idea, concept, emotion, desire, or feeling which a source desires to transmit to a destination.

Once a message has been selected, the transmitter is called into action. For the spoken word, the transmitter is the vocal mechanism of the sender. The transmission process in speech communication is accomplished in four steps: respiration, phonation, resonation, and articulation. Broadly speaking, *respiration* may be identified as the process of inhalation and exhalation which occurs in the bodily function we call breathing. A column of exhaled air literally is forced out of the lungs, up the tracheal passage (windpipe), and through the vocal folds within the larynx where the second step, *phonation,* occurs. As the folds are brought together, or "approximated," the column of air passes over them causing them to vibrate, and sound is produced.

Resonation occurs when the sound is amplified and modulated in the nasal and pharyngeal cavities. Although the resonance of one's voice is influenced also by the size and structure of the chest and trachea, as well as by the bones of the head, the principal resonating chambers are the nose, mouth, and throat.

The fourth and final step in the transmission phase of oral communication is that of *articulation.* The tongue, teeth, lips, and palate interrupt the flow of voiced air and shape it in such a manner as to produce identifiable speech sounds—consonants and vowels. In normal continuous speech, these four steps overlap, blending together in a smooth, continuous process to transmit the message. There are various types of systems of transmission to carry different kinds of signals. In the case of the spoken word, the transmission vehicle is the sound waves upon which vibrations are imposed. The sound waves travel through the air-space between the speaker and the listener. As the sound waves set in motion by the human voice cross the air-space and reach the receiver or "hearing mechanism" of another person, a very intricate and complicated process is set in motion. The *outer ear* collects the sound waves beamed at the receiver and passes them on to the *tympanic membrane* or "eardrum." Beyond this membrane lies the *middle ear.* As the sound waves strike the tympanic membrane, the pressure they create causes it to vibrate. These vibrations are then transmitted by a series of tiny bones in the middle ear to the *inner ear.* This chain of bones is in three parts: the *malleus* (hammer) which is attached directly to the tympanic membrane, the *incus* (anvil), and the *stapes* (stirrup) which connects to the inner ear. Once inside the inner ear, the sound waves are translated into nerve impulses and sent to the receiver's brain, or the *destination,* for decoding the message.

The factor of "noise" may occur anywhere along the communication line, and it may be physical, physiological, or psychological in nature. Examples of such interferences with speech communication might include: annoying vocal habits on the part of the speaker (excessive use of "and-uh," improper articulation, or lack of adequate projection of the voice), unfavorable speaking environment (a hot, poorly ventilated room, dim lighting, or poor seating arrangements), extraneous distractions (background noises, the shuffling of chairs, people passing outside a door or window, or whispering or coughing among the members of the audience) or poor listening (inattentiveness, lack of proper listener motivation, or physical defects in the hearing mechanism). These and literally hundreds more, either alone or in combination, may be present as "noise" and therefore may modify adversely or even totally change a message as it travels from source to destination.

In addition to the verbal message, the speaker may simultaneously send nonverbal signals (facial expressions, gestures, postural behavior, tonal expression, expression through touch, etc.). The message, then, consists of spoken words as well as additional stimuli.

Another element in the communication process that is represented in the model is feedback—an element omitted in the Shannon= Weaver model. Feedback is that integral part of the process of human communication allowing the speaker to monitor the process and to evaluate the success of his attempt to get the desired response from the receiver. Of course, feedback, or "return signals" have a regulatory effect upon the speaker since he must adjust to the feedback responses if he is to be successful. Feedback can be received from one's own speech mechanism and from the outside systems of transmission (the sound of his own voice, the appearance of his gesture), as well as from the verbal and nonverbal responses of the receiver. The responses of acceptance or rejection (inattention, smiles, nods of approval, frowns, and applause) indicate to the speaker the modifications he needs to make in subsequent communications.

Not all important variables are represented in the model (Figure 2). Beliefs, attitudes, images, values, social roles, and experience, are additional variables that determine what messages are constructed, how they are constructed, by what means they are sent, and to whom they are sent. The same variables operate in the receiver to determine what messages he selects, how he perceives them, interprets them, and reacts to them. Indeed, the process of communication is complex with many variables interacting within each communicator and among communicators. Yet, in all types and levels of communication, the basic elements identified in Figure 2 are present. These elements are selected arbitrarily as viewpoints or entry-points to the study of communication.

Levels of Speech Communication

Communication may be categorized in many ways. Dance has identified three levels of human communication: intrapersonal, interpersonal, and person-to-group;[4] Thayer has categorized human

4. Frank E. X. Dance, ed, *Human Communication Theory,* (New York: Holt, Rinehart and Winston, Inc., 1967), p. 298.

communication as intrapersonal, interpersonal, and organizational;[5] Barker and Wiseman have stated that the levels of communication are four: intrapersonal, interpersonal, mass, and cultural;[6] and Borden, Gregg, and Grove have discussed human communication in terms of three levels: intrapersonal, interpersonal, and public.[7] There is general agreement among communication scholars in regard to the labels for the first two levels, but different descriptions and labels are given to level three. In this book, speech communication is discussed in terms of intrapersonal, interpersonal, and public communication.

INTRAPERSONAL COMMUNICATION—Intrapersonal communication is that communication which takes place within an individual. It is the individual's communication system which may be thought of as a more or less complex, dynamic, open, purposive information processing and decision-making system, the basic operations of which are to convert raw data to information, to interpret and give meaning to that information, and to use such meaning as a basis for behavior. Intrapersonal communication is, for the most part, neurophysiological activity. It is also the level upon which an individual "talks to himself" and thus, handles events, ideas, and experiences. Intrapersonal communication is the base of operation for all communication levels. The patterns, rules, and skills one uses in interpersonal and public communication are formed on the intrapersonal communication level. Thus, this first level provides the base for speech communication behaviors that manifest themselves at levels two and three.

INTERPERSONAL COMMUNICATION—Interpersonal communication refers to that communication in which persons are engaged directly with each other in the overt transmission and reception of messages. It does not refer to communication situations in which the sender of a message cannot communicate *directly with an individual as a person,* with each aware of the other as a unique person. Interpersonal communication includes dyadic communication and small group communication. Dyadic communication may be formal or informal and includes situations such as two persons visiting over a cup of coffee, the job interview, the conference between subordinate and superior, the telephone conversation with one's girl. In each of these, two persons communicate directly with one another. Each is specifically aware of the other as a person—

5. Lee Thayer, "Communication and Organization Theory," in *Human Communication Theory,* ed. Frank E. X. Dance (New York: Holt, Rinehart and Winston, Inc., 1967), p. 87.
6. Gordon Wiseman and Larry Barker, *Speech—Interpersonal Communication* (San Francisco: Chandler Publishing Company, 1967), p. 7.
7. George A. Borden, Richard B. Gregg, and Theodore G. Grove, *Speech Behavior and Human Interaction* (Englewood Cliffs, New Jersey: Prentice-Hall, Inc., 1969), pp. 1–5.

an individual; each can send messages overtly to the other. There is a dialogue. Interpersonal communication is more dialogical than public communication; public communication is usually monological.

Of course, interpersonal communication also includes small group communication which, like dyadic communication, may be formal or informal. The difference between small group communication and dyadic communication lies in the number of participants. The small group may be three persons talking in the back yard, a committee of five persons planning the Homecoming activities, or a meeting of any problem-solving group. The essential element in interpersonal communication is that of direct, knowing, person-to-person interaction. The important characteristic is that of overt participation so that it is a *dialogical* communication situation.

Most of the communication that takes place every day for each of us is interpersonal communication. It is the level of communication at which many serious breakdowns occur.

PUBLIC COMMUNICATION—A third level of communication (public communication) is, for the most part, monological, and it is characterized by the sending of a message to a public. Although the group, audience, or crowd is made up of several persons, it is not as possible to know each specifically as an individual person as it is in the case of the small group and dyadic situations. Moreover, in public communication the audience, large group, assembly, or mass audience function primarily as receivers and responders. For example, although members of the audience may communicate with the speaker, he does most, if not all, of the speaking. He is labeled "speaker" indicating the *monological* characteristic of that communication situation.

Public communication includes speaker-audience communication and mass communication. Mass communication refers to the "mass" distribution of identical copies of the same message to persons or receivers unknown to the sender and unknown to each other in any sense of interaction. Mass communication is the extension of institutionalized public acculturation beyond the limits of face-to-face and any other personally mediated interaction. This becomes possible only when technological means are available and social organizations emerge for the mass production and distribution of messages. The key to the historic significance of mass communication does not rest on the usual concept of masses. There were "masses" (large groups of people) reached by other forms of public communication long before the advent of modern mass communication. But new means and institutions of production and distribution, the mass media, provided new ways of reaching people. *A Dictionary of the Social Sciences* defines mass media as "all the impersonal means of communication by which visual and/or auditory messages are transmitted directly to audiences. Included among the mass media are television, radio, motion pictures, newspapers, magazines, books, and billboards."[8] Mass communication is directed toward a relatively large, heterogeneous, and anonymous audience. Mass communication may be characterized as public, rapid, and transient. The communicator, or sender, in mass communication usually works through a complex corporate organization.

The three levels of communication as defined and used in this book are not clear-cut and absolute in their differentiation, and it should be recognized that all levels and kinds of communication are more similar than they are different. Some situations may not be easily categorized into a single level. Nevertheless, it will help us as we study communication behavior to focus on one general level at a time.

VI. Summary

The purpose of this chapter is to introduce you to the study of speech communication. In doing so, five concerns have received attention. Emphasis has been given to the purpose for communication, to the relationship between quality of communication and the enhancement of living, to the process characteristics and the major components or elements of communication, and to the levels of human communication.

In view of the significance of human communication behavior, it is hoped that you as a student in speech communication will make a commitment to acquire those understandings, intellectual skills, and behaviors that will enable you to communicate more effectively as you interact with other persons throughout your life. Recognizing that the foundation skills and behaviors for effective communication are intrapersonal ones, Part I of this book focuses on intrapersonal communication.

8. J. Gould and W. L. Kolb, eds., *A Dictionary of the Social Sciences* (New York: The Free Press of Glencoe, 1964), p. 413.

For Further Reading

1.   Burkhardt, Dietrich; Schleidt, Wolfgang; and Altner, Helmut. *Signals in the Animal World.* Translated by Kenneth Morgan. New York: McGraw-Hill Book Co., 1967.

2.   Berlo, David K. *The Process of Communication.* New York: Holt, Rinehart and Winston, Inc. 1960.

3.   Dance, Frank E. X., ed. *Human Communication Theory.* New York: Holt, Rinehart and Winston, Inc., 1967.

4.   Matson, Floyd W., and Montague, Ashley, eds. *The Human Dialogue: Perspectives on Communication.* New York: Free Press, 1967.

5.   Miller, George A. *Language and Communication.* New York: McGraw-Hill Book Co., 1951.

6.   Schramm, Wilbur, ed. *The Science of Human Communication.* New York: Basic Books, Inc., 1963.

7.   Shannon, Claude E., and Weaver, Warren. *The Mathematical Theory of Communication.* Urbana: The University of Illinois Press, 1949.

8.   Watzlawick, Paul; Beavin, Janet H.; and Jackson, Don D. *Pragmatics of Human Communication.* New York: W. W. Norton & Company, Inc. 1967.

Part I

Intrapersonal
Communication

Chapter 2

The Individual's Communication System

When we consider human communication, it is natural that we should think about social situations—a speaker addressing an audience, a committee seated around a table in conference, or persons engaged in conversation. However, at the center of all social communication situations are individuals, each with his own communication system. If we are to understand and improve our ability to function in social communication situations, we must first investigate the individual's communication system.

No individual can exist for any significant length of time without interacting with other human beings. Moreover, the quality of a person's interaction with others is, to a great extent, dependent upon the skills he has developed in intrapersonal communication. Intrapersonal communication refers to the creating, functioning, and evaluating of symbolic processes which operate within oneself.

The individual is a complete, self-contained communication system, able to receive messages from inside or outside himself. He can process the information; and he can respond by sending messages to himself or to destinations outside himself. The individual sees, hears, feels, smells, and tastes; he learns, remembers, and thinks; he speaks, writes, gestures, moves, and behaves. To better understand this self-contained system, let us consider the elements that comprise the system.

Basic Elements in the Individual's Communication System

The basic elements in the process of communication within the individual include receivers, an information-processing unit, and transmitters. The receivers, with which we are most concerned, are the five senses: sight, hearing, smell, taste, and touch. The information-processing unit is the central nervous system. The transmitters are the facilities used in speaking, writing, vocalizing, moving, gesturing, or posturing —the means whereby messages are sent. These three classes of elements—receivers, brain, and transmitters—function together interdependently to make possible intrapersonal communication. If any of the elements is defective or inefficient in its functioning, the quality of communication is similarly lower than it might otherwise be. The process of communication as carried out by the individual's communication system is complex, and there are natural and acquired limitations upon its efficiency. The information-processing subsystem is particularly highly complex. This system, composed of the brain, the hypothalamus, and the entire central nervous system, processes innumerable messages simultaneously. This system may be involved in receiving, interpreting, and regulating numerous internal messages through its responses, while at the same time it is receiving, processing, and responding to information from the outside environment. As Borden has stated:

The brain, being the data-processing center for both external and internal stimuli, has an extremely difficult job. It must, if it is really effective, separate these stimuli sufficiently to keep one set from affecting the processing of the other set. Couple with this the fact that we also have memories and imaginations active in this center, and you begin to see the complexity of the human communication process. It is not surprising that we can handle only a limited amount of information per unit of time, and that, if we are pressured to handle more, our nervous system breaks down.[1]

Perceiving, remembering, thinking—these are among the important processes carried out in the brain. This chapter is concerned with the process of receiving and processing information. Chapter 3 focuses on specific aspects of information processing—problems in using language and problems in thinking.

II The Information-Receiving Aspect of Intrapersonal Communication

There are two sources of information—internal and external. Information from internal sources may come from the brain and may be either verbal or nonverbal, or information may come internally from organs of the body in the form of nonverbal messages which may or may not be translated into language for intrapersonal communication purposes.

1. George A. Borden, Richard B. Gregg, and Theodore G. Grove, *Speech Behavior and Human Interaction* (Englewood Cliffs, New Jersey: Prentice-Hall, Inc., 1969), p. 9.

Similarly, external information may be verbal (primarily received by seeing or hearing), or it may be nonverbal.

Considerable research is being conducted, especially in medical science, to study the body and its organs as carriers of messages. Our interest in internal messages from body organs is limited, however, since our principal concern is with the process of receiving information from external sources.

Man possesses five primary senses: sight, hearing, touch, smell, and taste. The two latter senses are believed to be the oldest in the evolution of man. It is by means of smell and taste that many lower animals perceive changes in their environment and receive information which influences their behavior for survival. A great deal of animal behavior is related to the search for food, and in the chemical environment of lower animals, smell and taste are extremely important sources of information. Smell and taste are better developed in many animals than in man, and taste is also sharper in children than in adults. For man, seeing and hearing are the dominating avenues for receiving information. So powerful is sight that it tends to override touch. For example, if a person looks at a raised line through a tilting prism, the line will be "seen" as tilted; and if at the same time he feels the raised line, it will "feel" tilted. However, if one feels the line while *not* looking through the prism, it will *not* feel tilted. The seeing channel is so dominant in man that the impression yielded by the sense of touch is distorted to conform with the information received visually, even if the visual impression is incorrect.

The human eye is, in many ways, the most remarkable biological structure created by nature. O'Brien has referred to the eye as an "optical instrument, a chemical laboratory, and an electrical encoding-transmitting instrument."[2] Since so much of our information about the world around us is received through visual stimuli, we should know what the eye's limitations are, and how it contributes to the way we see the world.

Our eyes can be likened to twin television cameras. Each eye has a lens, just as a television camera has, and at the back of each eye is a light-sensitive screen which responds chemically and upon which is formed the images of everything we see. Each element of the screen is connected by transmission lines to the brain with more than a million of such lines available. The signals which travel along these lines are electro-chemical signals. Although the eye is like a television camera in many ways, it possesses even greater complexity and greater sensitivity.

2. Brian O'Brien, "How Much Can We See?" in *Contemporary Readings in General Psychology*, ed. Robert S. Daniel (Boston: Houghton Mifflin Company, 1959), p. 270.

Yet, there are limitations in "seeing," and these limitations and the reasons for them (as well as limitations in hearing or touch) are matters of interest in our study of intrapersonal communication. The fact is, we can communicate only the information we possess and the information we have comes to us through the process of perception.

PERCEPTION—The following story has been related many times to illustrate the fallibility of information received visually and aurally. It seems there was a meeting at Goettingen of psychologists and other scientists. In the midst of the meeting, a door was thrown open suddenly and a man wearing a clown's costume rushed in, followed by a black man wearing a black jacket, red tie, and white trousers. The men yelled at each other and scuffled on the floor. A shot rang out, and both men rushed back through the door and out of the room. The incident had been secretly planned, rehearsed, and photographed. The meeting chairman asked the scientists to write complete reports of what they had seen and heard, to be used in the police investigation which he said was sure to follow. Forty scientists wrote reports. None gave a complete description of what had happened, only six reports did not misstate facts, and twelve reports missed at least 50 per cent of what had happened. Only four stated that the Negro had no hat. Others wrote that the Negro had a derby, a high hat, a cap, etc. His suit was described as red, brown, black, striped, blue, and coffee-colored. The experiment demonstrated dramatically the fallibility of vision and hearing as avenues of information. Similar demonstrations have been made in numerous college speech and psychology classes since the original incident was carried out. Man does not *perceive* all he sees, nor does he necessarily perceive *accurately* what falls on the eye's screen; and yet, his intrapersonal communication is limited to and based on the information he has via the process of perception from all the senses. Specifically, what are some of these limitations in perception, whether from sight, hearing, or the other senses?

1.   One limitation is that of selective perception, i. e., although all the images within range of the lens may come on the screen of the eye, only some are in fact "seen." Certain stimuli are selected to be seen, while other stimuli are not perceived. Each of us has had the experience of a single face in a crowd or a familiar voice in a din of noisy conversation suddenly popping out into our consciousness. From among the many stimuli, we perceive one. It has been selected. There are other voices as loud and other faces as prominent, but we see one specific face rather than other faces or the entire crowd; we hear that special voice and none of the others. It is not simply a matter of being especially sensitive to some stimuli that are

stronger, for unselected stimuli may be stronger than those selected. Rather, selected stimuli invite our selecting them to be
perceived because they have special significance and meaning to
us. One of the most important sources of meaningfulness is past
experience.

2. *Experience affects perception*. The perceptual process is determined not only by the sensory input, but also by the organization
of the central mechanism—the brain. There is a general tendency,
therefore, to perceive (to see or hear) whatever one is already
looking or listening for and is expecting to see or hear. A mother
comes to recognize and respond to her baby's cry in the night,
while the father sleeps on peacefully, and the accomplished chef
learns to detect the missing spice in the complex aroma arising
from the stew. All of us are constantly receiving information col-
ored by our experiences.

3. Another fallacy (a visual one) in information received is the *optical
illusion*. Optical illusions cannot be explained on the basis of what
happens physically on the retinal image, since the image accurately
mirrors the objective state of affairs. Nor can they be explained in
terms of knowledge and its "derived expectancies." Optical illusions defy knowledge. For example, we know the two line segments in the familiar Muller-Lyer illusion are of equal length. We
can confirm that knowledge by measuring the lines with a ruler,
and we can then *know* and *expect* the lines to appear equal in
length. Yet when we add the "arrows" to the line segments, *the
lines will be perceived as unequal in length* (see Figure 3).

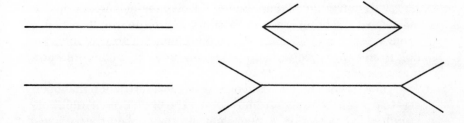

Figure 3

All optical illusions attest to the impotence of knowledge as a guarantee of accuracy in perceiving an object or situation. This does not
mean that perception cannot be affected by knowledge or experience, for it is, in some instances, as previously discussed. It does
mean, however, that *perception cannot be equated wholly with
knowledge;* perception cannot be reduced to knowledge only.

4. A fourth source of fallibility in receiving information is _neurological inhibition_. The neural networks, composed of many nerve cells, transmit messages to and from the higher centers of the nervous system. The messages, detected in the form of electrical impulses, may travel long distances involving the spinal column and several parts of the brain, or the circuit may be quite short as in the case of the reflex arc. The point at which nerve cells contact each other is called the _synapse._ At this juncture, the message (electrical impulses) may be stopped or sent on. At each synapse the impulse must be recreated if it is to be sent through the next nerve cell. The electrical impulse must be of sufficient strength to cause the adjoining nerve cell to re-create the impulse. Thus, each nerve cell acts as a relay station, receiving and sending signals. Only signals above a certain threshold of amplitude are received, however. If they are received, they are sent on at the same amplitude, for the impulse does not weaken as it travels over neural pathways; however, if the strength of the impulse is not great enough to trigger the next nerve, the message will be stopped. This process operates in the same manner for all five senses. Some incoming messages are stopped through neurological inhibition. At each junction (synapse) in the neural network are special nerve fibers that carry _inhibitory impulses._ Such impulses can act against incoming impulses by raising the threshold of the nerve cell to a point so high that the incoming impulse will not be strong enough to trigger the next nerve cell into re-creating and sending on the impulse. Rather, the incoming impulse is inhibited—stopped—and is prevented from reaching the brain. This chemical-electrical inhibiting process can act as a control on perception—a "preventer of perception." It means that the brain is not a repository for _all_ the stimuli available to our sensory organs. Neurological inhibition can prevent information from being received and, thus, can limit the amount of information passed on to the brain.

There is yet a second kind of neurological restriction that operates to prevent messages from reaching the brain even if inhibitory impulses fail to stop it. A neurological organ called the _reticular formation_ may prevent a message from reaching the brain. Apparently, there are impulses coming from the sensory organs not blocked out by inhibitory impulses that do not reach the brain. These impulses arrive at a point at which the neural pathway branches to become two pathways. One pathway leads to the reticular formation and the other leads to the cortex of the brain. "Messages" go down both pathways, but if the reticular formation ignores the message, so does the brain; and if the reticular formation heeds the message, it awakens the brain so that it will perceive the incoming message and interpret it. The functioning of the reticular formation in regard to intrapersonal communication relates to the ability of this unique apparatus to learn which stimuli are important and which are not. It may allow a mother to sleep regularly through the loud sounds of a train that passes by her bedroom window every night and yet awaken her immediately at the sound of her baby's cry. The reticular formation also permits one to concentrate for it shuts out all stimuli but those upon which the brain is concentrating. Thus, the reticular formation is the "High Command" of the central nervous system. It tells the brain which of the information passing through it it can perceive.

5. A fifth source of fallibility in information reception is that of the effect of *psychological and emotional states.* How does emotional and psychological stress (such as extreme fear) affect the process of receiving information? On the basis of research findings, it has been suggested that if an experience has intense psychological and emotional discomfort assigned to its interpretation, a neurological circuit may be set in motion whose purpose will be to prohibit the brain from receiving such a message again. Such messages will be blocked out entirely or distorted so as to be different messages. Not only do *those* messages not get in, but *other messages may also be unintentionally blocked out* in the process. Melzack explains how this process occurs:

Investigators in a number of countries have recently demonstrated the presence of systems of nerve fibers that run from the higher areas of the brain downward to make connection with the message-carrying nerve pathways in the spinal cord. Electrical activity induced in these higher brain areas is capable of suppressing or modifying the message; it may never get beyond the lower levels of the central nervous system or an entirely different message may reach the brain.

There is no longer any doubt that these message-modifying fibers exist; it has been found that electrical stimulation of widespread regions of the brain is able to modify the messages transmitted through every major sensory system. ... It is reasonable to speculate that the fibers provide the mechanism whereby higher brain activities such as memories, thoughts, and emotions can modify the sensory messages after injury. We can assume, moreover, that this modification can occur throughout the entire axis of the central nervous system, at every junction at which nerve messages are relayed from one neuron to the next in the course of their assent to the highest areas of the brain. If this view is right, we have a conceptual physiological model to account for the fact that psychological events play an essential role in determining the quality and intensity of the ultimate perceptual experience.[3]

3. Ronald Melzack, "The Perception of Pain," *Scientific American,* 204 (February 1961): 44.

The importance of psychological-emotional effects on perception and communication is that some informational messages are not allowed to enter the brain and other messages, when they are allowed to enter, are distorted so that the information received is erroneous. It is not difficult to understand that the operation of such *psychological sets* can affect intrapersonal communication. If the organism, through functioning psychological sets, can block or modify incoming messages from the senses, then the picture of reality that directs one's behavior can be false and the quality of intrapersonal communication can be adversely affected. Of course, it must be recognized that there may well be some positive aspects of this function that are also important to survival. The fact is, however, that each person's psychological-emotional makeup directly affects the information-receiving process and, for practical purposes, guarantees some distortion, omission, and falsity in information one possesses about himself and his environment. Such limitations invite mistakes and breakdowns in intrapersonal communication. For example, we may have a psychological set characterized by strong feeling for or against the specific concept, object, or situation. Let us suppose that the psychological-emotional set is associated with a particular attitudinal position on some topic. The moment we receive information that we recognize as unfavorable to our position, we may immediately distort it or shut it out entirely, along with other incoming messages.

Another way in which psychological set may affect information-reception is in the handling of competing messages or multi-messages coming in via two or more of the sensory channels. If the messages are contradictory, the brain must decide which to believe. Is the message that is being heard to be accepted while the message being seen is rejected? Psychological set is one of several factors directly related to the reception of information from multi-sensory channels.

6. Perception is also a function of *innate limitations and saliences.* For example, the ability of a musician to discriminate between tones is determined largely from the inherited structure of his ear. Thus, inherited traits affect perception.

Another example of inherited or natural forces affecting perception is what is known as the "releaser concept." Psychologists have discovered that a given behavior in man often is critically dependent on just one aspect of a stimulus situation that is perceived and responded to, while other equally perceivable qualities are without effect. The "releaser phenomenon" is commonly noticed in the animal world, too. For example, the red belly feathers of the male British robin will automatically trigger an attack by another male robin, while a dummy accurate in all ways except that the belly is not red, elicits no attack. Conversely, a small bundle of red feathers alone will release the attack behavior. There are many other examples of the releaser phenomenon operating in perception. These releasers do not have to be learned, and previous experience is not necessary—the "releaser phenomenon" appears to be innate. There is evidence indicating that some smells are related to releaser mechanisms in man. The smell of cooked cabbage was such a phenomenon for me, as a child. Many odors elicit strong emotional responses, with some smells repelling us and other brightening our outlook throughout the entire day. It may be that many of the feelings aroused daily in the odoriferous world of man are influenced in part by evolutionary memories recorded in the genes many ages ago.

In summary, there are several limitations upon the information-reception process, six of which have been identified and discussed. The important point, in terms of intrapersonal communication, is that the information received is not necessarily one-to-one with reality or with that received by others, a principle that will be stated several times throughout this book. An awareness of the limitations in the information-receiving process can help one improve the quality and efficiency of his intrapersonal communication.

III The Information-Processing Aspect of Intrapersonal Communication

Of the three components of the intrapersonal communication process (information reception, information processing, and information transmission), the remainder of this chapter, as well as Chapter 3, is concerned with information processing. The third component, information transmission, will not be discussed in Part I of this text.

Some factors discussed under information reception relate directly to information processing. It is difficult to "freeze" a process and to separate interrelated components into absolute entities, but for purposes of simplicity and clarity they have been arbitrarily separated here.

The information processing unit is composed of the brain and the central nervous system. The primary unit is the brain—the mind. No one has ever seen a mind. When one cuts into the brain, only nerves, tissue and blood vessels are seen. Recorded brain waves can show whether the brain is thinking or not, but they cannot show what is being thought. We cannot see the storing and interpreting of information, nor can we see the information being used in thinking. These information processing functions have been studied only indirectly. Nevertheless, considerable understanding has been acquired with regard to information processing in the brain.

The human brain is composed of some ten billion nerve cells.[4] Each cell contributes to mental activity by either firing or not firing impulses. What specifically occurs in neuronal activity involved in processing information—storing, recalling, thinking—is neither fully nor confidently understood. Some theories hold that the mechanism by which thought is carried on is chemical. Such theories suggest that since every type of cell of each individual has its own chemical personality —and since this differentiation of cells depends on proteins—memory, thought, and symbols may be associated with nerve protein characteristics.

Another theory, explained as follows by Gerard, suggests that intellectual activity produces structural changes in the brain:

> One observed change, already noted, is the swelling of fiber end-bulbs induced by activity. The swelling should favor the transmission of impulses . . . activity somehow causes a nerve fiber to sprout new twigs near its termination and so to increase its effective contact . . . the notoriously poor memory of old people for recent events might be attributed to the neurons' inability to grow more twigs or to accommodate more connections. . . .
>
> A given end-bulb of a neuron initially ineffective, can become and remain effective as a result of activity. Indeed, mathematical theories of the behavior of complex nerve nets demand only such an assumption to account for the basic properties of memory. Moreover, the total number of end-bulbs on the neurons of the brain, some 10 trillion, about matches the number of bits of information the brain may store during a lifetiime.[5]

The foregoing are only two of several theories of what happens in the brain during information processing, but regardless of the theory accepted, the single most important characteristic of the brain for information processing is its ability to deal with symbols. Symbolization is integral to the functioning of the brain for most of man's information processing. It is the single most important element in thinking.

The ability of the brain to represent an experience when the stimulus is absent, whether it is in the past or imagined in the future, is an extremely important step in mental evolution. When the brain can

4. Ralph W. Gerard, "What is Memory?" in *Contemporary Readings in General Psychology*, ed. Robert S. Daniel (Boston: Houghton Mifflin Company, 1959), p. 96.
5. Ibid., p. 97.

think of an object or an event, it can begin to solve problems by reasoning rather than by trial and error—it can process information in a way qualitatively different from the lower animals who do not possess such ability. In experiments with chickens, for example, if food is placed behind a glass, they fail to understand that it can be reached by going around the barrier. They may push against the glass, peck at it, and run around aimlessly; and they may accidentally come upon the food. However, if the test is repeated after they have come upon the food, the same trial-and-error behavior will again occur. Given enough trials, a chicken may learn to go around the barrier, but a chimpanzee can solve the problem without any trials. Primates can learn by observing. Chimpanzees have stacked boxes, climbed on them, and manufactured tools from sticks which they could then use to get bananas.

In maze experiments in which a *principle* must be learned, rats fail completely. After two thousand trials, a rat may have no more than chance probability of success. A raccoon or cat may learn the principle in from five hundred to eight hundred trials, and a chimp in one hundred trials or less. However, an adult human being will discover the principle in two or three trials. He will suddenly say, "Oh, I see. It's one to the right, three to the left, and one to the right." A child under three years of age cannot solve the problem. Until the child can begin to verbalize the situation, he can do no better than animals on the test. Even one of the most intelligent animals, the chimpanzee, cannot master language. It may be taught a few words (a limit of about five) which are conditioned responses to commands or to behavior associated with getting food, but it cannot acquire speech. One reason is that its brain does not have the necessary physical potential. The brain of an adult chimpanzee weighs about three pounds. The ratio of the chimp's brain weight to body weight is 1 to 150, but the ratio for human beings is 1 to 50. Also, the frontal area of the chimpanzee's brain, the area concerned with symbolic functions, is much smaller in relation to the rest of the brain than is the case for humans; and the chimpanzee lacks almost entirely the section in the left frontal lobe that is known to be involved in speech in the human brain. *It is the capacity of the human brain to symbolize—to acquire the ability to use words—that makes complex information processing possible.* The discovery that everything has a name opens a whole new world to the child. With language, the child begins to learn to think. Chapter 3 is concerned with using language and with thinking as especially important aspects of information processing in the individual's communication system. The remainder of this chapter is concerned with memory—an important element in intrapersonal communication.

IV Memory—the Storing and Recalling of Information

Without memory the past would disappear and man's ability to learn by experience would vanish. Memory is defined as the modification of behavior by experience. It is the making of an impression (fixation), its retention (storage), and its subsequent recall and recognition.

It is not necessary for the initial impression to enter one's awareness in order to be stored and recalled. Nor is consciousness necessary for information to be recalled from memory, for people can recall information under hypnosis. How much can be stored and how much can be recalled?

There is, apparently, no absolute limitation of the amount that can be stored in memory. Gerard has stated:

I have been told of a bricklayer who, under hypnosis, described correctly every bump and grain on the top surface of a brick he had laid in a wall 20 years before. Guesses have been made as to how many items might be accumulated in memory over a lifetime. Some tests of perception suggest that each tenth of a second is a single frame of experience for the human brain. In that tenth of a second it can receive perhaps a thousand units of information, called bits. In 70 years, not allowing for any reception during sleep, some 15 trillion bits might pour into the brain and perhaps be stored there.[6]

LIMITATIONS RELATED TO STORAGE OF INFORMATION—There are two major limitations related to storage of information—the inability to recall information and the inaccuracy of information recalled. Except when under hypnosis, one can recall only a small portion of the amount actually stored in memory. In one study, approximately 60 percent of verbal material was recalled after twenty minutes, 44 percent after an hour, 34 percent after a day, and a slowly shrinking percentage for each day thereafter. What are some of the factors related to whether or not information can be recalled?

One factor is time. For example, repeated experiences are more easily recalled than single experiences. Also, experiences in youth are more firmly fixed in memory and more easily recalled than are experiences in old age. Such experiences are the last to survive disruptive conditions such as brain damage, concussion, and deterioration from old age. These experiences are also the first to be recalled after a period of amnesia.

Another factor is the intensity or vividness of the experience. Early experiences in life that are also extremely vivid may sometimes remain to be easily recalled producing fear or other strong emotional responses

6. Ibid., p. 95.

years later. For example, an infant frightened by a particular sound or object may experience disabling fear of that sound or object throughout the rest of his life.

A third factor affecting recall is the *inhibitory function* of the brain. Even as incoming information can be inhibited or blocked in the information reception process, the recall of information can also be inhibited or blocked so that the organism is protected from the anguish of intense fear, shame, or pain. Although such experiences may be "forgotten" or "repressed" so that they are not subject to willful recall, they may reappear under the influence of pentathol, hypnosis, or in dreams.

Can information, once stored in memory, be genuinely erased? No confident answer is available at this time, but hypnotists can apparently "erase" from memory presuggested signals of instruction. Also, those persons who can glance through a book and then name any word on any line on any page claim that they can erase that mass of information at the end of their performance so that their memory will not be "cluttered." Whether or not experiences and information can be erased from memory, a more severe problem for most of us is that of being able to recall information from memory.

The second major limitation in the process of recall is that of inaccuracy of the information recalled. There is evidence that experiences can be altered over a period of time. Events, recalled from memory at intervals, may become more general and regular as details are lost and smoothed out; or events may change as they are recalled by becoming increasingly dominated by a salient detail or feature which becomes exaggerated and gains prominence. An object different from the original may ultimately emerge.

The inability to recall information and the inability to rely on information recalled as being accurate—these are the two major problems related to memory and information processing. What can be done to compensate for these limitations, and thus improve the information processing aspect of intrapersonal communication?

WAYS TO IMPROVE THE RECALL OF INFORMATION—The close relationship between memory and solving problems is demonstrated every time we cannot recall necessary information. Since our ability to remember directly limits our intelligence, we should try to handle the processing of information so as to facilitate recall. The following suggestions have been made by scientists and scholars who have studied memory.

One finding that has important implications for recall is that the human brain can efficiently handle only five or six items in either perception or thought processess. Miller has reviewed the history of this finding.

The first person to propose a test of man's instantaneous grasp seems to have been Sir William Hamilton, a 19th century Scottish metaphysician. He wrote: "If you throw a handful of marbles on the floor, you will find it difficult to view at once more than six or seven at most, without confusion. . . . In 1871 William Stanley Jevons reported that when he threw beans into a box, he never made a mistake when there were three or four, was sometimes wrong if the number was five, was right about half the time if the beans numbered 10 and was usually wrong when the number reached 15. . . ."

Experiments since have confirmed the fact that we perceive and handle in thought no more than six or seven items. . . .

We are justified in assuming that our memories are limited by the number of units or symbols we must master, and not by the amount of information that these symbols represent. Thus, it is helpful to organize material intelligently before we try to memorize it. The process of organization enables us to package the same total amount of information into far fewer symbols.[7]

As Miller points out, the organizing of material into related parts facilitates recall. De Cecco refers to this same technique as "chunking" material to be learned.

A second aid to remembering is that of rehearsal or repetition. Repetition not only brings the factor of time into memory, but has the important effect of organizing many separate items into a single unit, thus reducing the load the memory must carry. The technique is, in effect, like substituting a single symbol for a longer expression which would be difficult to write each time we wanted to use it.

In addition to these two suggestions are five more:

1. More is remembered if one consciously commits material to memory by reciting aloud rather than by just reading.
2. Material acquired through short study sessions with periodic review is more easily recalled than is material acquired in a single, long, cramming session.
3. We recall most easily those things that are of high interest and significance to us.
4. Information acquired under pleasant conditions or associated with pleasant emotions is more easily recalled than material acquired or associated with unpleasant conditions and emotions.
5. Visualization of materials to be remembered enhances their recall.[8]

7. George A. Miller, "Information and Memory," in *Contemporary Readings in General Psychology,* ed. Robert S. Daniel (Boston: Houghton Mifflin Company, 1959), pp. 106–8.
8. Robert G. Whalen, "Where Were You the Night of April 23, 1935?" in *Contemporary Readings in General Psychology,* ed. Robert S. Daniel (Boston: Houghton Mifflin Company, 1959), pp. 109–12.

Memory (the ability to retrieve relevant information) is an essential element in the process of thinking, i.e., the process of intrapersonal communication.

Ⅴ Summary

Recognizing that intrapersonal communication is involved basically in all levels and types of communication, this chapter has focused upon the communication system of the individual. The components comprising the individual's self-contained communication system have been identified as receiving units, an information-processing unit, and transmitting units. Receiving elements include: sight, hearing, touch, smell, and taste with seeing and hearing being the major avenues for receiving information. The unit in information-processing is the brain and the central nervous system; and the process of sending information includes speaking, writing, gesturing, moving, and other nonverbal behavior.

It has been noted in this chapter that the process of receiving information is subject to error. What one receives in the way of information is influenced by selective perception, the effect of past experiences, optional illusion, neurological inhibition, psychological and emotional states, and innate limitations and tendencies. What a given individual "receives" is not necessarily what is present in reality nor is it exactly what another individual "receives" from that reality.

As with reception, so the processing of information is somewhat unique for each individual. Important elements and functions in processing information include: recognizing, structuring, symbolizing, storing, and recalling. Memory, or information retrieval is an important part of information-processing. We have noted that repeated experiences, early experiences, and intense and vivid experiences are likely to be recalled more easily than are single, late-in-life, mild experiences; and we have noted, also, that the inhibitory function of the brain affects the recall of information. Because information retrieval is especially important to the process of information-processing, suggestions for improving one's ability to retrieve information were made.

Communication—conversation, marital communication, interviews, public speeches, television news reporting, picket-lines, demonstration marches, and all other forms of communication—involves the exchange of information that is sent, received, and responded to; and a major part, even a critical part, of that total process is what happens within the individual. Hence, it is important to investigate the individual's communication system. Now that we have looked at the individual's communication system from an overall perspective, let us look at a specific function, the use of language by the individual and how one's use of language is directly related to the quality of his thinking.

For Further Reading

1. Ashby, W. Ross. *Design for a Brain.* New York: John Wiley & Sons, Inc., 1952

2. Daniel, Robert S., ed. *Contemporary Readings in General Psychology.* Boston: Houghton Mifflin Company, 1959.

3. Fergus, R. H. *Perception.* New York: McGraw-Hill Book Co., 1966.

4. Magdalen, D. Vernon. *The Psychology of Perception.* Baltimore: Penguin Books, 1962.

5. Von Berkesy, George. *Sensory Inhibition.* Princeton, N.J.: Princeton University Press, 1966.

Chapter 3

Processing Information:
Language and Thinking

Man is the only language-manipulating animal; this fact is of decisive and central importance in the study of human communication; it makes possible those behaviors that are unique to man and that set him apart from other animals. The influence of language enables man to make cultural, intellectual, political, technological, and artistic accomplishments.

Pavlov, known primarily for his study of the conditioned response in his experimental work with dogs, also devoted considerable time to the study of human subjects and developed the concept of the "second signalling system." He contrasted the "second signalling system" (language behavior) with the "first signalling system" (simple sensory stimulation). Lower animals operate solely within the first signalling system, while man utilizes both signalling systems. When man learned to use language, he acquired the ability to register experiences and relationships. His behavior was no longer determined only by perception or unformulated emotional responses, but it could also be determined by reflection upon the past and prediction of future consequences and events—in short, by thinking.

Man has no greater need today than to improve his intrapersonal communication through an improved use of language, for as his use of language is faulty, so his thinking and living are deficient.

Thinking and Language

How we think is inextricably bound up with how we talk. Some scholars assert that all thought is subvocal speech, but we need not go that far to appreciate the importance of the observation of a relationship between using language and thinking. Certainly most of thought is a matter of talking to ourselves silently.

Language plays a decisive role in mental processes. By being given a name, an object is distinguished from other objects while at the same time it is related to other objects and its surrounding. Luria has stated:

... the fact that every word is a generalization is vitally important to the systematic reflection of the outside world, to the transition from sensation to thinking, and to the creation of new functional systems. Speech not only gives names to the objects of the outside world; it also distinguishes among their essential properties and includes them in a system of relationships to other objects. As a result of language, man can evoke an image of a particular object and use it in the absence of the original. At the same time, speech, differentiating among the essential signs and generalizing on the objects or phenomena denoted, facilitates deeper penetration of the environment. Human mental processes are thereby elevated to a new level and are given new powers of organization, and man is enabled to direct his mental processes.[1]

Thus, we can see that thinking (silent speech) is, for the most part, possible because of language. Of course, we can think to some extent without words, but we cannot entertain abstract ideas without using them. Mental activities such as memorizing, interpreting, and logical thinking are carried on through the use of language. Thought presupposes the existence of language, but there are many forms of behavior, the result of thinking, which do not require the intervention of a symbol. Percepts and emotions alone may determine the form of the response. We often act without thinking of ourselves as acting, or we respond without formulating beforehand the exact nature of the response to the conditions of the moment. Many actions in a game such as tennis or in driving a car belong in this category. Although the individual may be conscious of the result, he may be unable to recall the movements he has actually performed. It is correct, then, to say that man can think without language, but he cannot think at the sophisticated levels that characterize much of his thought without using language.

The direct relationship between thought and language has been stated strongly by Luria:

The sources of human development always include objective action and language. The latter, the basis of the second signal system, is not only a means of communication but also a powerful tool for the formation of human conscious processes. ... The fact that speech [language] processes taking part in intellectual operation are gradually condensed and converted into contracted internal verbal schemes has been demonstrated by several investigators. The essential

1. A. R. Luria, *Human Brain and Psychological Processes* (New York: Harper & Row, Publishers, 1966), p. 35.

role played by internal speech in the course of various intellectual operations was demonstrated some time ago by L. S. Vygotsky (1934, 1956) and has subsequently been described from different angles by a number of investigators.

A. N. Sokolov (1919), L. A. Novikova (1955), F. V. Bassin and E. S. Bein (1957) showed that nearly every intellectual operation is accompanied by a minutely determined innervation of the organs of speech, which may be detected by means of special electromyographic recording systems. . . .[2]

We begin by speaking as we think, we end by thinking as we speak, and both actions are shaped by language. Therefore, to improve our communication behavior at all levels—public, interpersonal, and cultural—we must understand the strengths and the problems inherent in using language; and we must become sensitive to the major pitfalls in using language. Man uses language in order to think and there is an important direct relationship between the two.

FOUR RELATIONSHIPS BETWEEN THINKING AND LANGUAGE—Language has four positive relationships to thinking. First, the use of symbols aids thinking and facilitates behavior by making unnecessary the trial-and-error process. Man can reason. He can "try ideas in the mind".

The second way in which the process of thinking is enhanced through language is through symbolization which enables us to detect likenesses and differences among objects and events perceived. This use of language is explained by Head:

When we are shown a pyramid, we recognise at once that it resembles an object of similar shape on the table and that it differs fundamentally from a cone. Most aphasics can carry out this test correctly because it is based on direct perceptual relations; no verbal symbol is required. But if, when shown a pyramid, the patient attempts in vain to name it before making his choice, he may subsequently be unable to select the object of the same shape from amongst those placed before him. Direct perception of the likeness of the two figures has now been complicated by failure to record their similarity by means of a name. On the other hand, in normal persons the power of recording likeness and difference by means of a symbol enormously extends the power of conceptual thinking. . . .[3]

A third relationship between symbol-utilization and thinking is that words connect and give permanence to non-verbal processes of thought which would otherwise be disjointed and momentary. This is especially true, for example, in the case of visual images. Such images would appear and then be lost if it were not for the fact that they can be symbolized, stored, and later recalled upon command. Without

2. Ibid., p. 117.
3. Henry Head, "Chapter 12: Language and Thinking" in *Readings in Social Psychology*, ed. Alfred R. Lindesmith and Anselm L. Strauss (New York: Holt, Rinehart and Winston, Inc. 1969), p. 104.

names, visual images would perish leaving behind no permanent addition to thought, and the relations among visual images in terms of time, space, essential likenesses, and critical differences could not be recorded.

A fourth advantage that accrues to man through symbol-utilization in thinking is that logical thinking (possible only through the use of verbal symbols) permits us to hold in check and to diminish emotional and intuitive responses. An animal—and man under certain conditions —tends to respond immediately and directly to the emotional aspects of a situation. Such responses were discussed in Chapter 2. Through the use of language, however, we can often check our emotional responses, submit them to logical analysis, and thereby gain the power to break up a situation for the purpose of selective action and rational control of our behavior.

Since man's communication (intrapersonal, interpersonal, and public) is so language-dependent, it is important to learn how we use language and how we can avoid the most common and dangerous misuses of language. In this chapter we will consider some of the basic principles underlying the use of language and identify some common problems or dangers in using language.

We have no greater need today than to improve communication with ourselves. We ourselves are often responsible for failures in communication. It is easier for us to stereotype and label persons than to think of them as individuals, and it is easier to talk about what *we* mean rather than what another person means. These problems center on language and how it is used intrapersonally. The functions of language, if they are to aid man, must affect the most basic need of any organism, survival. Darwin's thesis, that when the survival mechanism of any creature fails, that creature ceases to exist, applies to man as well as to all other animals. Language is man's chief means of survival. The ability to use language is the ability to transfer experience into symbols and, through symbols, to share experiences with one's fellow man.

Language and Speech

Language and speech are not identical. In order to differentiate language from speech, let us view language at two levels. The first level consists of the formal elements that are used for purposes of organization—syntactic devices and relational elements. There are rules that regulate the use of such elements. This first level is referred to as structure, and we can view language in terms of its structure. A second level consists of words and is called vocabulary. From this point of view, language is the totality of meanings evoked by words which carry objective reference. Putting the two levels together, language includes a set of symbols (words constituting a vocabulary), a meaningful method for combining these symbols (syntax), and a description of the structural relationships (grammar). The function of language is to elicit and express meanings. Language, then, represents the totality of options and rules for using words, a special type of symbol. Language symbolizes what can be done.

Speech is differentiated from language inasmuch as speech is constrained by the circumstances of the moment. *Speech exists in a social situation.* It symbolizes not *what can be done*, but *what is done*. Between language and speech is the social relationship. The social relationship affects or determines what is said. It regulates the options which speakers select at both the structural and vocabulary levels. Thus, the form of the social relationship establishes *coding principles* for the speakers. These coding principles guide speakers in their *encoding* of the message and listeners in their *decoding* of the messages. Different forms of social relationships create different speech systems or linguistics codes. The ghetto may have a different speech system than the wealthy suburbs. Children bring speech codes to school that symbolize their social identity. The child's code that has permitted him to relate to his family and local social relationships constitutes his world of reality.

Through language man symbolizes his experiences. Meaningful experiences result in learning, and as man shares experiences and learning he advances from generation to generation. Animals cannot learn or advance in the way man does: animals can learn to respond to *signs,* but only man can use *symbols.* The difference between signs and symbols is that signs *announce* but symbols *remind*.

Symbols may take any form; they may have the form of a material object, a color, a sound, an odor, the motion of an object, or a taste. The meaning of a symbol is in no instance derived from or determined by properties intrinsic in its form: the color for mourning might just as well have been red or green, for example.

Signs may be defined as physical things or events whose function is to indicate some other thing or event. The meaning of a sign may be in form only (the hurricane signal) or in form and context (the return of robins in the spring). Animals can emit and receive cries signifying food, sex, or danger, but no animal can think about the nature of food and decide to go on a diet. Another important difference between signs and symbols is in the number of possible responses elicited by each. An effective sign elicits only one response. It stands in a one-to-one relationship with an experience; a symbol is characterized by its ability to suggest several possible responses. To an animal, a sign of danger may automatically elicit one response—fleeing, changing its color, or some other response important to its survival. To man, however, the symbol *danger* may bring to mind a variety of responses. Symbols give man flexibility and time to consider possible responses before acting. To jump at every warning is to put man at the level of an animal. Mark Twain observed that people sometimes behave like animals when he stated:

We should be careful to get out of an experience only the wisdom that is in it —and stop there; lest we be like the cat that sits down on a hot stove lid. She will never sit down on a hot stove lid again, but also she will never sit down on a cold one anymore.[4]

Man uses both signs and symbols. The alarm clock's buzzing, the stop light, and the crack of the starter's gun in races are signs designed by man to elicit one appropriate and immediate response; but, as we shall discover later in this chapter, signal behavior that is inappropriate is one of man's most common sources of failure in communication. Man strives for the same ends as all other living creatures—preservation of the individual and the species—but man has symbolic and non-symbolic means to those ends. Man yawns, coughs, scratches, stretches, cries out in pain, bristles in anger, etc. He shares these non-symbolic behaviors with many animal species, but he also communicates verbally and non-verbally with himself, with others, and with the public. By using symbols, he contemplates, makes laws, resolves problems, confesses sins, observes social and cultural codes, establishes governments and institutions, remembers the past, and plans for the future. These kinds of behavior are possible because man can symbolize. In a way, a baby is not human until he begins to symbolize, for only then does he begin to enter the uniquely human world.

So important are the relationships among language, thought, and human behavior, that in the last few years a special area of study has developed—semantics and general semantics. *Semantics* is the study of the meanings of words and how persons respond to words; *general semantics* is the study of any behavior that results from language habits. While semantics is concerned with the relationship between a symbol and the thing it represents (its referent), general semantics has a broader concern, being concerned with all of human behavior as it relates to language. Count Alfred Korzybski, who coined the term general semantics, believed language to be a powerful influencer of our thinking and our behaving.[5] Mature, effective behavior is possible *only*

4. Bernard DeVoto, ed., *The Portable Mark Twain* (New York: Viking Press, 1946), p. 563.
5. Lord Alfred Korzybski, *Science and Sanity* (Lakeville, Connecticut: The International Non-Aristotelian Library, 1947).

if one can use language as he talks to himself, in an efficient way. Among those who have studied and written about improving behavior through a better use of language and thinking are Stuart Chase, S. I. Hayakawa, Wendell Johnson, Irving Lee, and Anatol Rapoport.

Six Principles in Using Language

Alfred Korzybski, trained as an engineer and mathematician, also devoted considerable time to the study of mental illness. His famous book, *Science and Sanity: An Introduction to Non-Aristotelian Systems and General Semantics*, is the result of his scientific and psychiatric studies and propounds the theme that the orientations of science and those resulting in sanity are the same. Korzybski advanced three basic principles: (1) the principle of non-identity, (2) the principle of non-allness, and (3) the principle of self-reflexiveness. From these are derived the six principles emphasized here.

PRINCIPLE NO. 1: WORDS SYMBOLIZE THINGS, BUT ARE NOT THOSE THINGS—In a way, man lives in two worlds—a world of words (a verbal world) and a world of things (objects, persons, etc.). Words are used to stand for , i.e., to symbolize, the world of things, but the words are not the things they represent.

One of the problems in using language is that sometimes one confuses the word with the thing the word represents. When a person fails to make that important distinction in his intrapersonal communication, he may arrive at conclusions that instigate inappropriate behavior. He may react signally rather than symbolically or rationally. He may react to the thing he has mistaken the word for. For example,

> A lady in Florida entertained a group of people for dinner. Everyone was delighted with the meal although no one could decide exactly what the main course was. After the dinner, a lady approached the hostess and said, "I enjoyed that food so much. I would like to learn to prepare it. Would you please tell me what we had?" The hostess turned to the lady and said, "Yes, of course. You just had the pleasure of eating *snake steaks*." Upon hearing that, the lady had the unfortunate experience of seeing her food for the second time.[6]

Obviously, the words (snake steak) evoked an unfortunate signal response. In order to avoid behavior that is immature, embarrassing, or destructive, we must learn not to react to words as though they really are the things they represent, but rather, to delay reacting and to evaluate the situation.

6. Sanford I. Berman, *Understanding and Being Understood* (San Diego, California: The International Communication Institute, 1965), p. 5. Used by permission.

Not infrequently people react to labels rather than to the person or object to which the label is attached. Labeling or name-calling, as used by unethical politicians, is an example of purposely attempting to get people to react to the word (the label or derogatory name) rather than to the person. One may vote against "Tricky Dick" without objective and logical consideration of his qualifications for office.

The means by which one can improve the quality of his intrapersonal communication in regard to this first principle (that the word is not the thing), as recommended by Korzybski, is to become *extensionally oriented* rather than intensionally (word) oriented. The extensionally oriented person relies on extensional knowledge as much as possible. Extensional knowledge includes statistics, factual descriptions, observations, and other data that can be called public knowledge since their validity can be checked by others. Intensional knowledge includes inferences, opinions, assumptions, judgments and generalizations. Such knowledge is made up of words about words. The extensionally oriented person does not rely on the words in an advertisement of the car he is interested in purchasing. "Cream puff," "slick," and "slightly used" are not the kind of data the extensionally oriented individual uses. He goes to look at the car, to listen to it, and to drive it, and he may have a mechanic check the car because he wants data that are factual, observable, and verifiable.

Principle No. 2: Meanings are in People, Not in Words—Words do not mean; people mean. Language, to be language, must have meaning, but meanings are not "out there"; meanings are not in words; meanings are in people. Even when words are not confused with things, there may be breakdowns in interpersonal communication because intrapersonally, meaning is assumed to be in the word. A sixteen year old that remarked to his grandfather that a certain television entertainer was *square* was left bewildered when his grandfather acknowledged that he, also, thought the entertainer was a person of honesty. The grandfather had one meaning for the word "square" (square shooter, square dealer, treat you square, i.e., honesty) and the grandson had another meaning (simple, old-fashioned, or outmoded). There is no natural or inherent meaning in any word, for a word is a symbol which has been arbitrarily assigned to stand for some object, person, or experience. Hayakawa says:

> Symbols and things symbolized are independent of each other; nevertheless, we all have a way of feeling as if, and sometimes acting as if, there were necessary connections. For example, there is the vague sense we all have that foreign languages are inherently absurd: foreigners have funny names for things, and why can't they call things by their right names? This feeling exhibits itself most strongly in those English and American tourists who seem to believe

that they can make the natives of any country understand English if they shout loud enough . . . they feel that the symbol is inherently connected in some way with the things symbolized.[7]

Not only are words arbitrarily assigned to objects and devoid of meaning until a user gives them meaning, but some words are often assigned to more than one object or situation. A single word, therefore, may stand for a variety of things. The 500 most-used words in the English language have at least fourteen thousand different definitions.[8] Hence, it should not be surprising that the meanings one person attaches to words are seldom identical to those attached to the same words by others. I ask my children, "Do you want a bottle of pop?" but my brother-in-law on the East Coast says, "How about a soda?" We are both referring to the same thing although soda to me has a different referent.

Because meanings are in *us* rather than in the word or message received, we project meaning into words. These projections are the consequences of each person's own experiences; each person, therefore, has his own unique personal meaning for any given word. Breakdowns in communication occur when we fail to realize that the *meaning intended* by the sender is not necessarily the projected meaning we give the word or message. Berman has given several examples of communication distorted because of projection.[9] He reports that The Lord's Prayer has had considerable abuse from children. One little boy was heard to pray, "Harold be thy name." The request of another was, "Give us this day our jelly bread." And a New York child petitioned, "Lead us not into Penn Station." There is little question but that projected meanings were imposed on these messages. Adults do the same thing. The story is told of an airline stewardess who looked over a passenger's shoulder as he was deeply engrossed in a book on the game of bridge and said as she moved away, "That must be a fascinating love story you are reading." Startled, the man looked at the chapter heading and noticed it was entitled, "Free Responses after the Original Pass."

In Quito, Ecuador, a young teacher substituted for a teacher friend who was taking a week's honeymoon. A month later at a party someone started to introduce the groom to her. "Oh," interrupted the groom, "I know Miss Rogers very well indeed. She substituted for my wife on our honeymoon."

---

7. S. I. Hayakawa, *Language in Thought and Action* (New York: Harcourt, Brace & Co., 1949), pp. 27–28.
8. Berman, *Understanding*, p. 14.
9. I am grateful for permission to use the examples given by Berman. They are taken from his book, *How To Lessen Misunderstandings* (San Diego, California: The International Communication Institute, 1969).

Not all examples of projection and of *assuming that a word means* are humorous. Some are serious and costly. To avoid miscommunication one must remember that meanings are in people, not in the words. It will help if we (1) are aware of the ambiguity of language, i.e., a word may stand for more than one thing, (2) are conscious that we learn meanings from our past experiences, and (3) are conscious of projecting our own meanings into what others say.

We can improve our use of words if we remember to be aware of the contexts which affect the meanings of words. Context can be a guide to the "intended meaning," and by observing the context we can check on the meaning we are assigning to the word. We need to become alert to words or phrases taken out of context. Skepticism, in regard to accepting words or phrases removed from their context, is a healthy characteristic of communicators.

We can also improve our behavior in regard to using language by developing a sensitivity to labeling, whether practiced by ourselves or others, and by developing the habit of not labeling and not assuming meanings automatically simply because they are attached to a given label.

PRINCIPLE NO. 3: AVOID SIGNAL RESPONSES TO SYMBOLS—A symbol is a perceivable stimulus which stands for or is used in reference to another object, person, or event which may or may not be perceivable. The relationships among symbols, signs, and signals was discussed in Chapter 2. Difficulty occurs in thinking when a person reacts to language symbols as though they were signals. If a person, upon hearing the word *airplane*, becomes airsick, he has reacted signally to a language symbol, the word airplane.

Signal responses, although they are not involuntary (e.g., reflex) responses, are quasi-automatic responses. The following example clearly illustrates the "automatic-ness" of signal responses.

> We enlisted men were at bat in a hotly-contested baseball game with our officers when a private hit what looked like a single to short right field. Instead of stopping at first, however, he foolishly started a wild dash for second. Realizing then, that he couldn't make it, he scrambled back toward first. Now he was being chased in a rundown between the lieutenant playing first and the colonel playing second. It looked like a sure out, but just as the lieutenant flipped the ball back to the colonel, the private snapped to attention saluting the colonel. Automatically, the colonel snapped the salute back and muffed the catch.[10]

It is important that a person learn to control his intrapersonal communication so that he avoids responding with signal reactions. Signal responses cause one to jump to erroneous conclusions that are not based

10. Cpl. Bill O'Brian in *True*, quoted in *Reader's Digest* (May 1958): 166.

upon observation of the facts. The method by which one avoids responding signally to symbols is to pause for a few crucial seconds to evaluate the situation. Of course, as stress and emotional states increase, it becomes more difficult to remain calm and to avoid responding signally. Man, however, can learn to control his behavior in stressful and emotional situations. Such control separates him from animals.

PRINCIPLE No. 4: IT IS IMPOSSIBLE TO KNOW EVERYTHING ABOUT ANYTHING—As previously noted, we do not "take in" all of the information available in the process of perception. Our interests, experiential history, psychological needs, physical capacities, and physical efficiencies operate to select and filter our information. The picture we get, then, is a partial one, and there is always some error in any perception or cognition. No matter how we describe the world, there will be some distortion.

One severe problem in intrapersonal communication is the failure to recognize that our picture of reality is partial. It is not *absolutely correct and complete*. Many people process information (decode and encode messages) from an allness frame of reference; they assume they "understand completely" and "know all about that." They are not aware that a multitude of factors can operate to obstruct and limit one's acquaintance with things—factors such as culture, language, education, interests, intellectual ability, and the knowledge one possesses. Not only do people assume that they know all there is to be known about an object, but they also assume that any other person knows the same thing about the object when, in fact, each person knows the object differently. The "assumption of certainty" causes one to overlook considering how messages he sends might be misunderstood, just as the same assumption prevents him from considering whether the messages he receives have the same meaning to the sender as they have to him, the receiver. When a person "automatically knows" what is meant, he does not question or verify his knowledge and understanding.

Marriage counselors agree that many arguments between otherwise happily married couples arise because certain words have contradictory meanings and each person believes his or her meaning is the *only meaning*. The picture of reality held by each is his own unique picture of reality—a *limited knowledge of that reality*—and each is unaware that he or she has only a partial picture of reality.

A study of what happens when the students and alumni of rival colleges watch a football game was made by Hastorf and Cantril. They describe how the opposing groups of people had different pictures of the reality. Princeton fans saw the Dartmouth players as playing dirty and the refereeing as unfair to Princeton, while Dartmouth fans saw an opposite picture. Hastorf and Cantril stated:

... the "thing" simply is *not* the same for different people whether the "thing" is a football game, a presidential candidate, Communism, or spinach. We do not simply "react to" a happening or to some impingement from the environment in a determined way (except in behavior that has become reflexive or habitual). We behave according to what we bring to the occasion, and what each of us brings to the occasion is more or less unique.[11]

All that we know is only a part of what is really there; and is, in fact, a distortion of the object or event. Even the scientist knows that he does not "know all" about an object. He does not see the world "as it really is." Condon has stated:

The scientist no more sees what is "really there" than does a mystic or poet or taxi driver. What the scientist does that most others do not is *to be aware of what he is doing*—at least to the best of his ability. Thus aware, he can tell others *how* he came to see what he saw and what they must do to see the world the same way. It is the rigor of the *method* of observation that distinguishes the tradition of science from other traditions that have made special claims for seeing the real world. The scientist is not blessed or superhuman; he is only careful. To this extent the study of semantics is an application of the scientist's attitude to our most common and important human behavior, speaking and thinking.[12]

Three devices to aid one in learning to apply the principle that not all about anything can be known are: (1) to me, (2) etc., and (3) quotation marks. A *to me* attitude acknowledges the understanding that others may have a different picture of reality. When we talk with others, we should speak more accurately by using self-qualifiers such as: it seems to me; in my opinion; the facts seem to indicate; apparently the evidence suggests; my impression is that. These are "to me" devices; they are useful in avoiding the assumption that the picture or understanding I have of reality is the same as that which the other person has of that reality.

Etc. helps one to understand that no matter how much he knows about an object something is left out because all cannot be known about anything. Similarly, mental quotation marks aid the communicator in knowing that most statements cannot be taken at face value. There is a chance for error and there are other possible meanings.

PRINCIPLE NO. 5: ALL THINGS CHANGE—Everything changes. This principle was discussed in Chapter 1 when the concept of process was explored. Our language, a product of centuries, and our vocabulary in

11. Albert H. Hastorf and Hadley Cantril, "They Saw a Game: A Case Study," *Journal of Abnormal and Social Psychology* 49 (January 1954): 133.
12. John C. Condon, Jr., *Semantics and Communication* (New York: The Macmillan Company, 1966), p. 23.

particular, tends to suggest a permanence about things when, in fact, the only thing that is permanent is change. Nothing is static. One can never step in the same river twice, for both he and the river have changed. A device suggested by general semanticists to help one avoid this danger is "dating." "Dating" shows that we are aware that everything in the world is constantly changing. The chair you are sitting on is changing, the friend you haven't seen for three years has changed, and you too are changing, as you can observe if you look at a picture of yourself taken a few years ago. America today is not America 1948; science today is not science ten years ago; and music today is not music 1940. By mentally dating things, we indicate that we are aware of the fact that old evaluations may be outdated and untrue now. If we assign to words understandings and meanings that are no longer true to reality, the conclusions we reach in intrapersonal communication may be erroneous and subsequent behavior may be harmful to ourselves and others.

When a person disregards changes in whatever he is judging (a person, group, situation, etc.) we say that he has frozen his evaluation. Frozen evaluations can be quite destructive. They are contradictory to the aging, growing, wearing out, eroding, learning, decaying, and regenerating processes that occur continuously.

Persons who have served a sentence in a penitentiary often discover that they are caught in "frozen evaluations" held by prospective employers, ex-friends, relatives, and others. Sometimes a student becomes the victim of a frozen evaluation held by a professor ever since the student did poorly in that professor's class two years earlier. Whenever non-change is assumed in reference to a person, to an organization, to a place, or to an event, erroneous, unproductive, and even harmful communication may result.

Our language reflects a static existence—one that strongly implies non-change and permanence—and so it is little wonder that we are enticed to overlook change. What one must do is to substitute the conscious premise of change for the unconscious premise of non-change; and when objects, persons, or places change, one's evaluation ought to change correspondingly.

PRINCIPLE NO. 6: AVOID RIGID, NON-PROCESS ORIENTATIONS—Problems are often created when we assume that things are either one extreme or the other, either black or white. One kind of rigid evaluation is the *one-valued orientation*, an over-generalized evaluation which we know as stereotyping.

Stereotypes admit to the possibility of only one category. Individual events, persons, or objects are grouped into a single class in which each has exactly the same characteristics as all the members of that class. "All blonds have more fun." "All redheads are quick-tempered." "All Mexicans are lazy." Persons who apply such evaluations indiscriminately, using such stereotypes, are guilty of using a one-valued orientation. They fail to recognize that a single label cannot accurately describe each individual member of the general class. People, objects and events vary; each is unique; each is constantly changing. Thinking improves as language is used in such a way as to avoid erroneous one-valued orientations.

A second type of rigid, non-process orientation is the either-or evaluation. Things are seen as either entirely one thing or entirely not that thing. Things are good or they are bad; they are black or they are white; they are wonderful or they are terrible. Rigid two-valued orientations leave no room for a middle ground. Persons who think from such an orientation cannot see that things may have some desirable characteristics and some undesirable characteristics, that some things have both good and bad elements, that some things are gray rather than black or white.

A student, upon receiving a mark on a single paper or test, sometimes reacts with a rigid, two-valued orientation. If the mark is lower than was expected, he may feel that he is a *total failure* in that class; or if the grade is high on that one paper, he may evaluate himself as *totally successful*. People often perceive themselves as *totally failing* or *totally succeeding* when, in fact, failure and success are seldom total. We fail and succeed a little each day.

There are events, of course, that seem to be either-or. Either one is alive or he is dead (although some prefer to think in terms of a "gray area" between the two); either there are sixteen students in the classroom or there are not; and either she is pregnant or she is not pregnant. Generally, however, we err in the direction of being too rigid in our orientation rather than being too flexible. Usually there are degrees of success and failure. Each paper, examination, or course of study is to some extent and in some ways successful and in other ways may be less successful.

We need to alert ourselves to words or phrases in the language we use that are too rigid in nature, whether they be one-valued or two-valued words or phrases. We need to learn to use language in our thinking that is conducive to a multi-valued orientation. We want to avoid using words such as *never, always, nobody, everybody, every, all* and *constantly*. What parent has not heard a son or daughter say, "But *everybody* is going," or "*Everybody* has one"; and what son or daughter hasn't heard a parent say, "You *always* stay out too late," or "You *never* turn off the lights." Rather than thinking with allness words and either-or words, we need to acquire the ability to think in terms of sometimes, occasionally, most, few, and *normally*.

A flexible orientation enabling one to avoid either-or and black or white classification is valuable not only in terms of making more accurate decisions, but also in fostering creativity, as indicated by available evidence. The most imaginative people are those who are not bound by a single classification for an object or situation. It has been theorized that children are often more creative than adults because, lacking a comprehensive vocabulary, they are freer to treat objects as objects, not as classifications.

Prejudice and stereotyped reactions to football players, blonds, women drivers, honor students, Democrats, Republicans, etc. are examples of the failure to avoid allness and either-or orientations. Football player 1 is not football player 2. Not all football players are dumb. Not all honor students are social introverts. Not all women drivers are naive drivers. Not all farmers are uneducated and simpletons. Each individual is unique, and to assign to any individual the stereotyped characteristics of a class is to run a great risk in reaching the decisions that determine one's behavior. Wendell Johnson indicated the importance of avoiding rigid orientations when he pointed out that healthy people are more comfortable with many classifications for acts and other people, whereas the disturbed person is happiest when he has only to choose between two possibilities.[13]

One of the devices, suggested by Korzybski, that may be used to avoid allness and either-or responses is *indexing*. Indexing (Negro 1 is not Negro 2, and white man 1 is not white man 2) relates similar things, but recognizes the uniqueness of each. With indexing in mind a communicator avoids two-valued and allness orientations.

The use of allness language tends to push one's thinking into set, rigid patterns. Using language in this way is dangerous because we live in a world in which things change constantly. When we fail to recognize the fact of change and fail to utilize the six principles related to using words, the quality of our intrapersonal and interpersonal communication deteriorates and we are led into trouble.

Not only do we fail to think effectively because of our misuse of language, but we also think poorly because we confuse facts, inferences, and judgments—types of outcomes or conclusions derived as a result of using language.

13. Wendell Johnson, *People in Quandaries* (New York: Harper & Brothers, 1946), pp. 294–335.

Fact-Inference-Judgment Confusion

As noted previously in this chapter, the principles that are followed in scientific study and those observed in effective thinking are similar. For example, in science we are interested in drawing inferences from observed data; but more than that, we are interested in *knowing* when we are making an observation and when we are drawing an inference, and under what conditions, and by what rules. We are interested in knowing what the probability is that the inference is valid. Science is based on observation, and from observations, inferences are drawn which are tested again and again. Similarly, we make observations and draw inferences in thinking as we communicate. We therefore need to acquire the ability to use the science-related principles of thinking if we are to improve our functioning as individuals in intrapersonal communication, as well as in interpersonal and public communication.

Consider the following statements:

1. The girl next to you is wearing a Mickey Mouse wrist watch.
2. The girl next to you is frightened.
3. The girl next to you is a dog.

All three of the statements begin with the same words, all use a common subject (girl), all have a common verb (is), and there are no significant grammatical, structural, or formal differences among the sentences. Yet each statement is different. The first is a statement of description, or fact; the second is an inference; the third statement is a value judgment.

Valid statements of fact or description are based on observation. We should be able to agree or disagree on the first statement by simply observing. The most accurate statements we can make are statements of description based on observation. Because of the limitations of any single individual, the more persons who can observe and agree on their observations, the more trust we can put into their common statements of description. Agreement alone, however, is not a sufficient criterion for believing a statement of fact; for agreement may be produced by pressures of habit, from authority, or from overt coercion. Another important criterion is that the persons must be capable of observing. Nevertheless, observation is the fundamental source of statements of fact or description, and such statements can be made only after observation—after one or more of the senses comes into direct contact with the non-verbal world. The non-verbal world that we see, feel, taste, etc., is the world of "facts."

The second sentence, "The girl next to you is frightened", is a statement of inference. Fear is not as easily observed as is a Mickey Mouse wrist watch; fear manifests itself in more ways than do wrist watches, and fear varies from person to person. Moreover, we conceptualize fear as an *internal state,* but a wrist watch is an *external phenomenon.* There are several observable (external or overt) actions and behaviors that might indicate to us that the girl is frightened or not frightened, but these observed actions are merely indicators. We have to interpret their meaning and their association with a particular internal state in this particular person. *We have to infer* that the girl is frightened. When we make a guess about the unknown on the basis of the known, we make a statement of inference. Statements of inference may be ranked according to their ability to be verified—some are immediately verifiable and some are unverifiable. You may infer that, because John's car is parked in front of his house, he is home. Such an inference might be verified by phoning and asking if he is home or by conducting a search through his house. You may also infer that driving an automobile gives John greater pleasure than does riding a cycle, but it may be difficult to verify that inference. Inferences may be true or they may be untrue. They may fall anywhere on a continuum covering a wide range of probability.

Most human thinking operates on the basis of statements of inference. This is true not only because anyone can create an inference at any time, but also because most of the time we do not have facts on which to base our thinking. This is both a beneficial and harmful capability of man, as we shall discover.

The third statement in the example used at the beginning of this section is a statement of judgment. Statements of judgment bring our values into consideration. To one person, the girl may be a dog, to another she may be a doll. Agreement proves very little in regard to statements of judgment except that there is agreement on values. Judgment statements have to do with goodness and badness, usefulness and uselessness, desirableness and undesirableness, and approval and disapproval. Judgment statements have a moral dimension and a preference or "taste" dimension. The important characteristic of statements of judgment, as we are using the term, is that they include value. They are *value judgments* rather than judgments as synonymous with inferences. Inferences do not indicate preferences; judgments do indicate preferences, and they are value oriented. A judgment is a personal evaluation of an object, event, or person, and it should be used with care.

Figure 4 provides a summary of the characteristics of the three types of statements.

At least two serious problems arise in thinking (and subsequently in interpersonal and public communication) that have to do with facts, inferences and judgments. One problem is that of "jumping to conclusions"—i.e., we make unwarranted inferences and judgments too quickly. We develop a habit of *operating only in terms of quick inferences and judgments*. Some persons find it difficult to restrain themselves from slipping away from observations and into inferences and judgments. Such persons seldom describe—they infer and judge. Probably one of the most difficult tasks for the student of communication is to learn to delay conclusion-reaching, to just "give the facts," to acquire the attitude and disposition necessary to observing and describing more and jumping to conclusions less. In the learning activities throughout this course (conferences, interviewing, group discussions, and persuasive speaking), you may observe this behavior operating to reduce the effectiveness of communication.

Facts	Statement of Fact	Inference	Judgment
World of Reality	1. Can be made only after observation.	1. Can be made any time—before after, during, or without observation.	1. Can be made any time.
Sensory	2. Does not go beyond what can be observed.	2. Goes beyond observation.	2. Goes beyond observation.
	3. Emphasizes denotative meaning.	3. Uses either denotative or conotative meaning.	3. Emphasizes conotative meaning.
	4. Intends to report.	4. Intends to interpret.	4. Intends to persuade or express an attitude.*
		5. May have low or high degree of probability.	5. May have low or high agreement.
			6. Utilizes values and preferences.

Figure 4   *Statements of fact also have in part a persuasive purpose. They direct attention, structure perception, and suggest a particular way of viewing physical reality. All language utterances have a persuasive dimension. No statement can be absolutely objective and nonpersuasive, but judgments *emphasize* the persuasive and attitudinal dimension.

Tests can be given to measure one's "inference proneness" or the degree to which one "jumps to erroneous conclusions." How can we stop jumping to conclusions? First, we can learn to recognize the difference between a statement of fact and one involving an inference or judgment. Further, as we learn to distinguish between these types of statements, we can, as senders of messages, develop an awareness of our own use of such statements. Further, as listeners we can practice recognizing these different types of statements when they are used by others. It is not possible, of course, for one to use only statements of observation and fact. We have to use inferences if we are to communicate, but it is possible *to be aware of what type of statement is being used,* and to know that each type of statement must be treated differently. One of the dangers created by confusing inferences, judgments, and facts is that all statements are acted upon as if they were facts. It is at this point that mis-communication and communication breakdowns occur. This is the second serious problem that arises in communication because of the inference-observation confusion.

Not only do we develop the habit of jumping to unwarranted conclusions (judgments and inferences), but we also act on those conclusions as though they were facts. Inferences and descriptions are on different orders of abstraction (see Figure 5). Inferences include guesses, opinions, estimations, and fiction, while descriptive statements are based on observations of the non-verbal world of reality.

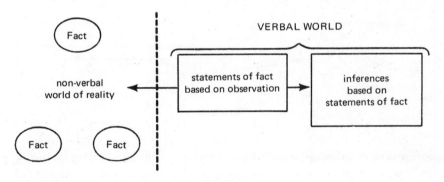

Figure 5

It takes relatively no time, energy, or thought to make inferences if one is willing to "leap to them"; but even when inferences are made with the utmost caution *they should be treated as tentative* and should be thought of in terms of probability rather than certainty. Descriptive statements, as we have already observed, are more certain, although there are errors in observing (as we learned in the discussion of perception) and in reporting. Yet, given enough capable observers, we can attain a relatively high probability of agreement. We create problems for ourselves, however, when we treat inferences and judgments with the same degree of certainty as that of the most agreed-on facts. We are too certain. And when, at a later time, results are different from what we predicted, we are frustrated and demoralized. Frustrations and defeats are invited when we treat inferences and judgments as though they were facts. The inference may be totally incorrect and judgments and values do vary. The judgment that we treat as fact may not be accepted by others as such. They may reject it as being untrue. While we cannot control all of the factors outside of us, we can exercise control over our own assumptions, and when we confuse inferences with facts, we too often act with an assumption of certainty. On the other hand, when we act on our inferences knowing they are inferences, we are able to operate with an assumption of probability rather than certainty. Our behavior becomes more scientific and, therefore, more intelligent. Figure 6 illustrates this second problem, i.e., operating on inferences as though they were facts.[14]

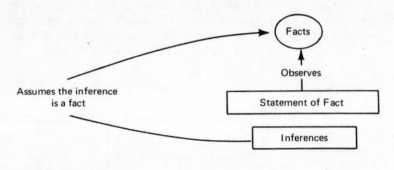

Figure 6

Inferences always contain an element of risk, but when we treat inferences as inferences we take a calculated risk, rather than an uncalculated risk (as is the case when we treat inferences as statements of fact), and we are in a better position to avoid the hazards, or at least to adjust to them should they occur. Haney gives an excellent example and explanation of the uncalculated risk-taking involved in treating inferences as facts.[15]

14. Sanford I. Berman, *Why Do We Jump to Conclusions?* (San Diego: International Communication Institute, 1965), p. 26. Reproduced by permission.
15. William V. Haney, *Communication: Patterns and Incidents* (Homewood, Ill.: Richard D. Irwin, Inc., 1960), p. 19. Reproduced by permission.

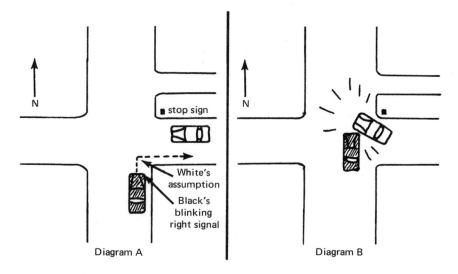

Figure 7

In Figure 7, Diagram A shows the driver of the white car stopped at a stop sign as the black car approaches the intersection from the south. White observes Black's right turn signal blinking and assumes Black is going to turn right at the intersection, and so White starts to cross the intersection. White is acting on the inference he has made *as if it were a fact.* Black does *not* turn, however, but continues straight through the intersection. A costly collision occurs (Diagram B). Black intended to turn right into a driveway a few feet *beyond* the intersection. White was held responsible for the personal injuries and property damage resulting from the accident.

White's behavior illustrates the *uncalculated* and *unknown* risks that are run when one acts on inferences as though they were facts true to the world of reality. White's crucial error occurred at the moment he treated the inference as if it were not an inference. It was at that moment that he took his uncalculated risk and, in doing so, failed to realize that he was in a situation involving a degree of uncertainty. He acted upon the situation out of an assumption of certainty rather than probability. (Haney has raised the question as to whether accident-prone drivers are unwittingly inference-prone persons.)[16]

Persons who experience either of the two problems related to facts, inferences, and judgments (jumping to conclusions or treating infer-

16. William V. Haney, "Are Accident-Prone Drivers Unconscious Inference-Prone?" *General Semantics Bulletin*, no. 20 (1957).

ences and judgments as facts) live in a world of uncalculated, unknown, and unnecessary risks. Although not all risks can be avoided, some can be, and many risks *can be known* and treated as such so that one can adapt to them more readily.

Life is basically lived on an inferential level, but we can learn to be aware that we are operating at an inferential level; we can learn to check and recheck our inferences against the facts, and we can attempt to use observation and description when it is possible to do so rather than jumping to conclusions.

The capacity to infer as accurately as possible is essential in the arts and sciences. Analysis, problem solving, criticism—all involve intelligent inferring. Our goal is not to avoid entirely making inferences; but, since we must make inferences, our goal is to be aware that we are making them and to calculate the risk or probability involved.

Thus far in this chapter we have been talking about problems in thinking and, more specifically, problems that arise from the misuse of language and from confusing facts, inferences, and judgments. Let us now focus, not on the problems or negative elements, but on the positive elements or principles involved in effective thinking. Moreover, we will now consider thinking from a wider, more general, viewpoint, and we shall consider factors other than the use of language and fact-inference-judgment confusions.

Guides to Effective Thinking

All purposive thinking is directed toward the solution of problems. For many of us the initial urge, when faced with a problem, is to dismiss the whole difficulty with some easy, impulsive solution. We like easy answers and we tend to substitute habitual responses for thinking whenever we can. But when problems persist in spite of our habitual responses and impulsive answers, we begin to apply purposive thinking.

Throughout the ages the wise man has been regarded as a special human being who gained his talent solely through a miraculous gift at birth. Teaching the rest of the people to think effectively was not considered, since the "thinking man was born, not made." Now, however, we have come to realize that clear thinking can be developed through proper instruction and experience. The ancient adage which limited wise decision-making and effective thinking to a talented few no longer applies.

CHARACTERISTICS OF EFFECTIVE THINKING—Before one can set out deliberately to improve his thinking he needs to know what behaviors are related to effective thinking. Problem-solving thinking, sometimes called critical thinking, has been the subject of much research and study. An abundance of evidence indicates that, since effective thinking is the product of many different skills or behaviors, the approach to improving thinking must be a multi-skills approach rather than a single formula. Critical thinking tests presumably based on the components involved in effective thinking contain sections labeled: inference, recognition of assumptions, deduction, interpretation, evaluation of strong and weak arguments;[17] and indication of attitudes, formulating the problem, analyzing the problem, evaluating evidence, and evaluating conclusions.[18] From these definitions and from the tests of critical thinking, we can identify the following components of effective thinking:

1. Classifying ability (seeing differences and likenesses)
2. Analyzing ability (breaking a problem into sub-problems and parts)
3. Inference-making ability (generalizing, inductive reasoning, interpreting data)
4. Ability to evaluate evidence
5. Ability to draw warranted conclusions
6. Using language accurately
7. Non-emotional attitude (control of emotions, curbing impulsiveness)
8. Scientific attitude (relies on probability rather than certainty and treats conclusions as tentative rather than absolute)
9. Attitude of flexibility (questions the traditional, looks at problems from new viewpoints, invents, and modifies)

In the previous sections of this chapter we considered the observation-inference-judgment confusion and the problem of using language effectively. Also, throughout this chapter and the preceding chapters, the role of attitude in communication has been emphasized. Now, we see that these skills are also related to critical thinking. We will not discuss items 6, 7, and 9 in the above list, therefore, asking instead that you recall the previous discussion of these factors. In the remainder of this chapter, we will consider the skills of classifying, analyzing, and evaluating evidence, and testing reasoning—skills that characterize the scientific attitude.

THE SCIENTIFIC ATTITUDE AND EFFECTIVE THINKING—In many science textbooks reference is made to a famous "science" incident which oc-

17. Goodwin Watson and Edward M. Glaser, *Watson-Glaser Critical Thinking Appraisal* (New York: Harcourt, Brace, & World, Inc., 1951).
18. Alma Johnson, "An Experimental Study in the Analysis and Measurement of Reflective Thinking," *Speech Monographs* 10 (1943): 83–96.

curred in Syracuse, Sicily, in the third century B.C., to one Archimedes, a mathematician. King Hiero of Syracuse had presented Archimedes with a problem that he was supposed to solve. It seems that the King had ordered a golden crown and it had been made and delivered to him, but he suspected that the goldsmith had cheated him by using some material less valuable than gold in the interior of the crown. Archimedes was ordered to prove that the crown was either solid gold or that it was not. It was this problem that Archimedes was contemplating as he stepped into his bath one day. Suddenly, when he noticed that his body caused some water to spill over, he realized that he had the solution to his problem: he would take the crown's weight in pure gold, put it in a tub full of water, and see whether the overflow was the same as that of the crown. Elated with the newly found solution to the problem, Archimedes leaped from the tub and ran home as he was, naked, shouting to the world: "Eureka! Eureka! I've found it! I've found it!"

This famous incident does illustrate some important characteristics of the scientific method, but in at least one way it is a contradiction of the scientific method. No scientist would feel so confident of an answer that he would shout to the world that he had "found it!" The attitude of science is opposite to Archimedes' attitude. The scientist is cautious in proclaiming answers. He tests his findings again and again and invites other scientists to replicate his study, to help him find the flaws or errors that will prove his hypothesis wrong. All findings are tentative to scientists as is indicated in Conant's definition of science as "an interconnected series of concepts and conceptual schemes that have developed as a result of experimentation and observation and are fruitful of further experimentation and observation."[19] Findings, then, are not absolute —they are the basis for further investigation. As in the case of science, effective thinking requires an attitude of tentativeness and probability rather than absoluteness. It is healthy skepticism or commitment to probability rather than certainty that causes the effective problem solver to evaluate evidence and to test conclusions rigorously. If one wants to improve his thinking, he should strive to develop the scientific attitude in processing information.

CLASSIFYING, ANALYZING, AND SYNTHESIZING—Other components of effective thinking are classifying, analyzing, and synthesizing. When problems persist, the effective thinker begins a process of analysis. He breaks the problem into parts and then deals with sub-difficulties. He defines the problem and identifies its several characteristics. As attention is focused on these fractional aspects, past experience with similar

19. James B. Conant, *Science and Common Sense* (New Haven: Yale University Press, 1951), p. 25.

problems becomes a source of suggestions for solutions. Invention also plays a role, so that from invention and past experiences solutions of these fractional or sub-problems are drawn together by a process of synthesis in which tentative answers to the original problem are constructed out of the solutions of its parts.

Two skills—comparing and inventing—are important to classifying, analyzing, and synthesizing. Comparison consists of seeking differences or similarities between two or more words, objects, or ideas, or between parts of a single object or idea. The search for differences is characteristic of analysis; the search for similarities leads to synthesis. Classification is a combination of both, for in classifying we put similar things together and keep dissimilar things apart. Invention consists of discovering a new element, word, object, idea, or relationship which will supplement a given situation. In invention we first analyze what we have, determine what we need, and then we make or find the new element which is needed to complete the synthesis.

Practice in classifying and the development of an awareness of the need to classify are important objectives for improving thinking. Experience in detecting differences and perceiving similarities improves thinking. It is not too late now for you, as a college student, to begin to sharpen your ability to classify—to see differences, similarities, and relationships. The development of such skills will improve your thinking ability. It is important, however, to remember that things classified are treated as *tentatively in that classification*.

EVALUATING EVIDENCE—Another component in effective thinking is the use and testing of evidence. Among the materials of evidence are facts and statistics, specific instances, and statements of authorities. Facts and statistics are based on observation. Statements of facts have to do with events, states, or descriptions accepted as true by the people with whom one is speaking. Statistics are facts in quantitative form. Specific instances include examples, illustrations, and descriptions. Finally, statements of authorities are used as evidence. The "knowledge explosion" of our times has made it impossible for each of us to have first-hand knowledge about all the issues or problems with which we are concerned. We have to rely on the research and knowledge of others —experts who are authorities in their respective fields.

The single point that must be emphasized in connection with evidence is that the effective thinker must acquire the habit of subjecting all these types of evidence to evaluation. Such behavior, when acquired as a part of one's processing of the messages he receives, can improve the quality of his thinking immeasurably.

The questions one asks when evaluating evidence include: (1) Is the person who is reporting a fact (making a statement of fact) competent to discover that fact? (2) Is the evidence first-hand, or is it second-third, or fourth-hand? (3) Does it appear that the speaker was in a position to have the evidence? Were the books and other sources of information available to and used by him? (4) Does the speaker seem to be free from attitudinal blind spots and biases? and (5) Is what he is labeling a fact really a statement of fact, or is it an inference?

Statements of authorities must be carefully evaluated, too. Authority should not be accepted uncritically. When the evidence is a quotation or statement of an authority, we should ask: (1) Is the authority *currently* an expert in the field involved? (2) Is he in a position to know the problem at hand? (3) Does he have a vested interest in any proposed solution? and (4) Does he have a reputation for being accurate and fair in his judgments? The critical thinker answers these questions as best he can before accepting the statements of authorities as evidence. Too many people fail to check authority. Too much of our knowledge is acquired by blind acceptance of conclusions reached by others. It would be foolish, of course, to refuse to accept all evidence that is not self-acquired, but we can develop the habit of subjecting authority-given answers to critical analysis. The danger (and usual state of affairs) is that we are more likely to be gullible than to be overcritical of authority.

EVALUATING REASONING—Suppose you say to your teacher, "All redheads have quick tempers," and your teacher replies, "You have known me only since I changed the color of my hair. Actually I'm a redhead." Such a remark may cause you to be quite embarrassed—it might cause you to blush, to stammer, to qualify your statement, to apologize, or to pass it off as a joke. Each of us has probably experienced a parallel situation. If so, why did we feel embarrassed? It was because our conclusion implied certain other inferences. In the hypothetical example above, when the teacher said, "I am a redhead," you had called her quick-tempered. It was a part of the stated conclusion. There are relationships between conclusions and supporting premises, and when we encode messages we must be careful that we really intend the implications contained in our statements. Similarly, when we decode messages we need to be aware of the logical implications in the message. In other words, we must check the validity of the reasoning. One important component of critical thinking is the ability to test reasoning—to evaluate the validity of conclusions. Reasoning is concerned with the connections and relationships between and among ideas. It is concerned with the movement from fact to fact, from fact to inference, from inference to inference, and from inference to judgments or conclusions.

Induction is a process characterizing one kind of connection or relationship. It means "to lead up to." Inductive reasoning requires the collection of data (specific examples or instances) which the person uses "to lead up to" an inference or generalization—a conclusion. *Deduction*, on the other hand, "leads down from" a generalization. In deductive reasoning a specific instance is shown to be a member of the "family" included in the generalization and, hence, has the same characteristics the "family members" have. For example, your teacher (in the hypothetical example) is quick-tempered because she is a redhead. Being a member of the family (all redheads), she has its characteristics of which one is quick-temperedness.

Deductive reasoning is sometimes studied in terms of the classical syllogism which has three parts:

Major Premise: All redheads are quick-tempered.

Minor Premise: Your teacher is really a redhead.

Conclusion: Your teacher is quick-tempered.

You will seldom hear a formal syllogism in either interpersonal communication or public speeches. They are found only in debate or logic textbooks. Rather, in interpersonal communication and in public communication, the syllogism usually appears in the form of the enthymeme—a telescoped or abbreviated syllogism such as, "Your teacher is quick-tempered because she is redheaded." One or more of the parts of the formal syllogism is missing, but it is possible to construct the syllogism that is implied in a particular enthymeme.

Although both induction and deduction are used in thinking, it is generally agreed that induction is the fundamental reasoning process. Even in deductive reasoning (the syllogism or enthymeme) the generalization, which provides the basis for the deduction, can be arrived at only through the process of inductive reasoning. Thus, the essential skill in reasoning is the ability to move from evidence to conclusion, or from a series of conclusions to a higher-order conclusion. Inductive reasoning, moving from the specific to a generalization or from several generalizations to a higher generalization linking them together, may occur in several patterns. In order to think more effectively, one must be aware of these patterns of inductive reasoning which include:

1. *Generalization.* As previously indicated, in reasoning by generalization one moves from specific items of information (evidence) to a logical conclusion (generalization). For example, if the cost of engagement rings has increased at the rate of 5 percent per year for the past ten years, there is reason to conclude that the cost of engagement rings next year will probably be 5 percent higher than they are this year. Again, if you know that a certain professor gave no A's last term, none in the term before, and none in any of the past twelve terms; and if your friend, who took the course from him

last semester, reported to you that the professor told the class that he had not given an A in all the years he had taught here, you could conclude that the probability is fairly high that this professor will give no A's this coming term.

2. *Comparison.* When one reasons by comparison, he brings two or more items in a class together to assess their similarities and differences. When differences are described, one is contrasting (contrasting is a type of comparison). If you wanted to buy a sports car, you probably would want to compare the models in which you were interested. You would make the contrast in terms of cost, speed, horsepower, design, etc. You would also be interested in knowing in what ways two models that are priced very differently are similar. If they are similar on those features important to you, but different in cost (one dealer will allow you $1200 on your old car and another will allow you $900 on your car), you may conclude that you will buy the one that permits you to save $300. In other words, when we reason by comparing, we are interested in similarities and in differences.

3. *Analogy.* In reasoning by analogy two items which are known to be alike in several details are assumed to be alike on the specific detail that is known about only one of the items. Through a process of induction in which the items are compared one against the other to determine that they are alike in all essential characteristics, one generalizes that the items are analogous. From that generalization one uses deductive reasoning to state that, since it is known that one of the two analogous items has characteristic A, the other item also has characteristic A. When one reasons by analogy he uses both inductive and deductive reasoning. As an example of reasoning by analogy, you may have heard someone say, "Since socialized medicine has worked well in Britain, it will work well in the United States."

One of the problems with analogies is that the two items may not be analogous. They may differ in many important ways so that they cannot be compared. If they are different in regard to several features that seem to be related to the feature under consideration, then the analogy has a low probability of being true; it is a false analogy because the two things cannot be compared. The effective thinker *checks analogies* rather than blindly accepting them. He questions the inductive process by which the conclusion (that the two items are exactly alike) was reached. Often the two items are more unalike than alike.

4.   *Causal Relations.* When one reasons from cause to effect or from effect to cause, the questions that one attempts to answer are why and what. Why has a certain thing occurred? What will be the result of this cause? If we do this, what will be the outcome? Some of the tests applied by the effective thinker, as a message sender or a message receiver, when he uses causal reasoning include the following: Is the cause too simple? (i.e., is *single* causation assumed?) Are there possible causes that are omitted or ignored? Are the alleged causes strong enough to produce the effects? Is the relationship or prediction consistent with past experience? Are there exceptions to this relationship? Is the relationship correlative rather than causal? Sometimes, things that are assumed to be related in a causative manner (one causing the other), are not related in that manner at all, but are related in a correlative manner (i.e., they are *always* present together or *never* present together, but both have a common causation source).

One of the serious weaknesses of cause-to-effect or effect-to-cause reasoning is the assumption of single causation. As previously emphasized in the earlier discussion of process, things are seldom related linearly. Rather, there are multiple factors and multiple relationships combining and interacting to produce a state characterized by dynamism.

Present in all of the patterns of inductive reasoning that we have discussed is the process of making inferences. Sometimes we make "hasty generalizations"—we jump to inferences and conclusions that are not warranted from the data. Sometimes our conclusions are too broad to be supported by the available evidence; there are too few instances to warrant the sweeping conclusion. In all these patterns of inductive reasoning, our thinking will be improved as we come to insist on evidence, to test the quality of the evidence, and to test the reasoning whereby conclusions are drawn.

Summary

This chapter was concerned with how we use language and how we think as we process information in intrapersonal communication. It is man's language-using ability that permits him to think, to reason, and to process information in a manner and at a level much higher qualitatively than that of other animals. Six principles for improving one's use of language have been identified: (1) words stand for things, but they are not those things; (2) meanings are in people, not in words; (3) avoid signal responses to symbols; (4) it is impossible to know everything about anything; (5) all things change; and (6) avoid rigid, non-process orientations. Problems related to statements of observation, inference, and judgment have been discussed, and the components of critical thinking (classifying, analyzing, inference-making, evaluating, drawing conclusions, and using language accurately) have been identified and problems related to each discussed. Suggestions and guidelines have been given that can be helpful to you in improving your thinking—in improving your intrapersonal communication.

For Further Reading

1. Berman, Sanford I. *Understanding and Being Understood*. San Diego, Calif.: The International Communication Institute, 1965.

2. Brown, Roger. *Words and Things: An Introduction to Language*. New York: Free Press, 1958.

3. Condon, John C., Jr. *Semantics and Communication*. New York: The Macmillan Company, 1966.

4. Duncan, Hugh Dalziel. *Symbols in Society*. Fair Lawn, N.J.: Oxford University Press, 1968.

5. Haney, William V. *Communication: Patterns and Incidents*. Homewood, Ill.: Richard D. Irwin, Inc., 1960.

6. Hayakawa, S. I. *Language in Thought and Action*. New York: Harcourt, Brace & Co., 1949.

7. Johnson, Wendell. *People in Quandaries*. New York: Harper & Brothers, 1946.

8. Korzybski, Lord Alfred. *Science and Sanity*. Lakeville, Conn.: The International Non-Aristotelian Library, 1947.

9. Lee, Irving, and Laura L. Lee. *Handling Barriers in Communication*. New York: Harper & Brothers, 1956.

10. Luria, A. R. *The Human Brain and Psychological Processes*. New York: Harper & Row, Publishers, 1966.

Chapter 4

Self-Concept
in Communication

Psychologists and educators are becoming increasingly aware that a person's idea of himself (self-concept) is intimately related to how he behaves. For example, if a student says, "I just can't give that speech! I just can't!" he is expressing something not only about his potential behavior, but also about his opinion of himself. All things being equal, chances are good that a student who feels this way about himself will not do well on his speech.

Research is teaching us that one's performance in a problem situation depends not only on how capable he actually is in relation to that problem but also on how capable he thinks he is. Indeed, classroom and clinical research evidence suggests that school or life success may depend less on those qualities a person has by way of genes or circumstances than on how he feels about those qualities.

No matter how we view the world, speech communication begins within the self. Skill in interpersonal communication, as well as in public communication, is closely associated with a useful and realistic perception of self. One's perception of self (self-concept) is the product of intrapersonal communication, according to Jung,[1] but the data one uses in intrapersonal communication to define his concept of himself is often data derived from interpersonal communication situations. The intrapersonal communication by which one constructs his self-concept may occur either simultaneously with or independently of interpersonal communication. The discussion of self-concept cannot be confined solely to either intrapersonal communication or to interpersonal communication. To adequately consider the role of self-concept in com-

1. Donald Washburn, "Intrapersonal Communication in a Jungian Perspective," *Journal of Communication* 14 (September 1964): 131–35.

munication, we must discuss important factors that cannot be confined to one level of communication or the other.

Self-Concept Defined

Each of us has certain beliefs about himself. Each person has a perception of his attractiveness or unattractiveness, of the sound of his voice, of his intellectual ability, of his ability to influence others, and so on. The collection of beliefs one has regarding his identity makes up his self-concept. Self-concept then, can be defined as *those physical, social, and psychological perceptions of ourselves that we have derived from experiences and our interaction with others*. Hall and Lindzey define self as "the awareness of one's being and functioning. In other words, it is the self-as-object, a set of experiences that have the same referent, namely the 'I' or the 'me.' "[2]

To understand ourselves, each of us must understand his own way of looking at the world; and, to understand others, we must, as best we can, understand how they see the world. Some perceptions we have of ourselves seem more satisfactory to us than others. All experiences do not have the same impact upon us, because some are accepted as consistent with our values and self-concepts, while others are seen as having no relationship to self and are therefore rejected and still others are rationalized to fit our needs and goals even though they may be inconsistent with our perceptions of ourselves. On the whole, a person's behavior provides clues to his self-concept.

Generally, we perceive experiences that do not fit our self-concepts, or that we cannot adjust to our self-concepts as personally dangerous, and we try to build defenses against them. Often, what is needed is not defenses, but a willingness to revise the self-concept to fit the actual experience. As we open up and become responsively aware of our sensory and physical experiences, we become more understanding and accepting of others. The acceptance of actual experiences and reactions into the self-concept will probably effect changes in previously held rigid value systems—thus we become more open to changing values and to changing concepts of ourselves. This is the *living recognition* of process in life.

How Self-Concept is Developed

How does self-concept develop? The young child is relatively neutral as to the kind of self-concept he develops, but as he begins to perceive

2. Calvin S. Hall and Gardner Lindzey, *Theories of Personality* (New York: John Wiley & Sons, 1957), p. 483.

the world around himself and comes to discover himself he starts to develop his self-concept. His discovery of the various parts of his body, the recognition of his own voice, and his viewing himself in a mirror are early beginnings of his awareness of personal properties and character-istics—of a concept of himself. Because one's concept of self tends to continue to develop in the direction in which it started, early childhood is a critical period in the development of self-concept. The child learns that words like cute, smart, good, bad, or dumb are attributed to him as a person, and gradually, he develops a picture of himself which he strives to maintain.

Self understanding is the basis of self-concept, but the primary means by which we acquire an understanding of ourselves is through our interactions with others and our subsequent perceptions and aware-nesses of how they see us—of how they react to us. Fritz Heider has pointed out that *other humans are the most significant agents of causal-ity for us*.[3] The first source of influence on self-concept that we will consider is *others*.

OTHERS—Self-concept develops within a social framework because we live in a social context. Personality characteristics such as shyness, extroversion, and introversion develop through social interaction. Simi-larly, our concept of self develops as a result of our incorporating how others feel about us, how others react to us, and what others expect of us. Throughout our lives *others* affect us—our success, security, happi-ness, and general well-being. So powerful is the influence of others on the development of one's self-concept, that some scholars maintain that *self-concept is the direct result of how significant others react to the individual*.[4]

The many others in our interpersonal communication situations and in public communication situations, through their reactions, tell us what we are like, whether we are good or bad, successful or unsuccess-ful, and liked or not liked. We use such data in "talking to ourselves" about who we are. Our deeds, ideas, words, and selves are constantly being evaluated by others through our interactions with them and, in turn, their evaluations influence the development of our self-concept.

REFERENCE GROUPS—A second source of information available to us

---

3. Fritz Heider, "Consciousness, the Perceptual World, and Communications with Oth-ers," in *Person Perception and Interpersonal Behavior*, ed. Renato Tagiuri and Luigi Petrullo (Stanford, California: Stanford University Press, 1958), pp. 27–31.

4. See: Harry Stack Sullivan, *The Interpersonal Theory of Psychiatry* (New York: W. W. Norton & Company, Inc., 1953); John J. Sherwood, "Self Identity and Referent Others," *Sociometry* 28 (1965): 66–81; and Carl Backman, Paul Secord, and Jerry Peirce, "Resist-ance to Change in the Self-Concept as a Function of Consensus Among Significant Oth-ers," in *Problems in Social Psychology*, ed. Carl Backman and Paul Secord (New York: McGraw-Hill Book Company, 1966), pp. 462–67.

for defining ourselves is reference groups. Reference groups are those groups in which we have membership or in which we want to have membership. Such groups approve certain values, attitudes, and behaviors and disapprove other values, attitudes and behaviors. If these groups are important to us (and by definition reference groups are important to us), then the way they evaluate us and react to us can be a powerful determiner of our self-concept. Research shows that how we evaluate ourselves is in part a function of how we are evaluated by reference groups.[5]   Ignoring one's presence, giving disapproving glances or approving nods, and direct statements are used to communicate the group's evaluation of and response to the individual's behavior. Such communication tells one "who he is" as perceived by the group.

VIEWING SELF AS AN OBJECT—A third source of information by which we develop our self-concept is that of viewing our "self" as an object of communication. We observe our phsycial behavior directly, and we relate this observed behavior to our internal psychological states, i.e., to our feelings, emotions, and attitudes. We come to associate certain aspects of our physical behavior with certain internal states. We develop a self-concept in part, then, based on our observation and interpretation of our own behavior.

ROLE-TAKING—A fourth phenomenon that relates to the development of one's self-concept is taking the roles of others.[6] Early in childhood, we learn to "role-play." We imitate the behavior of others, part of which is their behavior toward us. A baby's mother makes sounds to him, and he begins to imitate the sounds. His father smiles and makes facial movements, and these, too, are imitated. Through imitation the infant begins to act toward himself as others act toward him. This is the beginning of role-taking, and the beginning of the development of self-concept. Throughout childhood, as well as later in life, we engage in role-taking—often overtly in childhood, but covertly in adulthood. As children we imitate the behavior of others, and we are rewarded or punished for the "roles" we play. Thus, the child increasingly acts toward himself and sees himself in the same way that other people act toward and see him. By such a process he comes to understand what roles he can take. He begins to understand how others behave toward him, and he begins to put himself into other people's shoes and to look at himself in the same way as

5. See: Muzafer Sherif and Carolyn Sherif, *Reference Groups* (New York: Harper & Row, Publishers, 1964); and Alberta Siegel and Sidney Siegel. "Reference Groups, Membership Groups, and Attitude Change," in *Group Dynamics,* 2d ed., ed. Dorwin Cartwright and Alvin Zander (New York: Harper & Brothers, 1960), pp. 232–40.
6. The major source for this role-taking theory is George H. Mead, *Mind, Self, and Society* (Chicago: University of Chicago Press, 1934).

others look at him. So it is that he defines himself and develops his self-concept.

As adults, we role-play by hypothesizing the behavior of others. We infer their roles; we take their roles in our minds, rather than playing the roles physically, and, in so doing, we develop expectations about our own role and behavior. If we do a good job of role-taking, our predictions are validated. If we do a poor job, we are not rewarded and we are faced with problems of redefining our concept of self. In the latter situation, our set of expectations as to how we should behave are found to be inaccurate and unrewarding, and we must adjust our self-concept.

Through role-taking, self-assessment, interacting in reference groups, and interacting with others, each of us develops a concept of who he is. From the data secured from these sources we derive an understanding of our "self " and its relationship to the world. We are motivated to maintain, to enhance, and to strengthen the self.

The Many Selves

In order to better understand one's self, one should look at himself from several viewpoints. Each person has several dimensions to his existence, and there are several facets to any person's self-concept. In a manner of speaking we can say that there are many different selves.

There is the self as physical object. Each of us has a view of himself as a physical being. We see ourselves in the mirror; we feel the movement of ourselves as we walk; we see ourselves as attractive or unattractive, tall or short, well proportioned or ill proportioned. The perception I have of my physical self may differ from the perception of me physically that is held by others.

A second dimension of self is the dimension of ideas, feelings, and beliefs. Everyone has a perception of himself as a certain type of intellectual and emotional being.

Each of us also forms patterns of relationships with other people, and we develop a concept of the nature of these relationships. This is yet a third dimension of self. We view ourselves as being in certain locations in networks and at certain hierarchical levels. We have perceptions of ourselves in terms of how we get along with people and how we function in each group of which we are members. In the family we play one role and occupy a certain position; in the speech class our role may be different. This dimension of self—the self in relationship with others—is an important facet of one's self-concept.

Another viewpoint from which one may look at self-concept is in terms of private versus public self. In each of us there is the self that no one sees. Part of this self may be unknown even to the person himself, and part of one's private self, although known to the person himself, may be withheld and not disclosed to others. On the other hand, there is a public self—that self intentionally or unintentionally disclosed to others. All of these aspects of self—the public, the private, the known, and the unknown—are important selves one needs to understand if one is to discover himself and expand and improve his self-concept.

How Self-Concept Affects Communication

Communication is affected by self-concept in two ways: (1) in terms of self-fulfilling prophecy, and (2) in terms of selection of messages to be sent, or of messages to be selected and processed.

Each person behaves in a manner as consistent as possible with his self-concept: he acts like the sort of person he conceives himself to be. The student who has a concept of himself as a "failure-type student" can find plenty of excuses to avoid studying, reading, or participating in class discussion. Of course, at the end of the term he usually receives the low grade he predicted for himself. Similarly, the student who sees himself as a person nobody likes will usually find that he is not liked. He probably will not understand that it is his behaving in a manner consistent with his self-concept (his sour expression, his hostility, his refusal to be friendly or to participate) that invites rejection by others. It is quite important, therefore, whether one has a positive self-concept or a negative self-concept, since one tends to fulfull his prophecy, i.e., to be whatever he sees himself as being.

Negative self-concept (low self-esteem) is developed as the result of many negative experiences over a long period of time. Some of the characteristics or symptoms of negative self-concept are: (1) sensitivity to criticism, (2) over-responsiveness to praise, (3) hypercritical attitudes, (4) a feeling of "nobody likes me," and (5) a pessimistic attitude toward competition. On the other hand, the individual with a positive self-concept may be characterized as: (1) being confident of his ability to deal with problems, (2) feeling equal to other persons, (3) accepting praise without embarrassment, (4) admitting that he has a wide range of feelings, desires, and behaviors, some of which are socially approved and some of which are not, and (5) being able to improve himself, i.e., when he discovers an aspect of himself that he doesn't like, he sets out to change it.

It is unrealistic to attempt to classify each person as totally in one or the other category described above. As previously noted, there are many selves; furthermore, an individual may be in a middle-ground position rather than at one extreme or the other in regard to some of his selves. Nevertheless, it is a good objective to move away from those traits related to negative self-concept and toward those traits related to positive self-concept, because regardless of the *type* of concept one has of himself, the fact remains that self-concepts tend to be fulfilled.

One aspect of self-fulfilling prophecy is "living up to the label"— a concept closely related to our discussion of using language in Chapter 3. We have a tendency to live up to our labels whether given to us by others or selected by and for ourselves. Wendell Johnson, an expert scholar and researcher in the area of stuttering, has hypothesized that persons become stutterers only after they have been labeled "stutterers." Similarly, if you label yourself as "no good in music" or a "poor public speaker," you may prove this to be so. As Condon has stated: "Responding to such labels gives us direction, even if the direction is backwards; responding to such labels helps us decide what to do and what not to do, even if the choices are not the wisest."[7] For example, if you label yourself as unfriendly you will probably behave in a manner that is unfriendly. You will avoid opportunities to talk; you will refrain from smiling, and you will seek seclusion rather than the company of others.

One's expectation in regard to another person will often become a self-fulfilling prophecy for the other person. Such an expectation is communicated to the other person who then comes to define himself that way and to fulfill that expectation. Even when there is no verbal communication of that expectation, it is communicated. We know that nonverbal and unintentional communication between persons does take place, of course, and expectations are sometimes communicated indirectly. Rosenthal has discussed an interesting experiment in which elementary teachers were told that one group of children (the experimental group which was selected randomly from the classrooms) had scored exceptionally high on a test for "intellectual blooming." In reality, the children in the experimental group were no different from the control group in regard to their *real scores* on the test, but the *teachers believed they were different.*[8] The difference was in the minds of the teachers. The teachers *labeled the students as of high potential to bloom intellectually*, and apparently the students attached the label to themselves because, indeed, the experimental group fulfilled the prophecy. Other similar experiments, as reviewed by Rosenthal, have produced the same findings.[9] Labels are lived up to as self-fulfilling prophecies.

7. John C. Condon, Jr., *Semantics and Communication* (New York: The Macmillan Company, 1966), p. 60.
8. Robert Rosenthal, "Self-Fulfilling Prophecy," *Readings in Psychology Today* (Del Mar, California: CRM Books, 1967), pp. 466–71.
9. Ibid.

A second effect of self-concept on communication is that one tends to select messages to be sent or received that are consistent with his self-concept. One's self-concept influences the kinds of messages he creates and the treatment he gives them, just as his self-concept operates to select messages to which he will attend. Persons who watch only "soap opera" television shows probably have self-images different from those persons who watch only documentaries on television. Berlo has suggested that subscribers to *Harper's* may have self-images different from those of subscribers to *Reader's Digest* and that Republicans have different expectations about their behavior (self-concepts) than do Democrats.[10]   As sources and receivers, we use our self-concepts to direct our encoding, decoding, and responding to messages.

Improving Self-Concept

As noted in earlier chapters, there is a need to recognize change—especially true in terms of knowing one's self. One's self-concept is valuable to the extent that it is realistic, and it is realistic in terms of the environment in which it exists rather than in terms of an environment that has passed from existence. Frozen evaluations of one's environment or of one's self can cause one to develop an unrealistic picture of the world and his relation to it. It is true that some traits that we possess seem to remain reasonably consistent over a period of time, but it is equally true that many traits and aspects of one's self change. The evaluation of one's self as nonchanging can be harmful. Changes in our environment sometimes cause us to see a previously unseen aspect of self. Moving to a new city or going to a party where he is a stranger, one may notice qualities about himself he has never noticed before. We see portions of ourselves that the behavior of new "others" permits us to see. Through new interactions and new self-disclosures we know ourselves better.

If we are to improve our self-concepts, we must adapt to the environment as it changes, we must receive information from others so as to gain a greater understanding of self, and we must share ourselves with others. These three objectives are best met through an interpersonal process called self-disclosure. Since understanding ourselves is highly important to our speech communication, self-knowledge must be sought consciously and realistically through interpersonal self-disclosure.

10. David K. Berlo, "Interaction: The Goal of Interpersonal Communication," in *Dimensions in Communication,* ed. James H. Campbell and Hal W. Hepler (Belmont, California: Wadsworth Publishing Co., 1965), pp. 36–55.

THE PROCESS OF SELF-DISCLOSURE—Self-disclosure refers to an individual's explicitly communicating to one or more others some personal information he believes they would be unlikely to acquire unless he himself discloses it. This must be private personal information; i.e., of such a nature that it would not be disclosed to everyone who might inquire about it.

Self-disclosure is different from self-description which deals with information that is not personally private such as occupation, education, marital status, physical characteristics, and other information that is readily available to most people. Of course, self-information that is personally private for one person may not be personally private for another; self-information that one shares with most others may be a guarded secret to a specific other; and self-information that one person acknowledges may be vigorously denied or repressed by another.

Before one can disclose something about himself to others, he must know it about himself—he must become explicitly aware of that self-information. Self-disclosure does not occur without one's realization that he is disclosing.

We know more about others than just what they have made known to us through self-disclosure, and others' knowledge of us exceeds what we have self-disclosed. We know about each other those facts we can readily perceive. We know about each other through making assumptions from the information we have about each other, as well as from experiences with others who have the same or similar characteristics. Mutual acquaintances provide information to help us form our concept of the other person, who gets information from the same acquaintances to help him "know" us. Moreover, we view the words and behavior of the other person and make our own inferences about him—some true and some false. Indeed, we know more about some aspects of the other person than he knows about himself, and he may know some things about us that we do not know about ourselves. Many sources of information are used to form our concept of others and our self-concept. A useful framework for viewing self-concept and "other-concept," as well as for seeing how self-disclosure is useful, is the schema, known as the Johari Window.[11]

Area I, known to self and known to others, could be called the *public self*. Certainly self-description data are in this category. Area III, known to self but unknown to others, contains self-data that clearly have relevance for self-disclosure. By definition self-disclosure occurs when personally private (known only to self) data is explicitly made

11. J. Luft, *Group Process: An Introduction to Group Dynamics* (Palo Alto, California: National Press, 1963).

	Known to Self	Not Known to Self
Known to Others	I Free Area	II Blind Area
Not Known to Others	III Hidden Area	IV Unknown Area

Figure 8 The Johari Window

known to another. Information in area III is moved to area I in self-disclosure. Area II, unknown to self but known to others or another, could be involved in self-disclosure only if the self-data were made known by the other, or if—after an accidental slip—attention was called to this new data and the person realized it of himself and then acknowledged its disclosure to the other. Whether or not information in area II or area IV is self-disclosure information depends on the attitude and willingness of the person to receive self-data, to explore unknown self-material, and to acknowledge the information to others. The Johari Window illustrates not only the different selves, but it shows the various types of self-data that may be discovered and explicitly disclosed. One individual possesses as many Johari Windows are there are specific others who populate his life space at a given time. For example, one may disclose to his friend that he is making good grades through the use of an opportune short cut, but he is likely to conceal this fact from his teacher and his parents.

One's self-concept can be improved as the information contained in areas II, III, and IV of the Johari Window is diminished and moved into area I. Self-disclosure is a process that places data into area I from area III after it has moved from areas II and IV into area III. It is generally agreed that self-disclosure is valued positively and that it facilitates growth. Culbert, however, has pointed out that whether self-disclosure is beneficial or harmful depends on the state of the receiver and the relationship between the receiver and the discloser: "A more comprehensive position is that 'it depends'; for self-disclosure may also result in bad, negatively valued, growth-inhibiting outcomes."[12] Therefore, the role of the receiver must also be considered in this discussion of self-disclosure.

The receiver may be involved at one of four levels: (1) he may be a close friend who is *directly, closely, and empathically involved*— he may have asked a specific question which prompts the disclosure; (2) he

12. Samuel A. Culbert, *The Interpersonal Process of Self-Disclosure: It Takes Two to See One* (New York: Renaissance Editions, Inc., 1967), p. 6.

may be *less involved*, in that he is taking part in a conversation in which the need for the disclosure is limited to the fact that *the disclosure is relevant to that ongoing relationship or task*; (3) he may be rather uninvolved and *the self-disclosure represents a "getting-to-know-you" type*; and (4) he may be *quite uninvolved*, receiving a disclosure for which no solicitation has been made. The obligations the receiver feels upon receiving self-disclosed information may vary according to the level of involvement and the relationship that exists between the two persons. A "quite uninvolved" receiver may react with little concern, whereas an "empathically involved" receiver may feel obliged to help in supportive ways. With any self-disclosure there is some risk-taking. Risk-taking (opening one's self) demands trust in the receiver; it involves making an investment in the other person.

In some situations self-disclosure is engaged in quite conservatively. In the getting-acquainted process, for example, the person may begin with a strategy of minimal risks—the data disclosed initially may be of low intensity, relatively less important data than that disclosed later as a result of the establishment of acquaintanceship and trust. Rickers-Ovsiankina studied the relationship between self-disclosure and age differences; Jourard and Lasakow studied self-disclosure among strangers, acquaintances, and close friends.[13]   Both studies confirmed the hypothesis that the closer the relationship and age, the greater was the amount and intensity of self-disclosure. Bugental, Tannenbaum, and Bobele found that self-disclosure was also related to situational context, e.g., there was more self-disclosure to social acquaintances than to work associates.[14]

Institutionally, certain roles are defined as having relationships that are good or bad for self-disclosure. Clergymen, psychotherapists, counselors, and bartenders are examples of receivers who are expected to keep disclosures confidential and to make responses consistent with the best interests of the discloser. On the other hand, salesmen (especially used-car salesmen), it is said, are likely to treat self-disclosure in ways consistent with their own interests and objectives. Self-disclosure in the getting-to-know-you level, as well as in the levels characterized by more involvement, is facilitated by corresponding self-disclosures made by the receiver, for then the receiver and discloser enjoy a mutual exchange of roles. An understanding of this process is important to any communicator, for he needs to know his responsibilities as a receiver

13. See: Maria Rickers-Ovsiankina, "Social Accessibility in Three Age Groups," *Psychological Reporter* 2 (1956): 283–94; and S. M. Jourard and P. Lasakow, "Some Factors in Self-Disclosure," *Journal of Abnormal and Social Psychology* 56 (1958): 91–98.

14. Daphne E. Bugental, R. Tannenbaum, and H. K. Bobele, "Some Causes and Consequences in Self-Concealment" (Unpublished manuscript, University of California at Los Angeles, 1965).

of self-disclosure if he is to function in a helpful and cooperative way with others with whom he is involved. In addition, the receiver needs to understand the process of self-disclosure for the improvement of his own self-concept. Through such understanding, persons can interact to the mutual growth of both.

WHY SELF-DISCLOSE?—There are at least two important objectives of self-disclosure: (1) to acquire an improved relationship with the receiver of the self-disclosure, and (2) to fulfill a need of the discloser. Suppose a person is concerned about his ability to perform adequately (whether it is a task connected with a job or the task of doing well in a course as a student). If the person chooses to disclose this personally private information to a person at levels 1 or 2 in involvement, he does so because he wants a more helpful relationship to exist between himself and the receiver and because he seeks supportive help toward accomplishing the project or task. Without such self-disclosure and subsequently strengthened trust, he is forced to "go it alone." If one does not develop the ability to trust, to involve himself in risk-taking, to mutually share in self-disclosure with involved others, he will pass up situations where self-disclosure is in his own best interests.

There are many by-products of wholesome self-disclosure. Buber has written that the goals of greater self-experience derive from progressively intimate experiences one individual has with others.[15] In terms of this goal (self-experience and self-concept) the implications for self-disclosure are quite clear. Tillich emphasizes the necessity for the individual to have the courage to be his real-self in the presence of others.[16] Fromm has written of self-disclosure as the means whereby man may decrease his alienation from himself as well as from others, and of how societal forces have contributed to man's alienation by inhibiting the process of self-disclosure.[17] Rogers has written of man's need to accept his own self.[18] Self-disclosure serves that need. Jourard states that self-disclosure is important to better psychological adjustment.[19] Mowrer has formulated a theory of behavior pathology in

15. Martin Buber, *I and Thou* (New York: Charles Scribner's Sons, 1937).
16. Paul Tillich, *The Courage To Be* (New Haven: Yale University Press, 1952).
17. Erich Fromm, *The Sane Society* (New York: Rinehart and Co., 1955).
18. Carl R. Rogers, *Client-Centered Therapy*. (Boston: Houghton Mifflin Co., 1951).
19. S. M. Jourard, *The Transparent Self* (Princeton, N. J.: D. Van Nostrand Co., 1964), p.15.

which guilt from *not* self-disclosing is the underlying causal factor.[20] Insufficient self-disclosure is accompanied by insufficient reality testing and by a subsequent unrealistic and unuseful self-concept. Failure to disclose one's self to others impedes or prevents important opportunities for feedback. Moreover, Vosen concluded from his study that a self-perceived lack of self-disclosure results in reduced self-esteem.[21]

At the opposite ends of the self-disclosure continuum are *conceal-ers* and *revealers*. The concealer hides his feelings and responses. He keeps it all inside until he has mastered the interpersonal problem. The revealer, on the other hand, reacts immediately to a new situation by disclosing any and all self-information to any other person. The concealer runs the risk of insufficient external feedback, while the revealer runs the risk of overlabeling the elements present or of labeling them so early that their usefulness in the relationship is nullified. Too much or too little self-disclosure can be detrimental to reality testing. Keeping in mind the limitations imposed by the nature of the relationship that exists between persons, however, one should work toward self-disclosure so that he may come to know himself, accept himself, and grow into an improved self.

Summary

The disclosure of personal information is necessary to the establishment of strong, wholesome interpersonal relationships, and it is necessary for reality testing or for eliciting feedback that enables one to know himself. To know one's self is to develop a more realistic self-concept. It is also the means by which help and support are acquired so that one attains the objectives or the improved trait or behavior that makes him a more capable, more valued person—in other words, he has a more accurate picture of himself, he improves himself, and he has a better self-concept. With a healthier and more accurate self-concept, the individual can function more effectively in intrapersonal communication as well as in interpersonal and public communication situations.

20. O. H. Mowrer, *The New Group Theory* (Princeton, N. J.: D. Van Nostrand Co., 1964).
21. L. M. Vosen, "The Relationship Between Self-Disclosure and Self-Esteem" (Ph.D. diss., University of California at Los Angeles, 1966).

For Further Reading

1. Campbell, James H., and Hepler, Hal W., eds. *Dimensions in Communication.* Belmont, Calif.: Wadsworth Publishing Co. 1965.

2. Culbert, Samuel A. *The Interpersonal Process of Self-Disclosure: It Takes Two to See One.* New York: Renaissance Editions, Inc., 1967.

3. Jourard, S. M. *The Transparent Self.* Princeton, N.J.: D. Van Nostrand Co., 1964.

4. Laing, R. D. *The Politics of Experience.* New York: Random House, 1967.

5. Rogers, Carl R. *Client-Centered Therapy.* Boston: Houghton Mifflin Co., 1951.

6. Sullivan, Harry Stack. *The Interpersonal Theory of Psychiatry.* New York: W. W. Norton & Company, Inc., 1953.

7. Taguiri, Renato, and Petrullo, Luigi, eds. *Person Perception and Interpersonal Behavior.* Stanford, Calif.: Stanford University Press, 1958.

Part II

Interpersonal Communication

Chapter 5

Interpersonal
Communication Components

Part I of this book focused primarily on the communication behavior of the individual—how man collects, processes, remembers, and uses information. Communication, however, is *social* in nature, and when we study the individual's communication system we do so because of its inherent relationship to interpersonal and public communication. In this section, Part II, we focus on interpersonal communication. In Part I we were concerned with communication factors *within* the individual. Now we broaden our perspective to look at the needs, problems, and phenomena of two or more persons communicating with each other.

In past years speech was concerned only with learning to get up in front of an audience and deliver a one-way transmission of ideas. Today speech concerns include not only public speaking, but also interpersonal speech. The reason for this is that research has confirmed what we knew from experience—that all of us spend a high proportion of our speaking time in the more private, dialogical situation which we know as the interpersonal communication setting.

Interpersonal communication occurs when two or more persons are involved in an interaction that allows all participants to send overt verbal messages, i.e., a situation allowing each person to take an active part in speaking. Interviews, conversations, committee meetings, and group discussions are examples of interpersonal communication situations in that they are private, and dialogical in nature rather than monological. In public communication situations, as contrasted to interpersonal communication situations, there is an audience which is primarily a listening group and which does not perform in the same medium the speaker uses. The person sending the primary message is called the speaker because public communication situations are primarily monological. Although listeners in the public situation respond to the speaker, the symbols and behavior used in responding are different from those used in the private situation. Barnlund, in contrasting interpersonal communication with public communication, emphasizes the "private setting" versus the "public setting." He shares with Cooley, Sullivan, Simmel, and many others the conviction that the continuous, planned nature of discourse in public settings contrasts sharply with the episodic, impulsive, and fragmentary character of interpersonal interaction; and that the impersonality of public communication situations, the rigid control of channels, the calculated use of message cues, and the restrictions on communication roles create a highly structured social situation in which there is the expectation of unidirectional influence.[1]

In this section of the book we are concerned with those settings in which face-to-face dialogical communication occurs, and with some of the factors that appear to be extremely important in face-to-face communication. The problems discussed in Part I should be kept in mind as we move to another level of communication, that of interpersonal communication. In later chapters specific types of interpersonal communication situations—interviewing, social conversation, and problem-solving groups—will be discussed; but in this chapter we will investigate seven general factors that apply to *all* interpersonal communication situations and that are important in terms of influencing the outcomes of interpersonal communication.

Since communication is an extremely complex process, a limitless number of elements could be investigated and several different frameworks or viewpoints could be used to describe and explain interpersonal communication. The seven topics discussed in this chapter represent seven different ways of investigating interpersonal communication; hence, they are not absolutely independent topics—they overlap—yet each offers a somewhat unique contribution to our understanding of interpersonal communication.

Interpersonal Attraction

When we talk of interpersonal attraction we are referring to the attitudes that persons have toward each other, their liking or disliking of each other. The words like, dislike, love, and hate are among the most frequently used and easily understood words in the English language. Few persons need to ask what liking is; but a more important question is, "Why is it that one is attracted to a particular person?" Insightful

1. Dean C. Barnlund, *Interpersonal Communication: Survey and Studies* (Boston: Houghton Mifflin Co., 1968), p. 11.

observers and critics hundreds or thousands of years ago identified reasons which have been verified during the past few years by research.

It should be noted at the outset that not all of the determinants of one's liking of another person lie within the other person. Rather, some of the causes and correlates of interpersonal attraction lie within ourselves. Although the characteristics and behavior of another plays an important role in determining whether or not we find him attractive, researchers have found that liking often does lie in the eye of the beholder. Therefore, included in our consideration of interpersonal attraction are qualities of the attracted as well as qualities of the attractor.

One element that operates in interpersonal attraction is accidental happenings, either good or bad. Good happenings cause us to like the recipient of the happening, but bad happenings cause us to draw away from that person. Even when the thing that happens to another is beyond his control, it can affect our attitude toward him. There is evidence that we tend to like those who have succeeded (everybody likes a winner) and dislike those who have failed. One reason advanced to explain this phenomenon is that we want to believe that people get what they deserve, that people are responsible for their own fate, that the world is a predictable place. Walster's research reveals that persons who hear about an accident, for example, want to blame someone (preferably the victim) for the accident. Moreover, his research shows that the desire to hold the victim responsible increases proportionately with the severity of the consequences of the accident.[2] Lerner has conducted several experiments indicating that people convince themselves that chance occurrences to others are deserved.[3] So it is that persons who win, who are successful, and to whom good things happen are valued higher and admired more than persons who lose, who fail, and who have suffered unfortunate events.

A second factor in interpersonal attraction is that of unjust treatment of one by another and the effect produced by that unjust treatment. Tacitus enunciated this principle thousands of years ago when he stated: "It is a principle of human nature to hate those whom you have injured." Several recent experiments have demonstrated that persons who behave in a cruel or generous way toward another tend to change their attitude toward the recipient of their behavior so that it is consistent with their treatment of that person. The person who harms another tends to develop a dislike for the person he has harmed; and the person

2. E. Walster, "The Assignment of Responsibility for an Accident," *Journal of Personal Social Psychology* 3 (1966): 73–79.
3. M. J. Lerner, "Evaluation of Performance as a Function of Performer's Reward and Attractiveness," *Journal of Personal Social Psychology* 1 (1965): 355–60.

who does a favor for another tends to increase his liking for the other.[4]

Liking may also be produced by rewards provided by others. We like those who reward us and dislike those who punish us. Several researchers have suggested that interpersonal relationships always *cost* us something along with giving us something, and that liking is a function of comparing the cost to the reward (reward - cost = profit.)[5] If the relationship is profitable, or if mutually satisfying rewards are obtained, each from the other, interpersonal attraction is high.

Another factor related to interpersonal attraction is stress or anxiety. There is now considerable evidence indicating that when a person is under stress he desires the presence of other persons.[6] The evidence suggests that persons under stress prefer to be with those who are in the same situation as they are, or with whom they have had significant interaction previously. Persons often comfort and reassure each other. The mere presence of others appears to produce psychological and physiological responses helpful in reducing anxiety. Combat studies of bomber crews have shown that the presence of others does reduce anxiety created by severe battle stress.[7] Anxiety and stress motivate persons to seek and to be attracted to others.

Social isolation is a fifth element to be considered in interpersonal attraction. There is ample evidence that isolation alone creates a powerful desire for interpersonal contact and is a strong facilitator of interpersonal attraction. Man is a social creature, and social isolation for any prolonged period of time is a painful experience. As Schachter has pointed out, the autobiographical reports of criminals in solitary confinement in prison, of religious hermits, of prisoners of war, and of

4. See: K. E. Davis and E. E. Jones, "Changes in Interpersonal Perception as a Means of Reducing Cognitive Dissonance," *Journal of Abnormal Social Psychology* 61 (1960): 402–10; J. Davidson, "Cognitive Familiarity and Dissonance Reduction," in *Conflict, Decision, and Dissonance,* ed. Leon Festinger (Stanford, Calif.: Stanford University Press, 1968), pp. 45–60; D. C. Glass, "Changes in Liking as a Means of Reducing Cognitive Discrepancies Between Self-Esteem and Aggressiveness," *Journal of Personality* 32 (1964): 531–49; and T. C. Brock and A. H. Buss, "Effects of Justification for Aggression in Communication with the Victim on Post-Aggressiveness Dissonance," *Journal of Abnormal Social Psychology* 68 (1964): 403–12.

5. See: G. C. Homans, *Social Behavior: Its Elementary Forms* (New York: Harcourt, Brace, & World, 1961), p. 150; and J. W. Thibaut and H. H. Kelly, *The Social Psychology of Groups* (New York: Wiley & Sons, 1959), pp. 81–82.

6. See: S. Schachter, *The Psychology of Affiliation* (Stanford, Calif.: Stanford University Press, 1959); H. B. Gerard and J. M. Rabbie, "Fear and Social Comparisons," *Journal of Abnormal Social Psychology* 62 (1961): 586–92; I. Sarnoff and P. G. Zimbardo, "Anxiety, Fear, and Social Affiliation," *Journal of Abnormal Social Psychology* 62 (1961): 356–63; P. G. Zimbardo and R. Formica, "Emotional Comparison and Self-Esteem as Determinants of Affiliation," *Journal of Personality* 31 (1963): 141–62; and J. M. Darley and E. Aronson, "Self-Evaluation vs. Direct Anxiety Reduction as Determinants of the Fear-Affiliation Relationship," *Journal of Experimental Social Psychology Supplement* 1 (1966): 66–79.

7. D. G. Mandlebaum, *Soldier Groups and Negro Soldiers* (Berkeley: University of California Press, 1952), pp. 45–48.

castaways clearly reveal that isolation is devastating.[8] One of the rewards another person can provide to the lonely or isolated person is the sheer physical presence of a fellow human being.

6 Propinquity (proximity or distance between persons) has been shown to influence one's choice of friends. Simply stated, the finding is that, other things being equal, the closer two individuals are geographically to one another, the more likely it is that they will be attracted to each other. Studies supporting this finding are numerous and consistent. They have shown that proximity is directly related to friendship formation, to mate selection, and to a decrease in prejudice. It has been found that increased contact between white persons and Negroes results in a reduction of prejudice whether the contact is on the job,[9] in an integrated housing project,[10] in a university classroom,[11] or with policemen.[12] Clearly, propinquity is a factor in interpersonal attraction.

7 Another factor in liking and interpersonal attraction is similarity of personality. One hypothesis, supported by the findings of several studies, is that friends perceive each other as being more similar in personality than do non-friends.[13] Do persons who are attracted to each other actually possess similar personality characteristics? Research findings tend to support the folk-saying, "Birds of a feather flock together." Reader and English gave a battery of personality tests to friends and non-friends and found a significantly higher positive correlation between friends' personalities than between non-friends' personalities.[14] The finding of personality congruence should not be surprising inasmuch as it is consistent with other findings relative to the similarity of friends, i.e., that friends are similar on dimensions such as attitudes, socioeconomic class, religion, values, and beliefs. Whether friends *become* similar as a result of their associating together or become

8. Schachter, *Psychology of Affiliation*, p. 6.

9. E. B. Palmore, "The Introduction of Negroes into White Departments," *Human Origins* 14 (1955): 27–28.

10. M. Deutsch and M. E. Collins, "The Effect of Public Policy in Housing Projects Upon Interracial Attitudes," in *Readings in Social Psychology*, 3d ed., ed. Eleanor Mouoby, T. M. Newcomb, and E. L. Hartley (New York: Holt, Rinehart, and Winston, 1958), pp. 612–23.

11. J. H. Mann, "The Effect of Interracial Contact on Sociometric Choices and Perceptions," *Journal of Social Psychology* 50 (1959): 143–52.

12. William D. Brooks and Gustav W. Friedrich, "Police Image: An Exploratory Study," *Journal of Communication,* 20 (1970): 370–74.

13. See: E. G. Beier, A. M. Rossi, and R. L. Garfield, "Similarity plus Dissimilarity of Personality: Basis for Friendship," *Psychology Report* 8 (1961): 3–8; and J. A. Broxton, "A Test of Interpersonal Attraction Predictions Derived from Balance Theory," *Journal of Abnormal Social Psychology* 63 (1963): 394–97.

14. N. Reader and H. B. English, "Personality Factors in Adolescent Female Friendships," *Journal of Consulting Psychology* 11 (1947): 212–20.

friends because they are similar is not clearly known. Research findings on this question are contradictory.

⟨ A final element to be considered in interpersonal attraction is similarity of attitudes and beliefs. As is the situation with similarity of personality and attraction, so it is with similarity of attitudes and attraction, i.e., we do not know whether persons are attracted to each other because they have similar attitudes and beliefs; or whether, through their attraction and association, they come to have similar attitudes and beliefs. Perhaps it is some of both. We do know, however, that there is a tendency to make attitudes or orientations toward objects and ideas congruent with attitudes toward the other person in interpersonal communication. One of the best explanations of this phenomenon has been given by Heider.[15] His P-O-X balance theory explains how orientations held by each person toward the other are related in a balanced way to the orientations each holds toward the object of communication. In the model pictured (Fig. 9) "P" is the person perceiving, "O" is the other person, and "X" is the object of communication. If "+" indicates a positive attitude or evaluation toward the object of communication or a liking for the other person, and "-" indicates a negative attitude or evaluation toward the object of communication or a dislike of the other person, then "balanced situations" can be illustrated as follows:

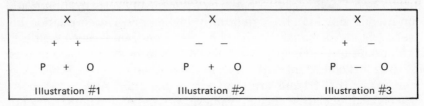

Figure 9

If the relationship between one person (P) and the other person (O) is positive (+) and P has a positive attitude (+) toward the object of social reality (X), then the other person will probably have a positive attitude toward the object of social reality, too (Illus. #1); or, if the persons have a positive relationship and one of them has a negative attitude toward the object, then the other one will probably also have a negative attitude toward the object (Illus. #2); and, if the relationship between P and O is negative and P has a positive evaluation of X, then P assumes that O has a negative evaluation of X (Illus. #3). The theory suggests that there is a tendency for people who like each other to share likes and dislikes and for people who dislike each other to disagree in likes and dislikes. Heider's balance theory not only recognizes that attitudes

15. Fritz Heider, *The Psychology of Interpersonal Relations* (New York: John Wiley & Sons, 1958).

between people as well as their attitudes toward common objects of
social reality are important factors in interpersonal communication, but
that the two factors are interrelated. Being aware of this relationship
may help one to better understand the behavior of other persons as well
as one's own behavior in certain communication situations.

We have discussed briefly eight factors that affect interpersonal
attraction, and we have found interpersonal attraction to exert a powerful influence on interpersonal communication. When there are strong,
positive relationships between persons, a high probability exists that
communication will be successful; but when there is a strong dislike
between persons, communication will be severly handicapped.

Role as a Factor in Interpersonal Communication

Communication creates norms, rules, and roles which in turn affect
subsequent communication. In the chapter on dyadic communication,
we shall see there are roles in the interview that impose certain expectations; however any human communication situation includes roles
and expectations if the participants are to send the messages required
of them and if they are to correctly interpret the messages of others.
One always speaks or listens from a particular position within a social
system—buyer, seller, father, son, employer, employee, male, female,
friend, stranger, husband, etc. To know what the other person's role is
—in what capacity he speaks—is to enhance the possibility for understanding his communication. Because two persons understand the role
each is playing does *not* mean that they will agree and that the communication will be successful, but it does mean that they are more likely
to interact with a minimum of confusion. If they do not understand the
role each is playing, however, they are not only likely to disagree about
the idea, but are apt to experience a frustrating and painful relationship.

A person may occupy several different roles and have an assort-
ment of behavior patterns associated with each role. There are certain
role expectations associated with being male and other role expectations associated with being female. With one person you are in a subordinate role, with another you are in a superior role, and with yet a third
you enjoy a close, coequal position. In one situation you are a jokester,
and in another a serious participant. Not only does each of us play
different roles as we are in different interpersonal situations, but our
role in any given situation may be temporary, changing over time as
others and the roles they play are constantly influencing the demands
and duties of the roles we possess. Each role requires the execution of
complimentary functions. There is no teacher role without students, no
buyers without sellers, no interviewer without a respondent.

When one is unacquainted with his role he may be anxious and unsure of what is expected of him, or if the role requirements or prohibitions are too demanding and rigid for the person, he may find the role difficult and uncomfortable. Some persons try to get by in life with a few unchanging, rigid roles. Other persons err in the other direction, i.e., they try to manipulate themselves to fit any and all of the thousands of expectations others have for them. Other persons follow a wiser course. They decide to choose their roles with care and to perform them as creatively and productively as possible. In any event, if one wants to improve his interpersonal communication behavior, he would do well to understand that roles are important "influencers" of communication. Some theorists have suggested (and research is tending to verify the hypotheses) that indifference to social roles, inaccurate perception of role cues, deficiency in role insight, stereotyping of others, and role rigidity are sources of interpersonal communication failures, of the socially inadequate. They are also characteristics of the mentally ill and the criminal. For example, when a person tries to behave uniformly in all situations disregarding the different responsibilities required by each situation, he is doomed to communication failure.

Interpersonal Bargaining and Goal Relationships

In any continuing interpersonal situation, each of the parties seeks rewards from the relationship. There are numerous types of rewards and we usually seek different rewards from different persons. We may want financial support from Dad but intellectual stimulation from a teacher, admiration and friendship from the girl seated in the next row but praise and recognition from a superior. Each person in communication has his own goals or anticipated rewards. Sometimes the goals of the two persons are interdependent but congruent, i.e., neither person can achieve his goal unless the other person also achieves his goal. Such a goal situation fosters cooperative behavior. On the other hand, the goals are sometimes interdependent, but *not* congruent, i.e., both persons are involved in the attainment of the same goal, but *only one of them can achieve that goal.* If one wins, the other must lose. To maximize one's own gain is to minimize the other person's gain. Such a goal situation fosters competitive behavior.

Brooks conducted a study in which several pairs of persons were asked to solve problems by communicating under different goal relationships.[16] Each member of the pair had three sets of cards: one set

16. William D. Brooks, "An Investigation of Three Goal Relationships Upon Communication Efficiency, Amount of Communication, and Honesty in Communication" (Unpublished Manuscript, University of Kansas, 1967).

possessed true information, another possessed false information, and the third set possessed true but irrelevant information. The sender knew which cards possessed what kind of information and he could exchange any card from any of the three sets for a card possessed by the other member of the pair. One goal relationship established for the pair was competitive in that one person could win only if the other person lost, a second goal relationship was congruent in that the two persons could win only if both cooperated and aided one other, and the third goal relationship was one of independent goals; i.e., either individual could win or lose regardless of the cooperativeness or participation of the other. Forty-five pairs of individuals participated in the experiment with each pair participating under each of the three-goal situations with the order of the goal situations being randomized. The results indicated that when the goals were congruent, cooperative behavior did follow. The efficiency of problem solving was higher in the congruent goal situations (mean time = 3 minutes and 10 seconds) than in the competitive goal situation (mean time = 12 minutes and 4 seconds) or in the independent goal situation (mean time = 6 minutes and 32 seconds). The amount of communication (number of cards exchanged) was highest in the congruent goal situation (mean = 18.2 exchanges). The mean number of exchanges in the competitive goal situation was 12.3, and in the independent goal situation the mean number of exchanges was 6.8. The third dependent variable was honesty in the communication. The participants could send false information, true but irrelevant information, or true relevant information. In the cooperative goal situation no false information was sent; in the independent goal situation, virtually no false information was sent (.02 percent of total messages sent); in the competitive goal situation, however, 68 percent of the messages sent were either knowingly false or knowingly irrelevant to the problem the receiver was trying to solve. Some persons who would not send false information did send irrelevant information, but most persons in the competitive situation sent a great amount of false information. Honesty in communication seemed to be more clearly related to goal relationships than to an absolute standard. The study indicates that goal relationships are related to honesty in communication, to amount and efficiency of communication. One must keep in mind that this experiment was a contrived game situation and any generalizing to the "real" world should be done with caution. The findings are in agreement with other studies, however, and do confirm the theoretical explanations of interpersonal bargaining behavior. In many interpersonal communication situations such as the problem solving group, the employment interview, and the committee meeting, the goal relationship is an important factor to consider; and attention to it can be quite valuable in understanding and improving the communication situation.

Of course, most interpersonal bargaining is complex rather than simple, involving several goals or anticipated rewards rather than just one for each communicator. Nevertheless, it is clear from numerous research studies that goal relationships are related to cooperative and competitive strategies; and it is also quite clear that cooperation vs. competition is a powerful element in determining the nature of interpersonal communication.

Defensive and Supportive Communication

Defensive communication is that behavior which occurs when a person perceives threat in a communication situation. The person who feels that he must defend himself devotes a high proportion of his time and energy not to the topic that is being discussed, but to how he appears to others, how he may be seen more favorably, how he may win, dominate, or impress, and how he may escape punishment or an anticipated attack. Gibb states:

Such inner feelings and outward acts tend to create similarly defensive postures in others; and, if unchecked, the ensuing circular response becomes increasingly destructive. Defensive behavior, in short, engenders defensive listening, and this in turn produces postural, facial, and verbal cues which raise the defense level of the original communicator.[17]

A defensive listener is apt to provide unclear and inconsistent feedback to the sender, thus making it difficult—and at times very nearly impossible—for the sender to evaluate the efficiency of his communication and to make the necessary adjustments to improve it. Also, the defensive listener tends to distort what he receives so that his feedback, although it is clear, is not based on accurate information. As the person becomes more defensive, he becomes less able to perceive accurately the motives and emotions of the sender as well as the cognitive meanings of the message. Gibb, after several years of research with hundreds of persons, found from his analysis of tape-recorded communications that increases in defensive communication were correlated positively with losses in efficiency in communication.[18]

As defensive communication tends to create a negative spiral en-

17. Jack R. Gibb, "Defensive Communication," *The Journal of Communication* 11 (September 1961): 141–48.
18. Jack R. Gibb, "Defense Level and Influence Potential in Small Groups," in *Leadership and Interpersonal Behavior,* ed. L. Petrullo and B. M. Bass (New York: Holt, Rinehart & Winston, Inc., 1961), pp. 66–81.

gendering greater defensive communication from the other person, *supportive communication* tends to create a positive spiral engendering greater trust and openness. Supportive behavior tends to create a climate in which tension and defensiveness are reduced—characterized by less distortion of the messages received and more concentration upon their content and cognitive meanings.

Gibb has identified six pairs of defensive and supportive categories of behavior from his research:[19]

Defensive Communication	Supportive Communication
1. Evaluation	1. Description
2. Control	2. Problem orientation
3. Strategy	3. Spontaniety
4. Neutrality	4. Empathy
5. Superiority	5. Equality
6. Certainty	6. Provisionalism

Figure 10

Defensive communication is characterized by messages which are evaluative. Whether by tone of voice, manner of speech, or the verbal content of the message, the speaker is engaged in pronouncing judgment. The effect of strong evaluation is that the listener may become defensive too, creating a climate of mistrust and suspicion. Moreover, the person who acquires the habit of sending "defensive" messages tends to regard almost any statement he receives as being evaluative in its intent. Even questions directed to the defensive person may be interpreted by him as full of accusations. With little effort the extraordinarily defensive person perceives virtually all speech as evaluative, judgmental, good or bad, and moral or immoral. On the other hand, messages which are descriptive tend to allay defensiveness, and foster a climate of trust. Listeners who are neither threatened nor defensive perceive requests for information as just that—requests for data—and not as questions with built-in accusations, or questions motivated by animosity. If, as senders of messages, we utilize description (statements of observation as discussed in a previous chapter) whenever possible rather than falling into the habit of using an evaluative or judgmental frame of reference for all our messages, we can foster a supportive climate rather than a threatening one for others.

Control, in the defensive communication column in Figure 10, refers to the attempt of one person to change the receiver's attitude,

19. Ibid.

to influence his behavior, or in some way to control the receiver. If a receiver believes the sender is attempting to do these things, he may become defensive and "on guard." There is some indication that a *perceived* "hidden attempt" produces defensiveness even more than does the open attempt to control. Implicit in all attempts to alter some aspect of another person is the assumption by the change agent that the person to be altered is inadequate.

The opposite of control behavior is problem oriented behavior. It focuses on the problem rather than on the person receiving the message. It focuses on the desire for cooperation from all the persons in the communication situation to define the problem, to discover its characteristics and causes, and to find and test solutions. Communication that is problem oriented tends to create the same orientation in the listener; permissiveness and supportiveness seem to emerge. If the sender is perceived as having a predetermined solution, method, or attitude, however, a receiver may regard the process as a hidden control effort and become defensive.

Strategy and spontaneity, the third pair of behaviors in Figure 10, refer to planned behavior versus "real" or genuine behavior. Any behavior that the receiver perceives as pre-planned in the sense of being a strategy may cause him to become defensive. Strategy is closely related to control behavior. Although the initiator of the strategy does not control the receiver, his ability to predict the receiver's behavior may be resented and may elicit defensiveness. On the other hand, behavior that is perceived as *genuine, real, spontaneous,* and *free of deception* tends to reduce defensiveness and creates a climate of trust.

The fourth pair of categories of behavior—neutrality and empathy —refers to communication without warmth or feeling as contrasted to communication that conveys warmth and empathy. Communication (verbal or nonverbal) that is empathic rather than coldly detached in an "uncaring" way tends to be strongly supportive.

The fifth pair of behaviors is superiority and equality. Gibb has found that when a person communicates superiority (power, wealth, physical characteristics, or intellectual ability) to another person, he arouses defensiveness. On the other hand, when a person communicates that he accepts the receiver as an equal, trust is created. If differences in ability, appearance, status, or power do exist but are unimportant, and if the fact that they are not important is communicated, then a supportive, wholesome climate is encouraged.

The last pair of behavior categories is certainty and provisionalism. Certainty is dogmatism. The dogmatic person produces defensiveness in others. Those who know the answers, who require no additional data, who know the exact procedure to be used—those persons arouse defensiveness in receivers. Conversely, the person who sees his "view of the world" as tentative and subject to error, who communicates that he is investigating rather than taking sides, and who appears genuinely willing to explore—that person diminishes defensiveness because others believe they can share in the quest.

Defensiveness is a serious handicap to interpersonal communication. Defensiveness in the sender means that ideas may not be conveyed clearly, feedback will be distorted, and the receiver will tend to become defensive, too. Defensiveness in the receiver will cause him to distort incoming information and to send multiple and contradictory feedback cues. An important goal in interpersonal communication, then, is that of creating a supportive climate. Supportive behavior, like defensive behavior, can be contagious—it can encourage that same kind of behavior from the receiver.

Hostility

Out of competitiveness engendered by goal relationships and from mistrust engendered by defensive communication comes hostility. When we become aware of hostility in another person, hostility directed toward us, most of us respond in kind or at least with a potential for hostility. Further, the blocking of any goal-directed behavior may arouse hostile and aggressive tendencies which are reflected in interpersonal communication. Statements indicating a wish or intention to commit a destructive act, statements attributing undesirable qualities or unfavorable characteristics to another person, and statements denying another person desirable qualities or favorable characteristics are examples of direct hostile communication. Indirect hostile and aggressive communication includes statements of strong disagreement and negative modeling. Hostile communication toward self includes statements that disparage self, condemn self, or inculpate self.

One of the major difficulties in handling hostility in interpersonal communication lies in providing opportunities for the release of that hostility. Unless some provision is made for their release, hostile feelings tend to be perpetuated so that the ultimate result is a total breakdown in communication. The problem is that as hostility increases, the tendency to withdraw or leave the scene also increases; thus, the means or opportunity for altering the attitude and reducing hostility is lost. Withdrawal is also accomplished by a cessation of talking and listening.

If the participants do not withdraw from the communication situation, some adjustive techniques for reducing hostility may be available to them. In the days of early man, hostile and aggressive feelings led to physical attack. Contemporary man has come to dissapprove of fighting as a means of handling hostility, although apparently there is still a social norm in the lower socio-economic strata that when someone makes you angry or insults you, you should punch him in the nose. This norm is not characteristic of other classes, however. For the most part, physical aggression as an adjustive technique is socially and legally rejected. There are other adjustive techniques available, however.

Verbal aggression. The fact that physical aggression is banned does not mean that acts of aggression are not available as responses to feelings of hostility. Aggression can take the verbal form. Verbal aggression is normally carried out in an indirect manner so as to conceal one's real motive, to protect his self-revealed image, and to preserve the approval of others; while at the same time it does harm to the person toward whom it is directed. Thus, a subtle and skillful adjustive behavior may be developed—the ability to respond to feelings of hostility toward another by using indirect verbal aggression. Verbal aggression, like hostility, is avoided by the good communicator. Nevertheless, when hostility occurs and the individual resorts to verbal aggression, you, as a knowledgeable communicator, can understand that the verbal aggression is an adjustive behavior—an outlet for the hostility. Further, you also know that the verbal aggression can have a cathartic, cleaning effect; it can result in reduced hostility. Your understanding of this process can permit you to help in the solution of the problem rather than "feeding the fire" that leads to total communication breakdown.

Rationalization. When an individual finds that he cannot achieve the goal he wants, he becomes frustrated and hostile. He sometimes restructures the situation so that he does not desire *that* goal anyway; rather he wants a different goal. In other words, if a goal is blocked, the individual adjusts to the situation by rationalizing—by speaking of the unattainable goal as an undesirable one. Such a public commitment of one's thinking tends to reassure him and to validate his inference. *By verbalizing the change of goals* he convinces himself that he is right. Thus, those statements which he *wants* to believe and *needs* to believe actually come to be believed. This is the process of rationalization—one of several processes whereby one adjusts to feelings of frustration, hostility, and aggression. Most of us have used rationalization many times.

Although rationalization may allow one to reduce his tensions and to allay hostility, it carries some dangers. We can do two things that will improve our communication effectiveness in connection with rationalization: (1) If we observe another engaged in rationalization, we can be wary of accepting the evaluations he makes; and (2) we can learn to identify our own rationalizations as such so that we break the habit of saying things we later regret.

Negativism. Another way one may react when experiencing hostility is to reject all or any part of proposals made to him. Some persons assume a general attitude of hostility and mistrust. They often give negative responses to almost all messages because that kind of response has become habitual. Such behavior indicates a general attitude of rigidity and fear of any new idea. There is some indication that extreme rigidity and negativism is associated with low intelligence, low ability in role-playing, and high generalized anxiety. Most of us, of course, react negatively once in a while because of a temporary mood or because the specific proposal or topic is fear-arousing. Sometimes a frozen evaluation underlies such fear. Earlier in this text, we discussed "frozen evaluations" and the need to update and constantly adjust our evaluation of the world about us. If someone makes a proposal that contradicts an outdated evaluation to which we have attached high salience, we may react negatively. Our reaction is not part of a rigid, generalized behavior, however; it is situation bound; i.e., it is related to that specific topic. For example, it is a common experience in many families that a son or daughter asks a parent for permission to go somewhere or do something, and the parent immediately says, "No!" The reason for the negative reaction may be that the parent has a "frozen evaluation" relative to this topic that is dated twenty-three years earlier than that evaluation held by the son or daughter. Of course, if the parent is flexible and can communicate effectively both intrapersonally and interpersonally, he may realize why he reacted negatively. The suggestion that was rejected immediately because it did not fit the orientation of the parent may, at a later time, be agreed to because it is then perceived differently. This does not mean that there should not be "no" answers, but such answers ought to be arrived at rationally rather than out of fear or hostility.

Facework

Each of us lives in a world where we are involved in face-to-face encounters with others. In each of these encounters, we act out what is called a *line*—i.e., a pattern of nonverbal and verbal behavior by which we express our view of a situation. Our view of a situation includes our perception and evaluation of the other participants in the encounter as well as the concept we have of ourselves and how we fit into this situation. Similarly, the other participants act out a line. They have formed impressions of us and of the relationship between themselves and us. Each person in the encounter presents himself in a certain manner in the group. He acts out his line—he *presents a face.* The term face may be defined as the positive social value a person claims for himself in an encounter.

If, in an interpersonal encounter, others accept, acknowledge, or confirm the image the person has of himself, then the person is *in face* or *maintains face.* If the behavior of others indicates that a higher social value is placed on the person than the person had expected, then he has *gained face* and he is likely to "feel good." Conversely, if his expectations are not fulfilled and he is evaluated lower than he expected, he *loses face* and he will "feel hurt." It is apparent that self-concept, person-perception, and the other elements we have discussed previously are directly related to facework in interpersonal communication. If the line a person takes presents an image of himself that is consistent, that is supported by judgments conveyed by other participants, and that is confirmed by the behavior of the persons in the encounter, face is maintained and effective and satisfying interpersonal communication can occur.

There must be consistency in the faces presented. There is an interdependent relationship between the face presented in encounter and all past faces that have been presented; and the face presented now affects the face that it will be possible to present in the future. In fact, a person is said to be *in the wrong face* when he finds himself presenting a face that is not consistent with what was expected. Sometimes the person is *out of face.* He has no face because he is in a new situation and does not know what face—role, position, or relationship—he can or should have. In short, he is out of touch with the situation; he has no face. Many practical jokes or pranks are designed to lead the victim into a situation in which he has no face or in which he will present a wrong face.

When a person is *in face,* he feels confident and assured. He openly presents himself to others with a sense of security; but when a person is *in the wrong face* or *out of face,* he feels inferior and is ashamed because his reputation suffers. Rather than finding the encounter supportive of the image he has of himself, he finds that image denied and feels threatened. Such lack of support and confirmation may confuse him and momentarily incapacitate him as a participant in the encounter. He may falter and be embarrassed, and others may perceive that he is flustered and that he is presenting no usable line. He may be not only out of face or in the wrong face, but he may become *shamefaced.* Poise can be defined as the capacity to suppress and conceal any tendency to become shamefaced during encounters with others.

In almost all cultures there is the expectancy that people should respect and help others save face in interpersonal communication situations. People do not like to witness the defacement of others, and the person who enjoys observing such defacement or causing it is considered heartless. There appears to be an unwritten law that *each person should conduct himself in interpersonal encounters in such a way as to maintain both his own face and the faces of the other participants.* This means that the line taken by each participant is allowed, if at all possible. There is a surface agreement and surface acceptance expected. It is, however, only a "working agreement" and not a "real agreement." This procedure creates a guarded or conservative climate in encounters, especially in first encounters. The line enacted and the face presented initially are allowed, and thereafter there is a striving to maintain that face. This striving to behave in a manner consistent with face is called *face-work.* Each person, subculture, and society develops its own face-work techniques. The knowledge and abilities one has in face-work is often called tact, diplomacy, or social skill. Face-work occurs in almost all interpersonal encounters, and thus, it cannot be ignored in the study of interpersonal communication.

KINDS OF FACE-WORK—Face is threatened in three ways. Sometimes, although a person acts innocently, his behavior or remark threatens the face of another person present. Those present perceive that his act was unintended and believe that he would have avoided it had he foreseen the consequences. Such behavior may be called a *boner, faux pas,* or *gaffe.* Second, the offending person may have acted maliciously with the intention of causing insult and loss of face, and third, the threat may arise incidentally as a result of actions of the participants. Regardless of how threat to face comes about, skill in face-work is necessary if communication is to continue successfully.

Avoidance. One technique for saving face is to avoid those situations and contacts in which threats are likely to occur. Avoidance behavior can be observed in all societies. One manifestation of the avoidance technique is the practice of using a go-between. It is not unusual in elementary school, for example, for John to use go-betweens to find out whether Mary likes him or not. The use of go-betweens among groups, organizations, or even nations is not uncommon. Avoidance practices are also used in the encounter by staying away from topics, changing the topic of conversation, or failing to see or recognize a loss-of-face situation.

Correction. When an event that is clearly inconsistent with face occurs despite efforts to avoid it, the participants will often acknowledge it as an incident and try to correct for its effects. Goffman has identified four moves in the typical corrective process.[20] First, the participants call attention to the misconduct; second, some sort of apology is offered (usually by the offender, but it might be offered by another person); third, the offended accepts the restitution as satisfactory; and finally, the offender conveys his thanks for being forgiven by the offended.

An offering or correction may take any of the following forms: the act was a joke not to be taken seriously ("I didn't mean it" or "I was joking"); it happened because of extenuating circumstances, the offender was under the influence of something and was not himself ("I'm just not myself today," "I'm tired," or "I've had a bad day"); the offender was under the command or influence of someone else (*"They* say that. I don't believe it."); compensation may be offered; or punishment and penance for the offender may be offered. All these forms serve the purpose of restoring the relationship so that communication may continue as before. If no corrective process is worked out, however, breakdown in communication is likely to occur. In rare situations the person (or persons) involved does not desire to help the offended save face. He may, in fact, engage in face-work negatively, using it as an instrument of aggression. He may purposefully introduce favorable facts about himself and unfavorable facts about others to put them down, or he may use snubs and digs to score points over others. This sort of motivation is often related to goal relationships, a factor discussed earlier in this chapter, as well as to personality factors and psychological characteristics of the individual. In any event, face-work is very directly related to interpersonal communication. An understanding of and skill in using face-work can be a helpful asset in interpersonal communication.

Feedback

A final element in interpersonal communication is feedback, the process by which we correct and adjust our messages so as to take into account the perceptions, values, wishes, and feelings of the other person. Through the proper use of feedback we establish a bond with the other person that enables the communication to be successful. By adjusting our messages we develop relationships enabling us to be understood and responded to as we desire. Only through utilizing the feedback process can there be a "sharing of meanings" of the persons involved. In communication both (or all) participants have an influence

20. Irving Goffman, "On Face-Work: An Analysis of Ritual Elements in Social Interaction," in *Readings in Social Psychology,* ed. Alfred R. Lindesmith and Anselm L. Strauss (New York: Holt, Rinehart and Winston, 1969), pp. 271–72.

in the outcome, and both (or all) participants need some system for correcting misconceptions, misunderstandings, and faulty responses. Each needs to find out if he is transmitting what he thinks he is transmitting.

The use of feedback is a requirement of all self-governing, goal-seeking systems, including mechanical devices, living organisms, and social organizations. For any system to seek a goal and to be self-governing in an environment, it must be able to have information about its relationship to the environment fed back into its regulatory unit. For example, the furnace in your home utilizes the feedback process as it receives information about the environment (how hot or how cold it is); that information is fed back into the system, and adjustments are made in the system to maintain the desired temperature. In the human physiological system oxygen, salt, hormones, etc. are controlled by automatic mechanisms that feed information back into the system so that beneficial adjustments can be made. In like manner, effective interpersonal communication involves the feeding back of information so that the two (or more) organisms can make the corrections that are necessary for clarity of understanding.

We obtain feedback from monitoring our own performance and by developing a sensitivity and receptiveness to information sent to us by the other person. When a person thinks about what he is saying as he encodes the message, or when he reflects about something he has just said, he is using *internal feedback;* but when he is observing the reactions of the other person to what he has said, or when he is listening to the verbal response of the other person, he is using *external feedback.* The person may also hear what he is saying as he says it and rephrase it to give it additional meaning. This is self-feedback as illustrated in Figure 2 on page 7.

Feedback can be *positive* or *negative.* Those responses that are perceived as rewarding (smiles, nods of agreement, high attentiveness) are labeled positive feedback, while punishing responses (inattention, frowns, yawns) are labeled negative feedback.[21] When a person receives rewarding feedback, he continues to produce the same kind of message; but when a person receives punishing feedback, he changes his message. The kind of feedback he gets affects subsequent behavior. When feedback indicates that one is successful in accomplishing his objective, he is encouraged to send more messages similarly encoded and similar in their purposes.

---

21. Gerald R. Miller, *Speech Communication: A Behavioral Approach* (Indianapolis: Bobbs-Merrill Co., 1966), p. 55.

Although feedback is present and is extremely important in the public speaking situation, it is not as free and complete as in the interpersonal situation. Feedback is even more limited in mass communication than it is in either public speaking or interpersonal communication, although it is present even in the large media systems such as television, radio, magazines, and newspapers. Public opinion polls, market research studies, fan mail, popularity ratings, and other surveys are used to get feedback in mass communication.

All responses can be considered feedback. Some feedback responses are nonpurposive and indirect responses; i.e., they are unintentional behaviors. Other feedback responses are purposive and direct, sent to check on the accuracy of the meaning that has been attached to the received message. Free, open, purposeful feedback is the most effective feedback; and when both the sender and the receiver are consciously and purposely trying to use feedback, communication is enhanced significantly. When the sender tries to discover whether the message he sent is the message received, and when the receiver purposefully attempts to check the meaning of the message, then feedback serves effectively to facilitate communication. Several studies of feedback have been conducted. A summary of these studies indicates support for the following hypotheses:

1. Lack of feedback tends to foster low confidence and hostility.
2. Free, open, and direct feedback tends to foster high confidence and friendliness.
3. Effective feedback is both positive and negative.
4. Effective feedback is positively related to interpersonal relations, the acquisition of new skills, and the development of new insights.
5. Unless feedback is interpreted accurately it has little value.
6. Feedback received immediately is more effective than delayed feedback.

It appears that timing, amount of feedback, the use of positive or negative feedback, the directness of feedback (use of questions, comments, corrections, and counter-arguments) and the accuracy of the interpretation of feedback have important effects on interpersonal communication outcomes. Two specific suggestions for acquiring effective feedback behavior and for translating the six principles above into action include: (1) develop the habit of checking on your understanding of what the other person means; and (2) check on your understanding of the meaning, not by asking a direct question, but by translating, paraphrasing, or telling the other person what you understand him to mean.

The effective communicator is aware of the need for feedback; he seeks feedback, he tries to send clear feedback, and he develops the ability to interpret feedback accurately. Too often we fail to see communication as a transactional process. We see only ourselves sending messages that we assume are understood.

Summary

To illustrate even more clearly the relationship between each of the seven factors discussed in this chapter and interpersonal communication, let us consider a real group of which you are a member—your speech class. Now, let us place this real group in a hypothetical situation. Let us assume that your speech class is a committee charged with managing the basic speech course for your college or university. This class or group of fifteen to twenty-five persons, as they pursue the task assigned to them, will engage, primarily, in interpersonal communication. Remember that we are not talking about this group as a speech class now—we are talking about it as an executive or administrative group. Your group must make decisions or policies that guide and determine the basic speech course. Such problem-solving will not be accomplished through viewing a television program, listening to the radio, observing a protest demonstration, or by taking turns giving public speeches—forms of public communication. The problem-solving tasks will be accomplished, rather, through discussion, conferences, interviews to get information and to persuade (interviews with the department chairman and the dean, for example) and through informal conversations—forms of interpersonal communication. How will interpersonal attraction, roles, goals, defensiveness, hostility, face-work, and feedback affect the degree of success of your group in accomplishing its task through communication? You can consider each of these factors for your class, a group of *real* persons. How much are the members of the group attracted to each other? Do they like each other, dislike each other, or just not care much? Are there some individuals who would play certain roles—leadership roles, peacemaker roles, etc? Is there hostility among members of the group? Do you notice an unusual amount of defensive communication, or has the group fostered and created a supportive climate? Has the group consciously sought and used feedback to improve its communication quality? As you answer these questions, you can possibly make some predictions about how the group will operate in terms of interpersonal communication, and, subsequently, in terms of accomplishing the task of administering the basic speech course.

Putting aside, for the moment, the *actual* characteristics of your class as a group, let us give them some hypothetical characteristics for the sake of illustration. Let us suppose that this is a class in which there is high interpersonal attraction. The members of this group are highly successful in college. They're *cool!* They know where the action is—and they're in it! They are smart, talented, good looking, and *tough!* They're *beautiful people!* Moreover, they have acquired this habit of helping each other, and realize considerable satisfaction (reward) from these experiences. Everyone is relaxed and happy—no anxiety or stress for members of this group. Further, the group members share not only their speech class, but several other classes as well. Finally, they have parties together and several strong friendships have developed. They have discovered that their attitudes in regard to political and social problems are similar. In short, here is a hypothetical group characterized by an unusually high degree of interpersonal attraction. This factor alone will exert a powerful influence upon their conversations, discussions, and conferences.

Let us suppose that, along with high interpersonal attraction, the individuals in this group are quite sophisticated with regard to role insight and ability to fulfill various needed roles. None of the individuals in the group is afflicted with "role-rigidity." Any member of this group can act as chairman, gadfly, resource person to do research (and furnish the group with data), or as the loyal opposition, etc . . .

A third characteristic of the group is that they understand that competitive goals can impair the group's efficiency. They are capable of defining or structuring goals so that the goals are interdependent and cooperative.

Because the individuals in this group like each other, have learned to help each other, are intelligent and capable, can play various roles efficiently as they are needed, and can shape situations in the way of being conducive to cooperation, it is no surprise that their communication climate is also supportive rather than guarded or defensive. Also, with such attraction, supportiveness, and cooperative goals, there is little reason for hostility or anger to develop. Finally, there is little need for face-work, and in the few instances when face-saving functions are needed, the individuals in this group are capable of performing them. If we add the ability to use feedback effectively in conferences, discussions, and interviews so as to correct messages and increase accuracy in understanding, we will have made of this hypothetical group a nearly perfect and utopian task force, for they are proficient in all the areas of interpersonal communication discussed in this chapter. No such perfect group exists, of course, but surely our description of this hypothetical group illustrates how the seven factors overlap and how they are factors that are extremely important in interpersonal communication. If we can play various roles, if we like the individuals with whom we are communicating, if goals are congruent—hostility, defensiveness, and loss of face are not likely to be significant problems. On the other hand, if our hypothetical group was comprised of individuals who hated each other, were jealous and envious of each other, who played rigid roles, who competed for the same leadership positions (had competitive goals), who vied with each other and had "done each other in" in previous encounters—then we could also expect high hostility, a need for an unbelievable amount of face-work, and an unusual amount of defensive communication. We know, also, that there would likely be problems in *intrapersonal* communication—in receiving and processing information accurately. It is not difficult to see that the interpersonal communication situations in which this second hypothetical group attempted to make decisions and administer the basic speech program, would be of a low quality and probably unproductive.

Although not all interpersonal communication situations will be comprised of individuals at one or the other of the two extremes described in our hypothetical groups, some groups in which you will participate will be of a higher quality, (in terms of the seven factors) than other groups. Some individuals will be better communicators than others.

As a student of communication your goals could include: (1) improving your own performance in these seven areas of interpersonal communication, (2) Acquiring skill in detecting these factors at work in interpersonal communication you observe and in which you participate, and (3) learning to influence interpersonal communication situations through adjusting to or correcting problems in these seven areas —particularly, in face-work and feedback.

For Further Reading

1. Barnlund, Dean C. *Interpersonal Communication: Survey and Studies.* Boston: Houghton Mifflin Company, 1968.

2. Campbell, James H., and Hepler, Hal W., eds. *Dimensions in Communication.* Belmont, Calif.: Wadsworth Publishing Co., 1965.

3. Gibb, Jack R. "Defensive Communication." *ETC* 22 (June 1965).

4. Miller, Gerald R. *Speech Communication: A Behavioral Approach.* Indianapolis: Bobbs-Merrill Co., 1966.

5. Smith, Alfred G., ed. *Communication and Culture.* New York: Holt, Rinehart & Winston, 1966.

6. Von Foerster, Heinz, ed. *Cybernetics: Circular Causal and Feedback Mechanisms in Biological and Social Systems.* Proceedings of the Ninth Conference on Cybernetics Sponsored by the Josiah Macy, Jr. Foundation, New York, 1953.

7. Weiner, Norbert. *The Human Use of Human Beings: Cybernetics and Society.* Garden City, N.Y.: Anchor Books, Doubleday & Co., Inc., 1954.

Chapter 6

Nonverbal Communication

Every message is put into a code. The codes to which we direct most of our attention are the spoken and written codes—verbal communication. Actually, verbal signals carry only a small part of the information that people exchange in everyday interaction. It has been estimated that in face-to-face communication no more than 35 percent of the social meaning is carried in the verbal message.[1] Still, we sometimes slip into the error of thinking that *all* communication must be verbal. Another code does exist, however—the nonverbal code, a relatively little studied but much used vehicle of communication. It includes the full range of human communication: tone of voice, gestures, posture, movement, and other signals which we call nonverbal communication. Many of the meanings generated in human encounters are elicited by touch, glance, vocal nuance, gesture, or facial expression. A good deal of this nonverbal communication goes on around us, and is important because we make decisions based on it and relate to each other through it. From nonverbal communication cues we make decisions to argue or agree, to laugh or blush, to relax or resist, to continue or end conversation. Many and sometimes most of the critical meanings in communication are transferred through the nonverbal codes. Although we do not always realize that we are sending and receiving messages nonverbally, the influence of nonverbal communication is always present in face-to-face communication situations. We gesture with our hands, raise our eyebrows, meet someone else's eyes and look away, and shift positions in a chair. Although the actions may seem random, researchers have discovered in recent years that there is a

---

1. Randall Harrison, "Nonverbal Communication: Exploration into Time, Space, Action, and Object," in *Dimensions in Communication*, ed. J. H. Campbell and H. W. Hepler (Belmont, Calif.: Wadsworth Publishing Co., 1965), p. 161.

system to them. Messages come across not only in words, but also in body language, and such nonverbal messages often get there faster than do the verbal messages.

Every culture has its own body language. A German talks and moves in German, while a Frenchman talks and moves in French. One's sex, ethnic background, and social class all influence his body language. Research has also shown that persons who are truly bilingual are also bilingual in body language. Politicians with a bi-cultured constituency are fortunate if they are truly bilingual, for they can campaign to each culture in the verbal and nonverbal languages of that culture. New York's famous mayor, Fiorello La Guardia, is said to have been able to campaign in English, Italian, and Yiddish. When films of his speeches are run without sound, it is not difficult to identify from his nonverbal communication the language he is speaking.

Many verbal expressions attest to the importance of nonverbal communication. We say "actions speak louder than words," or "one picture is worth a thousand words." Yet, in speech, we have placed great emphasis on verbal communication while giving little attention to nonverbal communication. The result is that some speakers too often display in interpersonal and public communication great skill in using words, but little understanding of, or a real feel for, the total phenomenon of communication itself. In this chapter we will describe the types of nonverbal communication, compare nonverbal communication with verbal communication, and identify some tentative principles of nonverbal communication. The direct relationship and application of nonverbal communication to specific forms of interpersonal and public communication will be discussed in later chapters. As you read this chapter, you will notice that nonverbal communication has a close relationship to topics discussed in previous chapters.

Types of Nonverbal Communication

Nonverbal communication, as we will discuss it in this chapter, falls into six categories: paralanguage (vocal nonverbal communication), sign language, gestures and body action, object language, tactile communication, and space and time as communication.

PARALANGUAGE—We have recognized for a long time that there is information included in words—i.e., that there are clear messages in the tone of the voice, in the emphasis or inflections given certain words, and in the pauses inserted in the sentence. We know from experience that a simple "yes" may express defiance, resignation, acknowledgment, interest, enthusiasm, or agreement, depending on tone and emphasis. Most of us, at one time or many times, have remarked, "It wasn't *what*

he said, but *how he said it* that made me angry!" We were referring
to the nonverbal, vocal phenomena—intonation, emphasis, stress, etc.
These vocal phenomena, often referred to as *paralanguage*, consist of
vocal modifiers, vocal differentiators, vocal identifiers, and a general
category called voice quality.

1.   *Vocal qualifiers.* One type of phenomena in paralanguage is
vocal qualifiers. Vocal qualifiers are usually thought of as *"tones of
voice."* Increasing loudness or increasing softness is one type of vocal
qualifier. The part of the utterance having the increasing loudness or
softness may be a single syllable, word, phrase, sentence, or a group of
sentences. Increasing loudness often expresses anger, hostility, or
alarm. If you will listen to someone in the midst of a heated argument,
you will often notice that the loudness of the speaking increases. Play-
wrights and fiction writers, as they have recorded man's behavior in
literature, have included "shouting at each other" in their descriptions
of hostile arguments and angry exchanges. On the other hand, increasing softness is often used to express disappointment. Loudness or softness is seldom used alone as a qualifier of the verbal message, but each
is used along with other techinques (pitch, voice quality, and rate) to
convey the message of anger or disappointment.

Loudness or softness may be used to give emphasis to certain words
—to make a particular word stand out from the others. In infinite and
subtle ways loudness (increasing or decreasing) can be used to add vocal
cues to verbal messages.

A second set of vocal qualifier is pitch: *raised pitch* or *lowered
pitch.* A raised pitch often accompanies loudness and can be used to
communicate alarm, annoyance, and anxiety. The whining, high-
pitched voice may tell a story of tenseness, fear, and anxiety that is as
revealing as the verbal message; or the relaxed, low-pitched voice may
communicate calm and relaxation.

We use pitch to indicate declarative messages and messages that
are questions. In fact, by using certain pitch patterns or inflections, we
can utter a statement constructed declaratively ("That was a basketball
game") as a question. Such is the capacity of pitch to qualify the meanings of verbal messages.

A third pair of vocal qualifiers—the *spread register* and the
squeezed register—refers to the spreading or compressing (lengthen-
ing and shortening) of the time interval between the pitches as one
speaks. Spread register is heard when you call to a person across the
street. You will tend to draw out the saying of the person's name over
a larger period of time ("Hey, Jim——my"). Squeezed register is the
opposite of spread register in that the intervals between the pitches are

shortened to give a monotone effect. You can hear the difference between spread register and squeezed register by listening to Jimmy's mother call to him from across the street and then, at a later time, listening to her scold him by saying his name when he is near her.

Rasp or *openness* is the fourth set of vocal qualifiers. Rasping is a function of the amount of muscular tension in the larynx. The strained or rasping quality is associated with tenseness. Openness, characterized by a hollowness or booming acoustic characteristic (and said to be associated with a lack of sincerity signaling that the speaker is of superordinate status, having the answers to one's problems), is often used by clergymen, politicians, and undertakers.[2] Between the extremes of hollowness and coarse raspiness is a wide range of characteristics of this phenomenon that are used to modify verbal messages.

Drawling or *clipping,* the fifth set of verbal qualifiers, have to do with the individual syllables. With clipping the syllable is chopped off or shortened, but with drawling the syllable is elongated and drawn out as with the stereotyped cowboy drawl.

Tempo, increased or decreased, is the last vocal qualifier to be discussed. Increased tempo or rate of speaking sometimes (especially as it is associated with other vocal qualifiers) indicates annoyance; at other times it may indicate anxiety; and it is sometimes associated with energy and intelligence. An extremely slow tempo often signals uncertainty.

Many psychiatrists and others skilled in communication rely heavily on the information in nonverbal messages. Through experience they have come to have confidence in the validity of the information received from vocal qualifiers.

2. *Vocal differentiators* constitute another class of voice phenomena. Among the most commonly used vocal differentiators are *crying, laughing*, and *breaking*. These types of communication are used according to the rules of each culture. In America, for example, women have more freedom to use crying to communicate than do men; while in Persia men are allowed to cry and, in fact, are expected to weep to convey certain messages. Laughing and crying may mean quite different things in different cultures. Custom may dictate who can cry and who cannot cry, how much they can cry, and what things can be meant by crying.

Breaking refers to speaking in broken, halting voice, or to some rigid and intermittent interruption of speaking. The nervous giggle, for example, is considered to be a form of breaking. The quavering voice

2. Robert E. Pittenger and Henry Lee Smith, Jr., "A Basis for Some Contributions of Linguistics to Psychiatry," *Psychiatry* 20 (1957): 61–78.

of emotion is another example of breaking. In our culture, breaking in any form communicates insecurity and loss of control. Laughing, crying, breaking—any one of these vocal differentiators—could be applied to the same verbal message at different times and under different circumstances to create totally different messages.

3. *Vocal identifiers*. This set of phenomena included in paralanguage consists of "un–huh" and "ah–hah" that mean yes, and "huh–uh" and "ah!–ah!" that mean no.

4. *Vocal quality*. A fourth set of phenomena, not yet researched fully so as to describe them systematically as is done for vocal qualifiers, vocal differentiators, and vocal identifiers, is the set called voice quality. Although specific elements have not yet been identified and shown to be predictively related to given meanings, we do know that meanings are conveyed and understood by others through voice quality. The anxious voice, the calm voice, the hostile voice, and other general emotional states have been identified with voice quality as a general characteristic. Psychiatrists, medical doctors, counselors, and teachers who are skilled in and sensitive to nonverbal communication messages make use of voice quality in interpreting messages.

Although each type of vocal communication has been discussed separately, it would be a mistake to think in terms of each operating separately and individually to communicate nonverbal messages. In practice, these phenomena are combined with each other in many different ways. Hence, people who do more than just react to nonverbal messages unintentionally—i.e., people who attempt to purposefully receive, interpret, and understand nonverbal messages—focus on the *general* or *multiple nonverbal factors* rather than first on one specific factor and then on a second, etc. Loudness, high pitch, rate, hollowness, and crying are more meaningful considered together than any one factor considered by itself.

SIGN LANGUAGE—Sign language includes all those forms of codification in which numbers, punctuation, and words have been supplanted by gestures. Examples range from the simple gesture of the hitchhiker to the complete sign language of the deaf. Other features, as well as posture, facial expressions, and body movements, are called action language, to be discussed as a third category of nonverbal communication.

Sign language gestures are believed to have been used by primitive man long before oral systems were developed. Sign languages were developed in various cultures throughout the world. There is evidence that some seven hundred thousand distinct and meaningful gestures can be and have been used by communicating man.[3] The North Ameri-

3. Mario Pei, *The Story of Language* (New York: Lippincott, 1949), p. 13.

can Indians, for example, were especially adept at sign language, with the Cheyennes having at least seven thousand symbols in their language. One advantage of the use of sign languages by the Indians was that any tribe could communicate at least grossly with any other tribe. One disadvantage, reported by Thomas in reference to the Bushmen, is that it is possible to have so many visual signals—and to rely only on them—that it is difficult to communicate in the dark.[4] Although the American culture does not rely exclusively on sign language, there is considerable use of sign language in our communication.

ACTION LANGUAGE—Action language includes all gestures, posture, facial expressions, and movements that are *not* used exclusively as substitutes for words. Walking, for example, serves the function of giving one mobility, but it may also communicate. Similarly, eating can be action language. Eating rapidly, for example, can communicate something about the person's hunger, upbringing, or emotional state.

It is useful to divide action language into two categories: (1) expressive actions which are unintentional, and (2) purposive actions which are intentional. The former are often subliminal while the latter are overt and identifiable by either the listener or the talker. Expressive actions are constantly adaptive, responding to feelings and needs of the moment, while overt actions are purposely communicative and instrumental. Expressive actions result in the message "given off," while purposive actions result in a given message. These two categories are not absolute; they do overlap at times. Some expressive actions are noticeable and some communicative gestures become so habitual that we use them almost unconsciously. It is not uncommon for a person to develop over a period of time certain habituated movements and gestures that are used regardless of whether they have any connection with the verbal message or not. Most public officials and entertainers have their idiosyncratic, habituated gestures, and these are often used by comedians who impersonate well known public figures.

As overt, intentional actions, gestures are used to locate, to describe, to emphasize, and even to express abstract concepts. As expressive, unintentional action, gestures, facial expression, posture, and movement reveal the personality and emotional states. We can observe in the musculature twitching, blotching, dilated pupils, rising hair, etc. the fear, nervousness, anger, joy, and other emotional states of the individual. We may not observe the individual cues, but rather probably observe the total visible pattern. We perceive the visual meaning as a configuration and interpret it almost instantly.

4. W. I. Thomas, *Source Book for Social Origins* (Chicago: University of Chicago Press, 1909), p. 706.

There is little doubt that we differ in our ability to send messages in the action language channel—both intentional and unintentional messages. Some people are more expressive than others in their visible behavior, and some people are more reserved and concealing in their visible behavior than are other people.

We vary greatly also in our ability to receive and interpret nonverbal messages. Some persons are keenly sensitive and accurate in understanding or reading the nonverbal signs, while other persons plunge ahead ignoring the nonverbal messages.

Coleman found that people vary in their ability to send visual cues and in their ability to interpret them. Not only is there a difference from person to person, but there appears to be a difference between men and women in their ability to use nonverbal communication. Women are better than men in sending nonverbal messages, but men are better than women in interpreting nonverbal messages.[5] Through the eyes, facial expression, gestures, and movement much meaning can be conveyed. The human body is a versatile instrument for expressing a wide range of ideas and feelings. One of the most potent elements in body language is eye behavior. Americans are careful about how and when they meet one another's eyes. In normal conversation, they allow each eye-contact to last only about a second, then one or both will look away. If they maintain eye-contact longer than that, emotions are heightened and the relationship takes on new dimensions. Hence, we avoid this except in appropriate circumstances. It should not be surprising that baseball pitchers, mothers, confidence men, and girl friends are capable of conveying much while saying little.

OBJECT LANGUAGE—Object language comprises the display of material things—art objects, clothes, the decoration of a room, hair style, implements, machines, and the human body. Engagement and wedding rings are examples of objects of communication, as is the American flag, a Peace decal, and the sports letter jacket. It is well known that the clothing one wears and its style and condition tell something about the person. We make inferences from the shine of the shoes, the cut of the hair, and other material things that reveal one's social sensitivity, associations, preferences, and values. Personal apparel seems to be a major source of information. Clothing, jewelry, cosmetics —these represent deliberate choices and are guides to personality. How one dresses, for example, shows sexual attraction and sexual interest, group identification, status, identification of role, and expression of self-concept. Compton's study is one of several that has found close relation-

5. James C. Coleman, "Facial Expression of Emotion," *Psychological Monographs* 63 (1949): 1–36.

ship between selection of clothing and expression of one's self, particularly between selection of clothing and personality and status.[6] Similarly the effect of wearing glasses has been shown to produce favorable judgments of intelligence and industriousness.[7]

TACTILE COMMUNICATION—Tactile communication is communication by touch, the earliest and most elementary mode of communication of the human organism. Tactual sensitivity is the most primitive sensory process in most lower organisms. Many sub-human organisms orient themselves to the world by their feelers or antennae. They literally *feel* their way through life. Tactile communication is also the primary mode of orientation to the world in organisms living underground, in fish, and probably in many reptiles.

Tactile communication is of special significance to human beings. It is the first form of communication experienced by the infant, and it is known that these early tactile experiences are crucial in later development of symbolic recognition and response. The infant's need for tactile contacts—nuzzling, cuddling, patting, feeling—and his quick response to and acceptance of tactile messages are well known facts. Parental care and love, through infancy and childhood, are largely matters of tactile communication—tactual contacts that comfort, reassure, express acceptance, give encouragement, and build confidence in the child. Moreover, the kind and duration of early tactile experiences wherein the infant or child can send and receive messages have an effect on early personality development.

Sometimes a small child will transfer tactile communication to objects other than his mother. A baby may become attached to the feel of a specific blanket (as is the case with the little comic character, Linus), a soft cuddly animal, or a toy and begin to enjoy these textures and tactile contacts. Denial or deprivation of early tactile experiences may inpair future learning such as speech, cognition, and symbolic recognition, as well as limit the individual's capacity for more mature tactile communication; for through early tactile experiences the infant begins to communicate, then gradually enlarges his communication as he develops capacities for other sensory perception and other forms of response. The foundation for these other forms of communication, both verbal and nonverbal, is tactile communication.

We need to note a second developmental stage in tactile communication because it too is related to subsequent adult tactile communication. This is the stage when the child learns that there are curtailments

6. N. Compton, "Personal Attributes of Color and Design Preferences in Clothing Fabrics," *Journal of Psychology* 54 (1962): 191–95.
7. G. Thornton, "The Effect of Wearing Glasses Upon Judgments of Personality Traits of Persons Seen Briefly," *Journal of Applied Psychology* 28 (1944): 203–7.

and prohibitions connected with tactile communication. He learns to define some things (property, sacred places, forbidden objects, persons, etc.) as untouchables except under certain conditions (when one has permission, has performed certain rituals, has made a purchase, etc.). Sometimes the child's naive use of tactile communication is prohibited with strong and painful punishment. The process of *socializing* the child with the rules of tactile communication may vary from successful to unsuccessful, i.e., accompanied by fears and strong inhibitions. Not only does it vary within cultures from person to person, but it also varies from culture to culture. Nevertheless, tactile communication experiences of the infant and the child are directly related to the effectiveness of adult interpersonal communication. Through the early tactile experiences of baby and mother, child and parents, child and others, the first patterns of interpersonal relations are established, and they will affect subsequent interpersonal relation patterns. These early tactile experiences are related to the individual's confidence in the world and trust in people.

For adults, tactile communication is a potent form of nonverbal communication. Tactile communication has at least four distinguishing characteristics: (1) tactile experience is ordinarily limited to two persons, (2) tactile experience is immediate and transitory, operating only as long as contact is maintained, (3) tactile communication is reciprocal in the sense that who or what a person touches also touches him, and (4) tactile communication takes place on the level of signals (direct stimulation through the sense of touch) rather than through symbolic mediation. Tactile experiences, as emotional and attitudinal messages and responses, are powerful, clear, and capable of an amazing variety of transformations in human communication. Through the touch of a hand one can feel fear, coldness, and anxiety, or love, warmth, and security. Tactile communication plays a pervasive role in human communication.

SPACE AND TIME—Space and time are types of nonverbal communication. Anthropologist Edward T. Hall has pointed out that cultures establish meanings that are related to distance or space, as well as meanings that are related to time.[8] In the United States the comfortable and appropriate distance to stand for conversation is about an arm's length. The Brazilian, as he talks with an American, moves in closer; the American is apt to interpret that space violation as pushy, overbearing, or aggressive; and, if the American backs away, the Brazilian is apt to think the American is being standoffish or cold.

The American and the Arab are even less compatible in terms of

8. Edward T. Hall, *The Silent Language* (New York: Doubleday & Co., Inc., 1959), p. 163.

space defined as appropriate for conversation. The Arab may stand quite close and look intently into the American's eyes as he talks. This space element and eye-contact behavior may be associated with sexual intimacy by the American, who consequently may find it disturbing in a nonsexual context. Hall believes that the space or distance between persons in communication is related to the nature of the messages. He has identified eight distances that may be indicative of certain types of messages. They include: (1) very close (3 to 6 inches)—soft whisper, top secret, or intimate information; (2) close (8 to 12 inches)—audible whisper, very confidential information; (3) near (12 to 20 inches)—soft voice, confidential; (4) neutral (20 to 36 inches)—soft voice, personal information; (5) neutral (4 1/2 to 5 feet)—full voice, non-personal; (6) public distance (5 1/2 to 8 feet)—full voice; (7) and (8) stretching the limits of distance (up to 100 feet)—hailing and departure distance.[9]

Birds, animals, and people mark out the territory they stand on as their own personal space. They let others approach, but not too closely. In one experiment, a person deliberately intruded on the personal space of female college students seated at study tables in a library. The intruder sat down right next to any coed sitting alone at a library table. The victims tried to restore an appropriate distance by moving their chairs further away, turning sideways and by building barriers of books, purses, and coats. The experimenter then pursued by moving his chair closer to the retreating victim. When all avoidance mechanisms failed, the victims took flight. Only one of the eighty invaded students asked the experimenter to move over. Personal space, like sex, seems to be one of those things we react to but do not acknowledge in words. The amount of space a person needs is influenced by his personality. Introverts, for example, seem to need more elbow room than extroverts. Mood is also indicated by space. We put more space between ourselves and those we dislike than between ourselves and those we like. Drawing away can communicate avoidance, rejection, or fear; while drawing closer can communicate acceptance, admiration, and liking. Space speaks.

It is said that each of us has a personal space that we carry around with us. Like a bubble that encloses us, it is our personal territory. Others may not enter it without permission or invitation. It has been discovered that placing physical barriers between persons to insure their territorial space improves morale in certain situations. Protective counters between waitresses and cooks have served such a function. Waist-high or shoulder-high partitions in large offices have had a similar effect. In ways other than through the erection of walls, counters, and

9. Edward T. Hall, *The Silent Language*, pp. 163-64.

partitions, we recognize the integrity of personal space. The butler or waitress does not listen to the conversations of guests, and the pedestrian avoids staring at the embracing couple.

The arrangement of furniture and distance between chairs utilizes space to communicate certain messages—messages having to do with rules, relationships, and status. It has been discovered, for example, that patients are more at ease with the doctor if the doctor is not behind a desk than if he is behind a desk. At one time, it was the practice for executives to communicate from behind their desks, but now one finds easy chairs, sofas, and coffee tables as integral parts of the executive furnishings.

As with space, so time is a type of nonverbal communication. Time talks. In America punctuality communicates respect, and tardiness can be an insult. In other cultures, however, being on time is an insult. In America a late message, whether term paper, business report, or press release, is likely to have undesirable consequences. Tardiness often communicates a low regard for the receiver and for the message. Many persons purposely use air mail only for their letters, believing that it builds credibility and respect by communicating a high regard.

If further evidence is needed to establish the fact that time talks, remember the telephone call you received at a very late hour, 2:30 A.M., for example. You probably felt some sense of urgency and importance, even danger, perhaps. It was the element of time that communicated the alarm.

In summary, we have identified six kinds of nonverbal communication—vocal elements, sign language, action language, object language, tactile communication, and communication by the use of space and time. Any of the codes, singularly or in combination, may be used to modify verbal messages—to reinforce, validate, or complement the verbal message, or to contradict and negate it; or nonverbal communication may be used in its own right, without accompanying verbal messages, to establish bonds and relationships necessary for survival.

Differences Between Verbal and Nonverbal Communication

The two systems, verbal and nonverbal, constitute *different languages* and operate according to different laws. When we talk face-to-face with another person we are sending discrete, digital, verbal symbols while at the same time sending him continuous, analogic, nonverbal cues. One of the differences between analogic and digital information, according to neurologists, is that the human nervous system handles the two kinds of cues differently. They travel over different neural pathways in the brain. The analogic travels over the older portions of the brain, those portions that develop in the infant months and years before words and numbers (digital information) are learned. Digital pathways lie in those parts of the brain which develop late in the child and which developed more slowly in the evolutionary growth of man. Medical science has shown that, in cases of brain pathology, the newer portions of the brain usually degenerate first, and so it is not unusual for the person to lose his ability to handle verbal symbols while retaining his ability to read visual and other nonverbal cues.

Another difference is that analogic messages are received rapidly while digital messages reach us more slowly and are processed more slowly. This means that the message sent by one's body is perceived and reacted to before the meaning of verbal messages are perceived. Hence, nonverbal messages often create in us a set that acts as a filter affecting our perception and reaction to verbal messages.

Yet another difference between digital and analogic messages is that words can and do represent abstractions such as love and hate, but nonverbal messages observed in one's behavior (expressive messages) are more likely to represent nothing but themselves. They are directly related to the feeling of the moment.

Finally, most verbal messages are governed by one's will—are constructed intentionally, while many nonverbal cues are not under one's control. One cannot so easily govern body movements and psychophysiological responses. The following table further compares verbal and nonverbal communication.

Because of these differences between nonverbal and verbal communication—because nonverbal communication has several unique characteristics—it is possible to suggest some tentative axioms or principles of nonverbal communication.

Three Principles of Nonverbal Communication

ONE CANNOT NOT COMMUNICATE—All observed behavior has message value. Behavior has no opposite. There is no such thing as nonbehavior. Hence, it follows that one cannot avoid communicating. One can avoid communicating verbally, but nonverbal communication cannot be avoided. Even inactivity and silence have message value. The mere absence of talking does not mean that there is no communication. Purposeful silence and avoidance of verbal communication is in itself communication. Sigmund Freud once wrote: "No mortal can keep a secret. If his lips are silent, he chatters with his finger tips; betrayal oozes out of him at every pore." Thus, an individual may appear calm and self-controlled—unaware that signs of tension and anxiety are leaking out in the tapping of his foot or the tenseness of his fingers.

Table 1

Verbal and Nonverbal Codification Differences*

Nonverbal Communication	Verbal Communication
Nonverbal communication is based on continuous functions; the hand is continuously involved in movement.	Verbal communication is based on discontinuous functions; sounds or letters have a discreet beginning and ending.
Nonverbal communication is regulated by principles governed by biological necessity.	Verbal communication is governed by arbitrary, man-made principles.
Nonverbal communication is international, intercultural, and interracial.	Verbal communication is culturally specific.
Nonverbal communication influences perception, coordination, and integration, and leads to the acquisition of skills.	Verbal communication influences thinking and leads to the acquisition of information.
Understanding of nonverbal detonation is based upon the participants' empathic assessment of biological similarity; no explanation is needed for understanding what pain is.	Understanding of verbal detonation is based on prior verbal agreement.
Nonverbal communication uses the old structures of the central and autonomic nervous systems.	Verbal communication uses younger structures, particularly the cortex.
Nonverbal communication is learned early in life.	Verbal communication is learned later in life.
Action and objects exist in their own right.	Words do not exist in their own right. They represent arbitrary symbols representing abstractions of events.
Nonverbal communication is emotional.	Verbal communication is intellectual.
Nonverbal communication represents an intimate language.	Verbal communication represents a distant language.

*It should be recognized that those differences are *not* absolute. There are exceptions and qualifications, but we are interested in calling attention to differences frequently found between verbal and nonverbal communication.

NONVERBAL CHANNELS ARE ESPECIALLY EFFECTIVE IN COMMUNICATING FEELINGS, ATTITUDES, AND RELATIONSHIPS—Man communicates verbally to share cognitive information and to transmit knowledge, but he relies heavily on nonverbal communication to share emotions, feelings, and attitudes. In fact, some nonverbal communication (tactile communication, for example) is used almost entirely to communicate non-cognitive in-formation. Watzlawick has stated that when relationship is the central concern of communication (superior-subordinate, leader-follower, helper-helped, etc.), verbal language is almost meaningless.[10] In courtship, love, or combat, nonverbal communication is the effective mode. One can, of course, verbally profess love or trust, but it is most meaningfully communicated through the nonverbal codes. The verbal channel has a high potential for carrying semantic information, but the nonverbal channel has a high potential for carrying affective information. The emotional side of the message is very often expressed by the nonverbal elements. When a person is liked or disliked, often it is a case of "not only what he said, but the way he said it."

Through the nonverbal codes (all the types we have identified—vocal, object, action, etc.) we communicate power, trustworthiness, status, affection, hostility, acceptance, and the full range of attitudes and feelings. From the student in conversation with the professor who holds his eyes with hers a little longer than usual to communicate admiration and affection, to the student who narrows his eyes and sharpens his voice as he communicates hostility to the professor, nonverbal communication makes its impact on interpersonal transactions.

Recent studies tend to show that attitudes are communicated nonverbally. Posture, for example, often reflects a person's attitude toward people he is with. One experiment indicates that when men are with other men whom they dislike, they either relax very much or are very rigid depending on how threatening they perceive the other man to be. Women in this experiment always signaled dislike with a very relaxed posture. Several studies have identified strong relationships between posture (particularly trunk and head positions) and attitudes, as well as between body movement (turning away or toward, moving nearer to or further from, etc.) and attitudes.[11] Four general postural attitudes have been identified—withdrawal, approach, expansion, and contraction. Therapists, psychiatrists, and others sensitive to nonverbal communication use these postures and other nonverbal cues to diagnose and understand persons whom they wish to help.

Not only posture, but also expressive gestures, facial expressions,

10. Paul Watzlawick, Janet Helmick Beavin, and Don D. Jackson, *The Pragmatics of Human Communication* (New York: W. W. Norton & Company, Inc., 1967), p. 63.

11. See: W. James, "A Study of the Expression of Bodily Posture," *Journal of General Psychology* 7 (1932): 405–36; F. Deutsch, "Analysis of Postural Behavior," *Psychoanalytic Quarterly* 16 (1947): 195–213; Howard M. Rosenfeld, "Instrumental Affiliative Functions of Facial and Gestural Expressions," *Journal of Personality and Social Psychology* 4 (1966): 65–72; and R. Taguiri, R. R. Blake, and J. S. Bruner, "Some Determinants of the Perception of Positive and Negative Feelings in Others," *Journal of Abnormal and Social Psychology* 48 (1953): 585–92.

and vocal cues communicate inner states and emotions. Autistic gestures (interlaced fingers, closed fist, finger on the lips, nose rubbing, ear pulling, etc.) have been found to be related to inner conflict states.[12] Other signals such as clearing the throat, closing the eyes, scratching, tapping the fingers or feet are related to attitudes and emotions.

The face (smiles, frowns, etc.) is often used to express affiliation, liking and approval, or disliking and disapproval. Nods of the head may be social reinforcers. Self manipulation has been found to be positively correlated with discomfort and negatively correlated with liking and approval. A continued exchange of glances may indicate a willingness and desire to be involved in ongoing interaction; while avoidance of eye-contact often is an indication of lack of interest and a desire to break away from interaction.[13]

It is apparent to the student of communication that the nonverbal codes are especially effective in communicating affective messages.

EXPRESSIONISTIC NONVERBAL MESSAGES ARE BELIEVED TO HAVE HIGH VALIDITY—When men interact, they rarely trust in words alone. They observe the shifting forward, withdrawing, frowning, smiling, speaking in strained or serious tones, the straightening of clothing, the manipulation of a cigarette, coffee cup, or pencil. Nonverbal cues are often used to determine the authenticity of verbal messages. Thus, the blush or the frown is likely to be taken as more reliable than the accompanying verbal reassurances. When verbal cues and the nonverbal cues tell different stories, the nonverbal story tends to be believed. Words can be chosen with care, but expressive nonverbal cues cannot be chosen. The body is not so easily governed. Further, because we are trained primarily in verbal communication and often disregard nonverbal communication, we are probably far less guarded even in our instrumental nonverbal behavior than in our verbal behavior, and hence we may reveal information nonverbally that we carefully control or censure in our verbal messages.

When we are able to communicate honestly, we do not send out contradictory messages. Some of the social games we play, however, force us to send verbal messages that are inconsistent with our true feelings which are revealed through nonverbal cues. We say: "Delighted that you could come," "We had a wonderful time," "Glad to meet you," etc. regardless of our feelings. Our real attitudes and emo-

12. See: M. Krout, "An Experimental Attempt to Produce Unconscious Manual Symbolic Movements," *Journal of General Psychology* 51 (1954): 93–120; and S. Feldman, *Mannerisms of Speech and Gesture in Everyday Life* (New York: International Press, 1959).
13. Ralph Exline, David Gray, and Dorothy Schuette, "Visual Behavior in a Dyad as Affected by Interview Content and Sex of Respondent," *Journal of Personality and Social Psychology* 1 (1965): 201–9.

tions are often communicated nonverbally, and when the nonverbal message contradicts the verbal, people tend to believe the nonverbal.[14] It has higher validity. Actions do speak louder than words. We rely on the nonverbal cues to gain our *real* impression of others. In one experiment perfect strangers described their impressions of each other based on observing the visual nonverbal cues (posture, movement, facial expression, clothing, etc.) with no verbal communication. Not only did each believe he could describe the other persons after observing them, but an analysis of their descriptions revealed exceptionally high agreement on many factors including submissiveness, assurance, friendliness, psychological state, and extroversion.[15] The validity of nonverbal messages that express feelings, emotions, and relationships has been demostrated by a number of scientists.[16] Labarre has noted that successful psychiatrists, artists, anthropologists, and teachers rely on the validity of nonverbal communication:

Dr. H. S. Sullivan, for example, is known to many for his acute understanding of the postural tonuses of his patients. Another psychiatrist, Dr. E. J. Kempf, evidences in the copious illustrations of his "Psychopathology" a highly cultivated sense of the kinaesthetic language of tonuses in painting and sculpture, and can undoubtedly discover a great deal about a patient merely by glancing at him. The linguist, Dr. Stanley Newman, has a preternatural skill in recognizing psychiatric syndromes through the individual styles of tempo, stress, and intonation. The gifted cartoonist, Mr. William Steig, has produced, in *The Lonely Ones*, highly sophisticated and authentic drawings of the postures and tonuses of schizophrenia, depression, mania, paranoia, hysteria, and in fact the whole gamut of psychiatric syndromes. Among anthropologists, Dr. W. H. Sheldon is peculiarly sensitive and alert to the emotional and temperamental significance of constitutional tonuses. I believe that it is by no means entirely an illusion that an experienced teacher can come into a classroom of new students and predict with some accuracy the probable quality of individual scholastic accomplishment—even as judged by other professors—by distinguishing the unreachable, unteachable, *Apperceptions Masse-less* sprawl of one student,

14. Albert Mehrabian, "Orientation Behaviors and Nonverbal Attitude Communication," *Journal of Communication* 17 (December 1967): 331
15. R. Barker, "The Social Interrelations of Strangers and Acquaintances," *Sociometry* 5 (1942): 169–79.
16. See: Charles Darwin, *The Expression of the Emotions in Man and Animals* (New York: D. Appleton & Company, 1862; reprint ed., Chicago: University of Chicago Press, 1965); Dr. Duchenne, *Micanisme de la Physionomie Humaine* (folio edition, 1862); Paul Ekman and Wallace V. Friesen, "Nonverbal Behavior in Psychotherapy Research," in *Research on Psychotherapy*, vol. 3, ed. J. Schlien (Washington, D.C.: American Psychological Association, 1967); and Clyde L. Rousey, *Diagnostic Implications of Speech Sounds* (Springfield, Ill.: Charles C. Thomas, Publisher, 1965).

from the edge-of-the-seat starved avidity and intentness of another. Likewise, an experienced lecturer can become acutely aware of the body language of his listeners and respond to it appropriately until the room fairly dances with communication and counter-communication, head-noddings, and the tenseness of listeners, soon to be prodded into public speech.[17]

Summary

In this chapter we have identified the types of nonverbal communication, we have compared nonverbal codification to verbal codification, we have discussed three principles that operate with regard to nonverbal communication, and we have emphasized how important and central nonverbal communication is to the total process of communication. In dyadic communication, small group communication, public communication, and mass communication, the nonverbal codes play a significant role. As each person increases his understanding of the roles and functions of nonverbal communication and improves his ability to use nonverbal communication both as a sender and as a receiver, he will increase his capacity to influence or adjust to his environment.

In the chapters to come, reference to and specific application of nonverbal communication will be made. We shall see that nonverbal messages are very much a part of interviewing, of public speaking, of mass communication, and of protest and demonstration.

17. Weston Labarre, "The Cultural Basis of Emotions and Gestures," *Journal of Personality* 16 (1947): 64, 65.

For Further Reading

1. Davitz, J. R. *The Communication of Emotional Meaning*. New York: McGraw-Hill, 1964.

2. Feldman, S. *Mannerisms of Speech and Gesture in Everyday Life*. New York: International Press, 1959.

3. Hall, Edward T. *The Silent Language*. New York: Doubleday & Co., Inc., 1959.

4. Harrison, Randall. "Nonverbal Communication: Exploration into Time, Space, Action, and Object." In *Dimensions in Communication*, edited by J. H. Campbell and H. W. Hepler. Belmont, Calif.: Wadsworth Publishing Co., 1965.

5. Mehrabian, Albert. "Orientation Behaviors and Nonverbal Attitude Communication." *Journal of Communication* 17 (December 1967): 331.

6. Pei, Mario. *The Story of Language*. New York: Lippincott, 1949.

7. Reusch, Jurgen, and Kees, Weldon. *Nonverbal Communication*. Berkeley: University of California Press, 1956.

8. Watzlawick, Paul; Beavin, Janet Helmick; and Jackson, Don D. *The Pragmatics of Human Communication*. New York: W. W. Norton & Company, Inc., 1967.

Chapter 7

Dyadic Communication

Unlike public communication which tends to be monological (a one-way transmission of ideas), dyadic communication is an interpersonal situation involving dialogue, or two-way interaction. In dyadic communication two persons initiate messages and responses as they mutually influence each other in a face-to-face communication situation. Each person alternately sends and receives information. This free interchange gives to dyadic communication a high potential for information-sharing and an opportunity for effective integration in which *each* source is influenced and changed by the other. Some of the most influential and important communication situations for many of us are dyadic situations.

Six forms of dyadic communication are identified in this chapter—five will be defined and described briefly and one (interviewing) will be discussed more extensively. The six forms are intimate interaction, social conversation, interrogation or examination, debate, the fight, and the interview.[1]

Intimate Interaction

One form of dyadic communication is that of intimate interaction. Included in this category of dyadic communication is communication with a close friend, communication within the family, and communication between husband and wife. These communication situations are characterized chiefly by their intimacy and comparative permanence of relationships. Cooley refers to such groups (marriage, family, friends)

1. W. Charles Redding is credited with having originated these classifications of dyadic communication in lectures he presented in his graduate course in interviewing at Purdue University in 1970.

as the "springs of life, not only for the individual but for social institutions."[2] With a close friend, the family, or one's spouse, one can communicate in a trusting and supportive environment.

The effect of intimate interaction in the marital relationship upon interpersonal perception, interpersonal understanding, and interpersonal acceptance is greater than in other communication situations. In marriage, for example, the effect of this strong interpersonal relationship is illustrated by the *honi phenomenon*. In 1949 a woman observed the faces of her husband and another man through a window of a specially constructed room having sloping floors and walls at odd angles. This room was constructed for the conducting of experiments. A person observed walking from one corner of the room to another corner would appear to grow or shrink in size depending upon the direction he was moving. When this woman observed her husband walking in the room, however, he did *not* shrink or grow in size, but the other man did change as he walked along with her husband. This unusual observation was named the honi phenomenon. Replications of this experiment have substantiated this 1949 finding—the finding that strong interpersonal relationships, which operate to influence perception, exist between those married which cannot be inferred from the relationships of those not married.[3] Married couples with a strong perception of each other are able to overcome the distorting influence of the physical background of the room. The honi phenomenon is illustrative of one of the many strong influences produced by intimate communication. Such influences occur not only in the area of perception but in many other areas discussed in our study of intrapersonal and interpersonal communication. The significant point to be made is that in intimate interaction situations such as those with a friend, in the family, and in marriage, communication has the opportunity to be the fullest and most accurate of all interpersonal communication situations. It should be stressed that the *opportunity* for such communication development is provided, but there is no absolute guarantee that it will develop. There are communication failures in marriage, there are parents and children who do not communicate with each other successfully, and broken friendships sometimes result. If one's intrapersonal communication is extremely inaccurate and ineffective, failure in intimate interaction situations is to be expected. Yet successful intimate interaction is communication at its best.

2. Charles H. Cooley, "Primary Group and Human Nature," in *Symbolic Interaction*, ed. Jerome G. Manis and Bernard N. Meltzer (Boston: Allyn and Bacon, Inc., 1967), p. 156.
3. Warren J. Wittreich, "The Honi Phenomenon: A Case of Selective Perceptual Distortion," in *Social Perception*, ed. Hans Toch and H. C. Clay (Princeton, N. J.: D. Van Nostrand Co., Inc., 1968), p. 82.

Social Conversation

Conversation is the most characteristic behavior of sociability. Social conversation is distinguished from other talk in that at a social gathering we talk merely for the sake of talk. It is consummatory talk (of no value except at the moment) rather than instrumental talk (used to accomplish a specific goal or to solve a specific problem). In social conversation talk is its own purpose. This does not mean that any kind of talk satisfies. There is a science and art of conversation with rules of its own, but the identifying characteristic of social conversation is its sociability—its existence for its own sake. Other forms of communication—the quarrel, debate, gossip, confessional, interrogation, public speech, interview, etc.—are used to obtain practical ends. If social conversation is to remain pleasurable, no content, idea, or theme can become dominant in its own right. As soon as the talk becomes objective, its purpose changes and it ceases to be social conversation.

Not all social conversation is dyadic. In fact, social conversation at a party or social gathering is usually *not* dyadic. One of the unwritten laws of the party is that conversation shall involve more than two persons. Two-person conversations at parties exist only temporarily, i.e., until a third person or more can be quickly brought in to the conversation. Although party conversation is not dyadic, it has the same elements as does dyadic social conversation and, hence, we will consider social conversation in the party context at this time. At parties we do not talk to decide, to judge, or to solve a problem, but to socialize, to engage in play interaction. Hence, we change topics easily and quickly. In social conversation we seek to achieve harmony, a consciousness of being together, and enjoyment of each other. We reject conversation that is "too intimate" and "too individual" because it cannot be shared by others. Those topics are appropriate in intimate interaction situations such as talk with a close friend or between husband and wife, but they are not appropriate in social conversation. That is why stories and jokes are common at parties—they provide a content that can be shared by the group.

At parties we are free to wander about and talk to whomever we wish. Groups form and reform throughout the duration of the party. The truly social situation becomes a "play of sociability." Not all play is constructive, however—some games have built-in destructive elements. Berne, among others, has observed and described some of these destructive party games.[4]

Not all social conversation is party conversation, but some social conversation is truly dyadic conversation. Such conversation may occur

4. Eric Berne, *Games People Play* (New York: Grove Press, Inc., 1964).

with a stranger or with a person one knows. An important element in social conversation with a stranger is the process of becoming acquainted. Usually the acquaintance process takes the form of a kind of verbal fencing in which each person "sizes up" the other person. Each tries to find out who this other person is while concealing himself until he knows something about the other person's identification, attitudes, and values. If he discovers that the other person has attitudes and beliefs like his own, and if he feels "safe" with the other person, he will reveal himself more freely. If, however, he is threatened or insecure with this stranger, he will reveal as little of himself as he can.

Even before the verbal fencing and innocuous exchanges, there is a general and immediate perceived "image" of the stranger that provides an almost instantaneous "definition" of who this stranger is. In research studies, two-second glimpses have been sufficient for a person to develop an image and general expectation of the person glanced at. Immediately, the stranger is perceived as a unit, as a whole. Specific traits fit together to form the almost instantaneous general impression.[5] Moreover, this general instantaneous impression exerts a powerful influence on subsequent communication with this person. Also, a single dominant or striking factor may heavily influence the general impression. A smile, frown, icy glance, bright color, etc. may be especially influential in the assignment of psychological and personality traits. Some traits are especially influential in their effect upon conversation. One of these is the warmth of the person.[6] If the person is perceived as "warm," then he is likely to be perceived as also being sincere, honest, generous, wise, and happy.[7] Interactions between physical and psychological traits also determine our impression of people. Psychological traits influence our perception of physical ones, and physical traits influence our impressions of psychological ones.[8] The *first* impressions are extremely important and, therefore, those things *first noticed*—those things determining first impressions—are of special significance. Social psychologists have found that physical appearance, what one first says, and what one first does are important determiners of another's first image of that person. Hence, gestures, posture, and rate of speech are important first indicators. Similarly, some unusual or especially significant physical appearance—unusual clothes, inappropriate dress, or bright lipstick may be powerful determiners of the

5. S. E. Asch, "Forming Impressions of Personality," *Journal of Abnormal Social Psychology* 41 (1946): 258–90.
6. H. C. Smith, "Sensitivity to People" in *Social Perception*, p. 14.
7. Ibid.
8. W. J. McKeachie, "Lipstick as a Determiner of First Impressions of Personality," in *Social Perception*, p. 33.

immediate image. In an experiment described by McKeachie, college girls who wore bright lipstick were perceived by college males as having different personalities than did the same girls when they did not wear lipstick. When the girls wore lipstick they were perceived as being more frivolous, anxious, and overtly interested in the opposite sex than when they did not wear lipstick.[9] This study showed, at the time it was conducted, that there existed a stereotype about girls who wore bright lipstick and it showed that first impressions can be heavily influenced by a single physical characteristic. In dyadic communication with a stranger, the first impression is an important determiner of the interaction that follows.

Social conversation with a person one knows has the same basic characteristics as social conversation at a party. It is consummatory light, unprepared, and has no pragmatic or instrumental purpose.

Interrogation, The Fight, and Debate

Three other types of dyadic communication situations are the interrogation, the fight, and the debate. The interrogation (a police interrogation of a suspect, for example) is characterized by its emphasis on a highly controlled, one-way, linear process rather than on an open, two-way, transactional process. The strategy in interrogation is for the interrogator to control the content, timing, and wording of the messages, the psychological climate, the physical conditions or environment, and any other elements that it seems wise to control. The person questioned is given a minimum of control and initiative in the interrogation. It is often the case that interrogation relies heavily on controlled manipulation of psychological states and of the logic and meaning of content.

The fight, on the other hand, is characterized by an absence of control and order. It is a situation in which there is no agreement on how to disagree, but there is disagreement and conflict. There are many kinds of disagreements and not all disagreements are fights. Some disagreements are controversies which are resolved rationally through communication. Other disagreements are resolved through standardized communication procedures involving rules that govern the conduct of the controversy. Debate is an example of such dyadic communication. The verbal fight, however, represents controversy in its most extreme form short of physical combat. As Anatol Rapoport has written: "In the fight there is no objective of integration, but the objective is annihilation. ... In a fight, the opponent is mainly a nuisance. ... He must be eliminated, made to disappear or cut down in size or

---

9. Ibid., p. 35.

importance. The object of the fight is to harm, destroy, subdue, or drive the opponent."[10] Not all conflict is harmful, but most fights are harmful. Conflicts can range along a continuum including contests, games, arguments, debates, fights, and wars. It is the last two, the verbal fight and overt aggression, that almost always have disastrous consequences. The fight is characterized by orders, commands, allegations, hostile statements, threats, charges, and countercharges. Hopefully, people will be skilled enough in communication to resolve differences before reaching the fight stage.

As already noted, debate is a formalized system for handling controversy that cannot be resolved through discussion. The dispute is submitted to adjudication by a third party who will resolve the controversy according to a set of rules agreed to by the parties involved in the controversy. The chief characteristic of debate is its provision to disagree according to established rules.

Although all these forms of dyadic communication are important, the type of dyadic communication on which this chapter focuses primarily is the interview, and the remainder of this chapter investigates communication in the interview setting.

The Interview

The interview is a form of dyadic communication involving two parties, at least one of whom has a preconceived and serious purpose, and both of whom speak and listen from time to time.[11] This definition indicates clearly that the interview is a *bi-polar communication situation*. Although it is possible to have more than two persons in an interview, i.e., the group interview, team interview, or board interview, yet even these interviews are essentially bi-polar: there are *two* parties. Thus, the interview is different from a small, problem-solving group in which three, four, five, or some limited number of persons present several points of view and then cooperate to find a satisfactory solution. The interview is also unlike debate, even though debate is dyadic and bi-polar, in that no third party renders a decision or acts as an arbiter in the interview, as is the case in debate.

A second element in the definition of the interview is that at least one person, and perhaps both, has a *preconceived and serious purpose*. Two persons getting together and talking with neither having thought in advance about the purpose or objective to be accomplished

10. Anatol Rapoport, *Fights, Games, and Debates* (Ann Arbor: University of Michigan Press, 1961), p. 9.
11. Robert S. Goyer, W. Charles Redding, and John T. Rickey, *Interviewing Principles and Techniques* (Dubuque, Iowa: Wm. C. Brown Book Company, 1968), p. 6.

does not constitute an interview. It might be social conversation, but it is not an interview. The word *serious* helps to differentiate the interview from social conversation for enjoyment.

The third element in the definition is: *both of whom speak and listen from time to time*. This places the interview clearly within the category of interpersonal communication. This element also emphasizes the constant two-way interaction that is a characteristic of any successful interview. The situation in which one person does almost all the talking is not an interview. It may be a private lecture, or an interrogation, but it fails to become an interview. When a "high-pressure" salesman delivers a memorized fifteen-minute presentation to a trapped customer, he is not engaged in a sales interview, but in a public speech since, like public speaking, it is a one-way form of communication with one initiator of messages. Goyer, et al. have stated: "Indeed, it is probably safe to suggest that if an expository interviewer finds himself talking uninterruptedly for as long as *two minutes*, he very likely is failing to 'get through' to his interviewee."[12]   Interviewing demands that each party be a skillful participator in both sending and receiving messages. Not only do both participants send and receive messages, but they are also constantly engaged in moment-to-moment adaptations—in checking on the meanings of messages through soliciting and sending feedback. The effective participant in interviewing cannot depend absolutely on an advance outline or memorized speech. Unlike the debate situation, the interviewer or interviewee cannot plan his response while his colleague talks. Neither can the participant in an interview stop the communication process while he interprets what the other person has said and its meaning. Nor can he depend on words alone. He must be sensitive to nonverbal communication, to feedback, to feelings and attitudes, to the interpersonal relationships that exist and are developing, and to his own accuracy and efficiency in *intrapersonal* communication. The interview is one of the most demanding and sophisticated forms of communication, as well as one of the most potentially productive forms of communication, and as such, it calls into practice all those elements of intrapersonal and interpersonal communication discussed in this text.

INTERVIEW PURPOSES—Interviews are of several types and take place in many different contexts with a variety of purposes. Nevertheless, it is possible to classify interviews in terms of the *dominant* purpose the interviewer (the person who has the chief responsibility for achieving a successful outcome) has in mind. Interviews have been classified into ten types: (1) information-getting, (2) information-giving, (3) advocat-

12. Goyer, Redding, and Rickey, *Interviewing*, p. 14.

ing, (4) problem-solving, (5) counseling, (6) application for employment or job, (7) receiving complaints, (8) reprimanding or correcting, (9) appraising, and (10) stress interviewing.[13]

In the information-getting interview, the objective is usually to obtain beliefs, attitudes, feelings, or other data from the interviewee. Public opinion poll and research surveys are typical well-known examples, but in fact, most people participate frequently in essentially the same kind of communication situation.

The purpose of the information-giving interview is to explain or instruct. Giving work instructions to a new employee or explaining the procedures and policies of the organization to a new member are examples of information-giving interviews.

Sometimes, a person wishes to modify the beliefs or attitudes of another person and attempts to do so through the persuasive interview. The sales interview is a typical example of the interviewer (the persuader or salesman) attempting to sway the interviewee (the respondent or customer) towards adopting his point of view. Another example of the advocating interview is the attempt of a subordinate to persuade his chairman, foreman, or boss to accept a proposal; or when you go to the bank to secure a loan you are a persuader engaged in a persuasive interview. Throughout life each of us engages in interviews in which we try to persuade another person to agree with us.

The problem-solving interview involves both information and persuasion just as does the problem-solving small group. In fact, the problem-solving interview could be classified as a two-person discussion or problem-solving group.

The counseling interview may be directly persuasive as one person tries to get the other to change his behavior in a prescribed manner, or it may be relatively non-persuasive (i.e., non-directive) in that its objective is to provide a situation in which the client can gain insight into his own problems. Counseling interviews focus on the *personal* problems of the person being advised. This type of interview requires a high degree of skill and psychological sophistication on the part of the counselor. It is far beyond the scope of the skills with which we are concerned in this chapter.

The employment interview, an interview in which virtually every member of society participates sooner or later, is a special type of interview that utilizes information-getting, information-giving, and persuasion as each party tries to get information from the other party and, perhaps, tries to persuade the other party.

Receiving complaints and reprimanding are specialized interviews which require the combination of several skills—persuading, problem-

13. Goyer, Redding, and Rickey, *Interviewing,* pp. 7–8.

solving, counseling, information-giving, and information-getting. The purpose of the receiver of complaints is to do as much as possible to satisfy grievances. The purpose of the reprimand interview is to change the behavior of the interviewee favorably by helping him acquire new insight and motivation.

The appraising interview aims to inform the interviewee as to how well he is doing at his job and to give guidelines relative to his future performance. This interview of appraisal is related, in part, to the counseling interview.

Stress interviewing is often used as a testing procedure in which an opportunity is provided to observe how the interviewee reacts or behaves under pressure. This chapter is not concerned with stress interview or with appraisal, reprimand, complaint, and counseling interviews. We will focus our attention on two kinds of interviews—the information-getting interview, and the employment interview.

PARTICIPANTS IN THE INTERVIEW—The participants in interviews generally are most commonly referred to as *interviewer* and *interviewee*, although these terms are not the most appropriate for some interview situations. Terms such as counselor/counselee or persuader/persuadee are, for example, better terms for the counseling situation and the persuasive interview. However, regardless of the term used—counselor, persuader, or interviewer—it refers to the party that carries the chief responsibility for achieving a successful outcome of the interview. It should be recognized, of course, that in many interviews both parties accept a responsibility for the successful outcome of the interview. This is especially true of the employment interview in which the employer wishes to "sell" his company and the applicant attempts to "sell" his qualifications.

The interviewee in most interview situations has the power of decision. In the information-getting interview the respondent (interviewee) decides whether to provide the information or not; in the reprimand and appraisal interviews the interviewee decides whether he will accept the correction or evaluation; and in the persuasive interview the respondent has the power of accepting or rejecting the persuasive attempt. In the employment interview, however, both parties share the decision-making power.

There are role-relationships in every interview as there are in other communication situations. Normally, it is the responsibility of the interviewer to take the initiative in the interview and to clarify role-relationships if such clarification is needed. It is not unusual in the employment interview for roles to change as the interview develops: e.g., at one time the applicant is the respondent and at another time the employer is the respondent. Since the functions of each interview participant vary widely among types of interviews as well as from specific interview to specific interview, it is unwise to think in terms of rigid, universal duties.

THE INFORMATIONAL INTERVIEW—There are two general methods of conducting the informational interview—direct and nondirect. With the direct method, the interviewer decides what question will be asked, what topics will be covered, the sequence of the topics and questions, and the over-all procedure that will be followed in the interview. In the nondirective approach, the interviewer allows the interviewee to make almost all of these decisions. The interviewee is reinforced and encouraged to talk about whatever he wishes to. These two kinds of approaches are not absolutely exclusive; rather, there is often some of both in most information-getting interviews. The interviewer usually has a plan in which topics are identified and ordered and in which specific questions are indicated and ordered, but he is sensitive enough to the dynamics and interpersonal relationships of the situation to operate nondirectively in certain phases or places during the interview when it seems wise to do so. When interviews are used for research purposes, of course, it may be necessary to standardize the procedure so that there can be a basis for response comparisons; but if the purpose is to get information from the one interviewee in a non-research situation, then a flexible, alert approach may be profitably used.

Interviews may be classified as standardized or nonstandardized, i.e., as structured or nonstructured. Any interview that is directive is standardized or structured, and any interview that is nondirective is nonstandardized or nonstructured. The terms directive, standardized, and structured are often used interchangeably, as are the terms nondirective, nonstandardized, and nonstructured.

There are two kinds of standardized interviews, the schedule standardized interview and the nonschedule standardized interview. The schedule standardized interview is one in which wording and sequence of questions are determined in advance by the interviewer and the questions on the schedule are asked of all respondents in exactly the same way. This kind of interview is sometimes used to gather data in research projects. The nonschedule standardized interview seeks to gather information on the same topics from all the respondents, but it does not use a rigid set of questions that are presented to all respondents. Rather, the interviewer is thoroughly familiar with what he wants to investigate and with the areas to be covered, but he phrases the questions and arranges the sequence of questions and topics to fit the interviewee and the interview situation as it evolves. He can vary the wording and sequence of questions for maximal effectiveness with individual respondents. If the respondent does not understand a question, the interviewer can rephrase it; if the respondent indicates he is fearful on a certain topic, the interviewer can drop the topic and go to another topic for the moment. The nonschedule standardized interview attempts to cover the same topics for all respondents, but it allows flexibility and adaptation in order to facilitate the acquisition of the information. It is apparent that the nonschedule standardized approach is especially advantageous for the two kinds of interviews studied in this chapter.

The nonstandardized interview is especially useful in counseling interviews, some sales interviews, and some stress interviews, but we shall not be as concerned with this method as with the nonschedule standardized approach. Again, we should keep in mind the fact that these approaches are not necessarily independent of one another. On the contrary, all three forms may be utilized in an interview. In one area of the interview, the interviewer may desire to present each interviewee with exactly the same questions (worded and arranged alike) so that the comparisons of the responses can be precise; in another area of the interview, although the interviewer may want to secure the same information from all respondents, he may see fit to adjust the questions to the individual and ask the questions at appropriate times regardless of the point at which those opportunities appear in the interview; and, in yet another area of the interview, the interviewer may wish to be quite nondirective as he follows a nonstandardized procedure.

THE QUESTION–ANSWER PROCESS—The information-getting interview relies in great measure upon the question–answer process. There are many ways of classifying the various types of questions. Regardless of the classification system used, it appears to be a useful first step in developing skill in the question–answer process to be able to identify types of questions and their uses as well as types of answers. Our system calls for classifying interview questions into five basic types: open, closed, mirroring, probing, and leading.

Open questions. Open questions call for a response of more than a few words. One type of open question, the open-ended question, is extremely vague in that it may do nothing more than specify a topic and ask the respondent to talk. An example is "What do you think about life?" or "Tell me a little about yourself."

A second kind of open question is more direct in that it identifies a more restricted topic area and asks for a reply on that restricted topic. In some classification systems this question is classified separately from open questions and is called the direct question. An example is "What did you do on your weekends last winter?"

Closed question. A second category of questions is the closed question. The closed question calls for a specific response of a few words. One type of closed question is the yes-no, or bipolar question. It calls for a "yes" or a "no" answer—or, perhaps, an "I don't know" reply. "Did you attend the last home basketball game last winter?" is a closed question. Similarly, "What two courses did you like most, and what two courses did you like least in high school?" is a closed question, though not a yes-no question.

One important principle related to the use of open or closed questions is that these types of questions tend to influence the length of the interviewee's responses. Open questions encourage the respondent to talk more, while closed questions discourage participation by the respondent.[14] Since one of the problems in most interviews is getting the interviewee to become freely involved and to participate in the interview, it is unwise for the interviewer to plan and use only closed questions. Neither should an interviewer in the informative, persuasive, or employment interview rely solely on open questions. Doing so, he may discover that, even though the interviewee does talk a lot he gives up very little specific information about himself. Further, the exclusive use of open questions often results in covering fewer topics than might have been possible with more direction and specificity. It is desirable to learn to use both types of questions. Generally speaking, open questions are more likely to be used in the early part of the interview or at the introduction of each new topic area, while closed questions are used as follow-ups for the responses to open questions.

Mirror questions. Mirror questions are nondirective techniques. The reason for using a mirror question is to encourage the interviewee to expand on a response that the interviewer believes was incomplete. Mirror questions are often restatements of what the interviewee has just said. If the interviewee has said: "I don't approve of legalizing abortion," a mirror question might be: "You say that abortion should not be legalized?" Closely related to the mirror question is the probe.

Probing questions. Some questions are asked in order to probe more deeply into the reasons for an attitude or belief, or to elicit more specific information. Not all probes are questions of *why* or *how*, although those are common probing questions. There are a variety of other vocalizations that act effectively as probes and encouragements. Brief sounds or phrases such as "Uh-huh," "I see," "That's interesting," "Oh?" "Good," "I understand," and "Go on" have the effect of requesting further comment from the respondent. Probes and encouragements are introduced at any time—

---

14. Stephen A. Richardson, Barbara S. Dohrenwend, and David Klein, *Interviewing: Its Forms and Functions* (New York: Basic Books, Inc., 1965), p. 147.

during pauses or while the interviewee is speaking. They indicate careful attention and interest, and they have the function of encouraging the respondent to "tell more" without specifying in a closed way the further response. It is important that an interviewer avoid the habit of relying on one reinforcing or probing word.

Equally as important as direct probing questions and sounds or phrases of encouragement is the use of silence. As indicated in Chapter 6 in the discussion of nonverbal communication, silence communicates. The inexperienced interviewer is often afraid of pauses and silences. He tends to fill every silence, and so doing, rushes through the interview. Sometimes, if the respondent is slow in answering a question, the inexperienced interviewer may rush in to rephrase the question or to ask a new question. With experience, interviewers can learn when to use silence as a means of communication—as a probe, for example. Silences, if they are effective as probes, must be terminated by the respondent. Research findings indicate that silences of three to six seconds are most effective in getting the respondent to provide more information.[15] If the respondent does not terminate the silence within that time, the chances of his remaining silent increase. This means not only that the interviewer will have to speak, but that the use of silence will have been ineffective and that it will have had a damaging effect upon the interview situation. Hence, when one uses silence as a probe, he should be prepared to terminate the silence within six seconds or at such time as it seems destined to fail as a probing technique.

Leading questions. Leading questions strongly imply or encourage a specific answer. They "lead" the respondent to an answer the interviewer expects. The leading question can be quite *detrimental* to the interview when used for the wrong reasons. If the interviewer wants straightforward, valid, and reliable information from the respondent, he will want to carefully avoid using leading questions. Cannell and Kahn state: "Questions should be phrased so that they contain no suggestion as to the most appropriate response,"[16] and Bingham, Moore, and Gustad state: "Avoid implying the answer to your own question."[17] If, however, the interviewer wishes to *test* the respondent, to see if he *really* under-

15. See: R. L. Gordon, "An Interaction Analysis of the Depth-Interview" (Ph.D. diss., University of Chicago, 1954); and G. Saslow et al. "Test–Retest Stability of Interaction Patterns During Interviews Conducted One Week Apart," *Journal of Abnormal Social Psychology* 54 (1957): 295–302.
16. C. F. Cannell and R. L. Kahn, "The Collection of Data by Interviewing," in *Research Methods in the Behavioral Sciences*, ed. L. Festinger and D. Katz (New York: Dryden Press, 1953), p. 346.
17. W. V. D. Bingham, B. V. Moore, and J. W. Gustad, "How to Interview" (New York: Harper & Brothers, 1959), p. 74.

stands, or is *genuinely* committed, then the leading question may be quite useful. For example, when the speech therapist asks the mother of a stuttering child, "You are slapping his hands every time he starts to stutter, aren't you?" he is leading her to an incorrect answer unless she clearly understands that slapping the child for stuttering is inappropriate behavior. When this tactic is taken by the interviewer, he is sometimes referred to as the *devil's advocate*.

One type of leading question is the *yes-response* question, or the *no-response* question. "Naturally, you agreed with the decision, didn't you?" is an example of a yes-response question. One of the components of leading questions is *expectation*. If the interviewer asks, "Are you twenty-one years old?" the question is a direct, closed question, but it is not leading. If the interviewer, however, asks, "Of course, you are twenty-one years old, aren't you?" he indicates an expectation. Expectations can be identified by the syntax and logic of the question, but, as noted in Chapter 6 on nonverbal communication, intonation can communicate doubt, confidence, and *expectation*. Through intonation and emphasis one might make the question, "Did *you* agree with that decision?" a leading question. The intonation and emphasis could register surprise and incredulity at anything other than the expected answer.

Another form of the leading question is the loaded question, which uses loaded words and has high emotional connotations. It reaches "touchy spots" and strikes strong feelings. It may present a dilemma from which it is difficult for the respondent to escape. Questions that are not stated objectively are considered loaded. Various techniques are used to indicate the bias or expectation. Prestige may be used. "The President of the United States believes that the problem is serious. Do you agree?" is an example of using prestige to indicate the bias. The interviewer may also associate positive stereotypes with responses that are desired or negative stereotypes with responses that are not desired. It is apparent that loaded questions should be used with extreme caution, and probably not at all by the inexperienced interviewer. When used by an insightful and skilled interviewer, the loaded question may uncover important hidden information, attitudes, or feelings.

To gain an understanding of the question-answer process, one needs to become familiar with and be able to recognize the various types of questions that may be used. Through guided practice, he can develop skill in using questions. He must also develop skill in recognizing inadequate answers to his questions.

Inadequate answers. One kind of inadequate response is the *oververbalized response*. In one trial situation, the lawyer asked a witness how she came to be at a certain place at 1:30 A.M. She proceeded to tell in detail how she had spent the preceding twenty-four hours. After five minutes in relating what she had done between 7:00 A.M. and noon, the attorney was finally successful in interrupting her and requesting her to skip those details and tell why she was at that certain place at 1:30.

Another kind of inadequate response is the *irrelevant answer*. It simply has nothing to do with the question asked. It has no bearing on the subject or purpose of the interview.

A third unacceptable response is the *inaccurate response*. The information may be purposely or accidentally false, but it is inaccurate, detrimental, and unacceptable. Inaccurate responses are often difficult to detect, but when inaccuracy is suspected related questions and delayed, repeated questions may be asked to check consistency.

The *partial response* is a fourth kind of inadequate answer. Partial responses are easily detected if the interviewer is alert and thinking. If the interviewer is hastily taking the first small answer and rushing on to his next question, he may settle for partial responses when he should have probed and elicited more information.

Nonresponse is the fifth inadequate response. It is a rather serious response which may be ignored and the question dropped, or which may be probed if the interviewer thinks it would be profitable to do so. One of the most common weaknesses related to using questions in the interview is the tendency to take too much for granted, i.e., the interviewer too easily assumes that his interpretation of the interviewee's responses are accurate. He jumps to conclusions too quickly. He fails to check the meanings of the messages. The interviewer also assumes too quickly that the interviewee understands the question—that the respondent has the same frame of reference as does the interviewer. Such assumptions are not warranted, as has been stressed throughout this text. As interviewers and as interviewees we need to develop a critical attitude toward our questions and answers. We must curb the tendency to accept the first meaning that pops into our heads. The tendency to take things for granted, to presume, is not easy to correct. It is a common characteristic we all share. It is a subtle fault, and for this reason, we need to discipline ourselves—to stop and ask ourselves, "Now, what am I taking for granted here?" Successful interviewing requires effective interpersonal and intrapersonal communication.

We must remember that in the informational interview, information is forfeited when we omit data and meanings, when we distort statements (sometimes we mistake qualified statements for definite statements), and when we make additions to what the other person has said. We can prevent some of this forfeiting of information if we are systematic, if we employ verbal emphasis and attention factors, if we encourage and use feedback, if we summarize frequently, and if we are sensitive to the other person's viewpoint, frame of reference, experience, and intended meaning. We must remember that role differences, interpersonal attraction, thinking habits, attitudes, and poor listening habits can act as barriers to effective informational interviewing.

Interviewing is a complex, but potentially richly rewarding communication experience. It requires critical ability within the context of a noncritical attitude, emotional control, and skill in communication.

THE STRUCTURE OF THE INFORMATIVE INTERVIEW—There are at least three parts to all interviews—the opening, the substantive part, and the closing. The initial stage, opening the interview, is quite important, for during this time the relationship between the interviewer and the respondent is established. The objectives of the opening are to establish confidence, trust, clarity of the purpose of the interview, and the identification of mutual goals. Rapport, an important element throughout the interview, is largely established in the opening stage of the interview. Some pre-interview acts also relate to the establishment of rapport. The request for an interview should *never* be made in terms that alarm or threaten the interviewee, for example; and the place selected for the interview should be private, comfortable, and conducive to a smooth and satisfactory interview operation. In addition to pre-interview planning, certain behavior during the opening of the interview can help to establish good rapport, confidence, and relaxation for the interview. The purpose of the interview should be clearly explained and the procedures indicated and mutually agreed to or adjusted.

The second phase of the interview is the substantive part of the interview that relies heavily upon the question-answer process previously discussed.

The final part of the interview is the closing. Some interviews come to natural closings as a result of the nature of the progress of the discussion or as a result of the inclination of the participants. Other interviews need to be continued, but circumstances dictate that they must be closed. Still other interviews could be continued profitably because things are going so well, but time dictates that they must be ended. Regardless of the reasons or conditions, the interview closing ought to contain a short summary by the interviewer, an opportunity for the interviewee to make additions and corrections, and an indication of the next steps, or where-to-go-from-here.

THE EMPLOYMENT INTERVIEW—The employment interview combines several purposes—to inform, to get information, and to persuade; and the employment interview is unique, also, in that both the applicant and the employer enjoy a power of decision. Generally, the applicant should consider the employment interview as a situation in which he is in the position of persuading the prospective employer that he (the applicant) represents a good investment for the employer, but sometimes situations arise in which the procedure is reversed and the primary burden is upon the employer to sell the job to the applicant.

The employment interview represents a communication situation in which almost every person in college will participate sooner or later —an extraordinarily important communication situation. An understanding of and skill in interpersonal communication can enhance one's performance in the interview. Consider, therefore, three topics that can be of particular value: they deal with special understanding relative to personal conduct, to what the typical interviewer wants to know about the applicant, and to what the applicant needs to learn about the position.

Personal conduct in the employment interview. The following six elements are important as far as personal conduct in the interview is concerned. From these behaviours, appearances, and physical traits, the interviewee is judged and his image constructed. Whether employer or applicant, you should be concerned with these factors. They are set forth here as a convenient checklist rather than for discussion of each item.

1. Dress, appearance, and physical bearing
2. Bodily behavior during the interview
   a. Walking (entering and exiting)
   b. Shaking hands
   c. Posture
   d. Facial expression and eye-contact
   e. General animation
   f. Mannerisms indicating tension; or aimless movements
3. Use of the voice
   a. Quality of voice
   b. Pitch level
   c. Audibility
   d. Intelligibility (rate, phrasing, and articulation)
   e. Expressiveness
4. Use of language
   a. Vocabulary
   b. Oral grammar
   c. Slang and triteness
5. Attitudes (minimum essentials for the average interview)

     a.   Directness—not withdrawal (revealed in eye-contact, body-tone, and posture)
     b.   Responsiveness—actively participates
     c.   Mental alertness
     d.   Sincerity
     e.   Emotional control (poised, controlled, open, but no cockiness)
     f.   Honesty
6.   Ability to listen

Using this checklist and applying the principles and concepts discussed in the chapters on interpersonal communication and nonverbal communication, one can describe, evaluate, and establish self-improvement objectives for participation in employment interviews.

What the typical employer wants to know about the applicant. The results of several studies of employment interviews indicate that the major areas of concern to the interviewer are the applicant's ability, desire to work, social-emotional maturity, and character. An applicant, knowing that these areas are important to the interviewer, would be wise to give some thought to these questions so that he can provide full and accurate information in an effective manner.

In terms of *ability*, interviewers are especially interested in the applicant's vocational and avocational experiences. It is wise for the applicant to know in substance how these experiences contribute toward making him capable for the position he is seeking. It is to the advantage of the applicant to be able to point out such relationships or applications rather than leaving them to the imagination or "assumed knowledge" of the interviewer.

Education and training, both formal and informal, are part of one's ability, and should be fully explored in the employment interview. Similarly, intelligence—as revealed through grades in school, activities, honors, recognitions, and conduct during the interview—is related to ability. The questions asked by the interviewee, as well as the responses he makes to questions asked by the interviewer are used to evaluate his intelligence and general ability.

A second area of major concern is *desire to work.* Studies of interviewing show that questions and information relating to three areas—past record of changes in jobs, schools or majors, applicant's reasons for wanting the job for which he is applying, and his knowledge of this company or organization—are used to evaluate the applicant's desire to work.

The third major area of concern for the employer is the social-emotional level of maturity of the applicant. The typical interviewer may attempt to discover the applicant's personal goals, his measures of independence, self-reliance, creativity, and imagination; also his ability to exercise authority and to take orders or be corrected.

Finally, the character of the applicant is of importance to the interviewer. His character may be judged on the basis of his personal behavior, honesty, history of financial responsibility or irresponsibility, and the accuracy and objectivity of his self-reports (the things he divulges about himself during the interview). As we shall note again, later, dishonesty, sham, and boastfulness are extremely detrimental and even disastrous in the employment interview.

What the applicant should know about the position. Not only should the applicant be concerned and prepared to satisfy the employer in terms of what the employer wants to know, but it is also necessary that the applicant systematically and thoroughly discover some things that he needs to know.

One of the most important areas of concern is that of job expectation or requirements beyond the brief job description. There is a history of sad stories about jobs that were not at all what the applicants assumed or understood them to be when they accepted the positions. Careful thought and effort should be given to understanding and fully satisfying one's self as to what the job entails.

A second area is that of discovering who one's co-workers are. A common background in education, values, philosophy, and training will enhance the relationship one has with his co-workers and increase his potential satisfaction with the job.

The applicant should also be concerned with the opportunities and policies for advancement. Other items of information that are needed include information on benefits, hours, pay, job security, and working conditions. It is helpful for the applicant to have these areas clearly in mind during the interview so that he can secure the information necessary for a good decision.

Specific suggestions for the applicant and the interviewer. The following list of suggestions for interviewers and interviewees in the employment interview should be considered as general guidelines.[18]

Suggestions for the applicant:
1. Clarify the job requirements.
2. State why you are applying for this job with this company.
3. Present your qualifications in terms of having something of value to offer the company. Deal as much as possible in specific details and examples— job experiences, avocations, travel, activities, offices held, organizations, and school work.

18. Adapted from Goyer, Redding, and Rickey, *Interviewing*, pp. 23–25.

4. Do not hesitate to *admit potential "weaknesses."* Under no circumstances should you attempt to bluff or fake on these but wherever possible, *make a transition from a "weakness" to a strength*; or at least, when the facts justify it, show some good *extenuating circumstance* for the "weakness." (This does NOT mean supplying alibis or excuses!)
5. DO NOT depend merely on a "smooth front" (appearance and smile) to "sell yourself." Provide full information to the prospective employer.
6. Get as much information as possible on such "sensitive" matters as *salary* (usually in terms of a *range*, or of the *"going average"*).
7. Let the employer set the "tone" or atmosphere of the interview. Be a *little* more formal than usual—but not a stuffed shirt! Be cautious about jokes, wisecracks, sarcastic asides, etc.!
8. Watch the opening moments of the interview. Avoid making remarks that create a *"negative set"* for the rest of the interview. Avoid starting the interview with a remark such as: "I'm really not sure that my background will be appropriate for your company, or for this job." Or: "I'm sorry to say I haven't had any experience along these lines."
9. *Be informed on the company:* its history, geographical locations, general methods of doing business, reputation, etc.
10. Try never to have an interview concluded without *some* sort of *understanding about where you stand*, what is to happen next, who is to contact whom, etc. This does *not* mean you are to push the employer against the wall and force a definite commitment!

Suggestions for the employer:
1. Take the initiative in getting the interview under way; don't just sit back and stare at the applicant. Offer your hand first. Ask him to be seated. Establish "rapport" *before* probing for information about him!
2. Make an easy, casual, smooth *transition* from opening greetings to the first serious topic of the interview.
3. *Start off with "easy" materials* and aspects on the applicant's background that are not sensitive areas. Encourage him to talk freely about something which, on the application blank, should be easy for him to discuss with specific details and examples.
4. Don't give a "sales pitch."
5. Do more listening than talking. Encourage the applicant to "open up." Listen carefully—including "between the lines." Insert brief "prompters" to encourage more talk; use "mirror" ("turn-back") techniques.
6. Don't exaggerate the benefits of the company or the job! Create confidence and trust by being honest about potential or actual drawbacks.
7. *Avoid evaluative comments on the applicant's answers* such as "that's too bad," or "I'm certainly glad you said that!"
8. *Without being mechanical* about it, try to cover topics in a *systematic* order. Your objective is not only to avoid hit-and-miss jumping around, but also to avoid giving the impression you're engaging in an oral examination!
9. Be alert to "cues" in the applicant's answers and behavior. Adapt immediately to what he says so that you can *"follow up a promising lead."* Probe suspected weaknesses.
10. Ask questions which will reveal the applicant's *attitudes* and *personality* in terms of the job's *total* requirements.

Common mistakes and irritating factors in the employment interview. Goetzinger's study of irritating factors in employment interviews consisted of 479 questionnaires returned by personnel men engaged in employment interviewing on campuses. Of the almost 100 factors identified by the professional interviewers as irritating, 23 were considerably more irritating than the others. These 23 are listed here in order of seriousness (as rated in questionnaires by respondents), not in order of frequency.[19]

The applicant:
1. Is caught lying
2. Has alcohol on his breath
3. Is rude or impolite
4. Shows a lack of interest in the interview
5. Has a belligerent attitude
6. Puts his feet on the desk
7. Doesn't want to fill out the application blank
8. Lacks sincerity
9. Is evasive concerning information about himself
10. Is concerned only about the pay
11. Seems unable to follow instructions
12. Tries to bluff during the interview
13. Isn't able to concentrate
14. Displays a lack of initiative
15. Is indecisive
16. Has an arrogant attitude
17. Has a persecuted attitude
18. Wants to start in an executive position
19. Has dirty hands or face
20. Tries to use "pull" to get the job
21. Wants the job in order to stay out of the armed forces
22. Wears his hat during the interview
23. Has an offensive body odor

The employment interview is a give-and-take process, highly dynamic and rich in its informational and persuasive potential. The communication skills involved are varied and include those examined in this text in intrapersonal and interpersonal communication. The person who desires to improve his behavior as an interviewer or interviewee must learn to be extremely perceptive and accurate in his observation and understanding of the other person and in his relationship with that person during the interview situation.

19. Charles S. Goetzinger, "An Analysis of Irritating Factors in Initial Employment Interviews of Male College Graduates" (Ph.D. diss., Purdue University, 1959).

Summary

This chapter has focused on dyadic communication. We have identified six types of dyadic communication and have discussed in considerable detail one form of dyadic communication, the interview. In each of these forms of dyadic communication, the skills and understandings acquired in both intrapersonal and interpersonal communication must be used if the purposes of these communication situations are to be realized. Accuracy in perceiving, receiving, and processing information, in using language, and in thinking (intrapersonal communication skills) are very much a part of interpersonal communication. In marital communication (or other intimate communication), in social conversation, in interviewing, and in other types of dyadic communication, deficiencies in intrapersonal communication figure prominently in breakdowns and failures. Similarly, as we will discover later, public communication and protest communication are influenced significantly by intrapersonal and interpersonal communication factors.

For Further Reading

1. Berne, Eric. *Games People Play*. New York: Grove Press, Inc., 1964.

2. Bingham, W. V. D.; Moore, B. V.; and Gustad, J. W. *How to Interview*. New York: Harper & Brothers, 1959.

3. Kahn, Robert L., and Cannell, Charles F., *The Dynamics of Interviewing*. New York: John Wiley & Sons, 1957.

4. Rapoport, Anatol. *Fights, Games, and Debates*. Ann Arbor: University of Michigan Press, 1961.

5. Richardson, Stephen A.; Dohrenwend, Barbara S.; and Klein, David. *Interviewing: Its Forms and Functions*. New York: Basic Books, Inc., 1965.

6. Smith, H. C., and Toch, Hans, eds. *Social Perception*. Princeton, N.J.: D. Van Nostrand Co., Inc., 1968.

Chapter 8

Small Group Communication

The small group has become the most common setting for speech communication. One social scientist has stated that the key to understanding our society and its problems is the unit of human interaction known as the *small group*.[1] Small groups operate in every organized human activity. As a student, you have participated in innumerable problem-solving small groups; the average professional man or businessman attends as many as two or three luncheons or evening meetings a week, in addition to the many conferences and committee meetings in which he takes part during his regular working hours; and representatives in government carry on most of the work of solving problems and making decisions in small groups. Most people participate in small groups, formally and informally. Since it is virtually impossible for an educated person in a responsible position to avoid participation, understanding how small groups function is essential.

In order to understand how small groups function, we must examine the nature of the small group. The small group has a powerful potential for action. When people come together in a group, friendships or hostilities can develop. Decisions can be made and problems can be solved. Many people, however, are not able to participate in decision-making effectively in our society because they do not understand the nature of the small group or their role in a small group.

The Nature of the Small Group

Homans has defined a group as "a number of persons who communicate with one another often over a span of time, and who are few enough

1. Gerald M. Phillips, *Communication and the Small Group* (Indianapolis: The Bobbs-Merrill Co., 1966), p. 3.

143

so that each person is able to communicate with all the others, not at
secondhand, through other people, but face-to-face. . . . A chance meeting of casual acquaintances does not count as a group for us."[2] Neither
does the collection of people at a basketball game constitute a group.
They are an aggregation, but not a group in the sense we will use the
term. Congregations, aggregations, audiences, and other collections of
a large number of individuals are not groups. They cannot communicate with each other (any individual with all the others) face-to-face. A
member of an aggregation or collection of people cannot interact with
all the others. A group involves two or more persons interacting rele-
vantly.

It is through significant interaction with others that a *Homo sapiens*
becomes a human being with specific identity. It is in the context of
groups that the human infant develops his humanness. To be isolated
from human interaction is to not become fully human.

When there is a band of communication established between two
or more, a group is created. A group is the antithesis of *aloneness*, but
being in a collection of people does not guarantee that one is not alone.
Most of us have had the experience of being jostled and bumped in the
congested crowds on busy sidewalks, at the state fair, at sports events,
or in the large stores during the Christmas shopping rush—the experience of being "inundated" by people, and yet feeling very much alone.
Conversely, we have also had the experience of being alone and yet not
really feeling alone. Aloneness does not necessarily destroy the bond of
communication. The letters, the telephone calls, the knowing that
another or others are thinking of us—these bonds defy being alone as
being one-to-one equated with loneliness and isolation from others.
One may be by himself, but not alone; and one may be surrounded by
people, but be very much alone. It is the bond of communication,
relevant interaction, that is a key element—an essential characteristic
of groups. When there is no relevant interaction and cohesiveness,
groups disintegrate.

Types of Groups

There are essentially five kinds of small groups: primary groups, casual
groups, problem-solving groups, educational groups, and therapeutic
groups.

PRIMARY GROUPS—Primary groups, the first that every human being
experiences, are *primary* in the sense that they give the individual his

2. George C. Homans, *The Human Group* (New York: Harcourt, Brace & World, Inc.,
1950), p. 1.

earliest, most basic, and most complete experience of social unity. The individual's first primary group is the family. It is one of the most elaborate, complex, intimate, and influential groups we experience, and it gives us our first training in social behavior and interpersonal relationships.

During early preschool years, each of us probably began playing with other children, and a second primary group was formed—the peer group. As we grew older, we became involved with other peer groups and even now we have membership in peer groups composed of friends, work colleagues, church groups, etc. These are primary groups and they exert a strong influence upon our lives.

CASUAL GROUPS—The coffee group, bull sessions, and social gatherings are examples of casual groups. These groups do not exist to solve specific problems although they may, from time to time, hash out problems or get into heated discussions on important issues. Rather, they exist to exchange ideas, to enjoy interacting with one another, and to extend the warmth of companionship. Conversation may ramble over many topics. There is no specified agenda; no requirement to stay on the subject. The members of such groups have as their goal friendly companionship.

EDUCATIONAL GROUPS—A third type of group is the educational group, the purpose of which is to instruct, to teach, or to learn. There are any number of adult study clubs; for example, the Great Books Club and the League of Women Voters. In classrooms, the small-group format is often used as a vehicle for instruction and learning.

THERAPEUTIC GROUPS—The small group is widely used in therapy. Social workers, psychiatrists, and psychologists are employing small group techniques in increasing numbers. The therapeutic group is interested in personal improvement—changes in behavior, values, or attitudes of the individual. There is no collective group goal; rather, each member seeks solutions to his own problems. The group is a vehicle used to aid in the discovery of solutions and new insights, as well as to facilitate mutual interpersonal support.

Problem-solving groups, education groups, or casual groups can also have therapeutic effects on the individual, but that is not their primary purpose as is the case for therapeutic groups. Apparently there is something about the atmosphere of the small group that makes it conducive to individual and group problem solving.

PROBLEM-SOLVING GROUPS—The focus of this chapter is on the problem-solving group. Most of us belong to groups that have specific tasks assigned to them. Unlike the casual group or the therapeutic group, the problem-solving group has a particular *group goal* involving some anticipated action. Although the difference in goals distinguishes the five types of groups, all five kinds contain the essence of the group process —face-to-face interaction that is relevant to all members.

Committees (except for committees of the whole) are small groups, and some conferences are small groups, except when we use the term conference as synonymous with convention or large meeting.

Some small groups are on-going groups in the sense that they have permanent membership over an extended period of time, and they have problem-solving objectives—administrating, decision-making, policy-making—that are on-going. The staff meeting is an on-going group meeting, for example. Permanent committees are also examples of on-going groups. Other small, problem-solving groups are appointment groups. The temporary committee and ad hoc committee are examples of appointment groups. Their task is specific and when it is completed the group ceases to function. The decorations committee for the Homecoming Dance is an example of a temporary small group.

In order to understand how small groups function, we must examine the behavior of individuals in groups and the behavior of the group as a whole. We also need to examine the process of problem-solving intrinsically (problem problems—the agenda) and extrinsically (people problems—the hidden agenda). A small group is an entity with a style and personality of its own, and although made up of individuals, each of whom brings his own personality, values, feelings, skills, and life history to the group, the small group becomes something *more than the sum total of individual behaviors*. Not only does each member influence the group, but the group also influences each member. Several factors including individual personalities, communication skills, leadership, and group size influence the productivity of the group. We now examine some of the important factors or problems related to the individual.

Problems Related to the Individual

If one is to become effective as a participant in small groups, he needs to develop a sensitivity to himself and his behavior as a member of the group. Each person, when he joins a new group, encounters some common problems: belonging, taking a role, gaining identity and status, developing affection, and developing a sensitivity to group processes. These five factors are extremely important to each individual, and the successful group member understands these problems and functions effectively as he resolves or copes intelligently with each.

BELONGING—One of the first issues one must face on becoming a member of a small group is "Do I want to be a member of this group?" Sometimes, of course, one is arbitrarily or automatically a member of a group. He is appointed to the committee and born into the family; yet even in these groups a person can decide that he would just as soon not belong, or he can decide that he is glad that he does belong—he wants to belong, to be involved. That decision, to want to belong or to become genuinely involved, is a critical factor in the ability of the individual to become a constructive member of the group. If this question is not resolved affirmatively (i.e., wanting to belong and to be involved), then the individual may contribute nothing more than his name on the membership list of the group. Worse than that, he may create interpersonal problems that sabotage the best efforts of other group members. If, on the other hand, the person perceives that his needs can be met by belonging and by becoming involved—if he wants to contribute to the group, then his time, energy, and best motives will be dedicated to the work of the group.

Each of us belongs to many groups and, while we may not have the same degree of commitment to all, we should understand that the commitment we have has a direct effect on our functioning in the group; and to the extent that we can, we need to develop an honest involvement in the group and its objectives. The problem lies with the individual, and only he can resolve it.

TAKING A ROLE—In Chapter 5 we discussed several factors in interpersonal communication of which one was role-taking. The problem of the individual's discovering and taking a role is as important in the small group situation as in any other interpersonal communication situation.

Some individuals have a strong desire to be the leader in every group in which they have membership. They see themselves in that role only. They expect to exert influence over all other persons in all groups in which they have membership. They want to control the group. Such rigidity and narrowness in the ability to take different roles is a serious obstacle to the effectiveness of that individual in small groups.

Other persons may err in the other direction—i.e., they perceive themselves as not competent to fulfill the leadership role; consequently, they cling rigidly to an attitude of being unwilling to assume leadership responsibilities regardless of the group in which they have membership.

Most of us are somewhat flexible in our role-taking—perhaps not as flexible as we ought to be, but at least we do vary our roles some. In one group we take a leadership role, while in another group, having no desire to assume a leadership role, we are happy to cooperate in other ways. The point is that each of us, sooner or later, faces the problem of making a decision about whether we want to lead, whether we will accept leadership, or whether we can be content to be led. The question of whether or how much we desire to lead and to control the group will have an effect on our behavior in the group. Unfortunately, some groups fail to achieve their objectives because individuals are unwilling or unable to take the roles that are needed by the group.

The nature of the role that one takes in a group is determined by several factors—the pressures of the other group members for us to behave in a certain way, our own desire to perform in a certain way, and our abilities to fulfill a specific function. Sometimes the group exerts pressure on us to assume a certain role while we have in mind another role. We want to do things in the group that the group rejects and will not allow us to do; or the group wants us to perform certain functions. Such conflict can seriously impair the operation of the group. The first step in coping with such a situation is to learn to "know thyself" and then "know the group"; i.e., to develop the sensitivity that enables us to see ourselves and what we are expecting of ourselves and to perceive what others are expecting of us. Once we perceive these situations and expectations (conflicting role pressures) we can attempt to solve the problem by making the differences known to the group (getting them out into the open), by adjusting our own desires and behavior, or by developing defense systems. The most desirable solution to problems in conflicting roles is through direct, open communication by all the group members.

STATUS AND IDENTITY—A third problem relating to the individual is his status and identity in the group. Recognition and attention from a group is related to identification. If the individual's participation is to be sought by the group, he must be known as a specific individual; he must have a *particular identity*.

The point was made in the chapter on self-concept that we have many selves, and we do not reveal the same self to all groups in which we have membership. One self is revealed in one group while another self is revealed in another group. Further, our perception of our self is not always the same as the group's perception of us. Our identity in our own eyes may differ from the identity perceived by others. The point is that the kind of identity the group assigns to us is directly related to the role expectations and functions they have in mind for us. Because we soon learn that "who we are" in the group (our identity or self as perceived by others) is very important to our functioning in that group, we are concerned with the kind of identity we have in the eyes of our colleagues. When we enter a new group, we often attempt to establish an identity that will enable others to "know" us and that will make us useful and wanted in the group.

Some identities carry higher status than other identities. When the status of each member is equal to that of all other members, communication is generally about equal among the members of the group; and when one person (or two persons) achieve higher status than the other members of the group, communication generally takes place between equals or flows downward from high status persons to lower status persons. Rarely do those of lower status initiate a significant number of messages to those in higher status. Higher-status individuals normally initiate messages more often than those at lower levels.

Who we are, as perceived by the group and by ourselves, is an important factor in small group functioning. Who we are in terms of knowledge, attitudes, communication skill, listening skill, popularity, position, age, reputation, and power is the problem of identity and status—a problem that must be resolved by every individual in the group as well as the group before the group can function effectively.

AFFECTION—Liking and disliking was discussed in Chapter 5 as one of the important elements in interpersonal communication. Hence, it is important in the small group. Personal emotional feelings are very much a part of one's participation in a small group. Interpersonal attraction or unattraction are powerful elements in groups, but the issue of affection or liking usually is not resolved until the problems of *belonging*, *control*, *role-taking*, and *identity* have been resolved. Shutz suggests that the development of affection is usually the last phase in the development of an interpersonal relationship.[3] After persons have encountered each other, have defined each other and their relationship, bonds of affection can develop.

The importance of affection as a factor in group functioning lies in the fact that each individual determines whether, or to what extent, he will permit bonds of affection to develop and to be a part of his relationship with group members and with the group. If he develops a dislike for members of the group, or if he experiences too little affection or refuses to allow the development of affection, he will be "standoffish"; he will maintain an emotional distance between himself and others. On the other hand, if he develops close, emotional relationships with others in the group, he will find the group satisfying and his behavior productive to the group. When the individual resolves the affection problem, a significant obstacle to group productivity is removed.

UNDERSTANDING OF AND SENSITIVITY TO GROUP PROCESSES—A final problem related to the individual is his understanding of and sensitivity to group processes. If an individual is to be a productive group member and if he is to find group work satisfying, he must be able to cope satisfactorily with the group situation. To do that, he must have a knowl-

3. William C. Shutz, *The Interpersonal Underworld* (Palo Alto, Calif.: Science & Behavior Books, Inc., 1966), pp. 21–23.

edge of the factors that operate in the group process—i.e., factors relating to the individual (belonging, identity and status, role-taking, and affection) and factors related to the processes of group discussion and problem-solving.

Problems Related to the Group

The following five problems are no less important to group productivity than are the problems of individuals, but they are group problems and they must be resolved by the group rather than by individuals.

LEADERSHIP SKILL—Leadership has been defined as:

Interpersonal influence, . . . through the communication process, toward the attainment of a specified goal or goals. Leadership always involves attempts on the part of a *leader* (influencer) to affect (influence) the behavior of a *follower* (Influencee) or followed in a *situation*.[4]

The situation, customs of the group, goals, and personal attributes all affect leadership. At the beginning of a discussion, the problem must be defined, interest and concern need to be generated, and procedures and tasks must be identified. Later in the discussion heated arguments may need to be cooled and resolved, or other problems may arise creating needs for other leadership influences.

Leadership may vary from group to group. With one group permissive leadership in which the leader acts as a central point for communication exchange is needed. In another group democratic leadership with its reliance upon guiding the group is most effective; and in yet another group, a more directive, controlling type of leadership is needed.

In any problem-solving group situation certain needs must be met. Plans should be made for seating arrangement, agenda, having materials available, seeing that participants become acquainted with each other, getting the discussion started, keeping the group moving toward the goal, defining tasks and objectives, and creating a positive interpersonal environment. It is not always possible for one person to handle all these needs; he may not have abilities in all these areas. It is not uncommon, therefore, for leadership to be shared at times among various members of the group. But whether leadership is shared or resides in one person, it is an important factor in the functioning of the small group. The effective group utilizes its available leadership as efficiently and smoothly as it is possible to do. The effective group meets the needs

4. Robert Tannenbaum, Irving R. Weschler, and Fred Massarik, *Leadership and Organization* (New York: McGraw-Hill Book Co., 1961), p. 24.

it has for leadership by discovering the best leadership resources in the group and facilitating their growth and development.

DECISION-MAKING SKILL—A second problem in the small group, decision-making, should not be confused with problem-solving. One can make a decision that fails to solve the problem. Decision-making is commitment to a future action, policy, or attitude. In small group discussion there are many decisions to make—decisions on what problems are to be tackled, when they are to be placed on the agenda, how they are to be handled. How much participation is wanted, what action the group should be taking, when discussions should be stopped, whether a topic is or is not germane to the discussion, and what goal the group should be seeking now: Such decisions involving procedures and subject matter must be made, and the ability of the group to develop a skill in making them jointly is vitally important to the group's productivity. From selecting the chairman to answering questions that arise in discussion, decisions have to be made. A group decision is nothing more than several individuals' decisions that coincide to the degree necessary to allow a choice to prevail. Each member of the group is constantly involved in making decisions for himself, (personal decisions), but some decisions must necessarily be made by the group, either by having the chairman or another individual make them or by allowing the group as a whole to make them. Group decisions fall into two categories—those having to do with group process, i.e., the establishment or modification of procedures for dealing with the task at hand; and those related to the task, i.e., the fundamental decisions necessary to reach the specific objective of the group.

Group decisions may be made by authority (the chairman or one or two dominant members of the group), by majority vote, or by consensus. Group decisions made by the chairman or by a single individual and then forced upon the members of the group by manipulation, persuasion, or the influence or raw power of the decision-maker usually have the effect of destroying group decision-making ability and group morale. The single exception may be the conference situation in which it is clearly understood that the chairman has the responsibility for making the decisions and the group serves consultative, advisory, and sounding-board functions. Studies have shown that some 60 percent of business and professional people who hold regular conferences with their staffs said that the actual decision-making did not occur in the conference, but was made by the chairman back in his own office at a later time.[5] This procedure for making decisions may be satisfactory

---

5. Martin Kriesberg, "Executives Evaluate Administrative Conferences," *Advanced Management* 15 (March 1950).

when the climate, policies of the organization, and procedures are clearly understood and accepted. When that is not the case, autocratic decision-making will have disastrous effects upon the group. Figure 11 illustrates the leader-group relationship in decision-making.

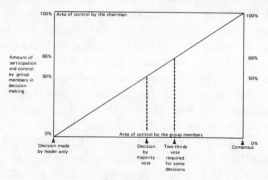

Figure 11

Two other methods of making decisions that are more satisfactory to the group are consensus and majority vote. The one-man, one-vote majority-rule procedure for making decisions has been the foundation of our democratic process. According to Phillips, however, this system is satisfactory only for final decisions in the small group. Before such final decisions are made, issues must be raised and proposals devised and developed. These phases include decisions that are better made through consensus.[6] It would seem, however, that at whatever level the decision was being made, true consensus would be the method of greatest merit; and, when the situation is such that the total human resources of the group and the fullest cooperation of all group members are necessary to the successful fulfillment of the commitment made by the decision, then consensus is the only satisfactory decision-making procedure. If, however, it is sufficient that only a majority of the group be involved in the decision, the majority-vote method may be used. The majority-vote procedure permits the group to arrive at a decision even though some individuals are not in agreement with that decision, and it reduces the time necessary to arrive at a decision when there are different opinions. One of the major weaknesses of making decisions by majority vote is that it tends to force division and polarization, thus leaving some members uncommitted to the policy or action.

Consensus occurs when everyone in the group agrees to the decision. The strength of consensus is in its total support of the decision, but

6. Phillips, *Communication and the Small Group*, p. 7.

when consensus does not exist, the decision must be postponed until agreement is reached. Another danger in relying on consensus is that persons are pressured to "give in," to capitulate so that consensus can be achieved. This often results in phony consensus and is ultimately detrimental to the group.

Consensus is the result of careful and effective interpersonal communication. When consensus can be achieved it is the best decision-making procedure. When it cannot be achieved the group must pay the price of delayed action while attempts at understanding, persuasion, and integration are made, or the group must rely on majority vote to resolve differences and make decisions.

PROBLEM-SOLVING SKILL—A third factor related to the group is problem-solving ability. Problem-solving is composed of six steps or components: (1) definition and analysis of the problem, (2) establishment of criteria or standards for the solution, (3) discovery of possible solutions, (4) evaluation of each solution, (5) selection of a solution, and (6) implementation of the solution. When a problem is encountered, there is an awareness of a goal (something wanted, including escape from punishment, pain, or the uncomfortable) and of a barrier to that goal. The first step in problem-solving includes the specific identification of the goal and the obstacles to it. The best way to understand a problem is to analyze it thoroughly: to define the problem, to discover its qualities, characteristics, and elements, to compare it to other problems, and to study its relationships to other entities and ideas of numerous kinds. Included in this first phase of group problem-solving is the clear specification of the problem—the phrasing of the question. It should usually be phrased in the form of an open-ended question that is neither too narrow nor too broad. Open-ended questions do not restrict the number of choices to two. "Should the voting age be lowered to eighteen?" offers only two alternatives and therefore is too narrow for effective problem-solving through discussion. Equally detrimental to discussion is the question which is phrased too broadly. "What should be done about voting?" is so broad that almost any topic may be discussed. A narrower, yet not unduly restrictive question could be, "What is the best voting age requirement?" Once the problem has been phrased the group needs to check their agreement on the meanings of the terms in the question as well as terms that are apt to be used in the discussion.

Other aspects of the first step in problem-solving are fact-finding (What are the facts? What are the available statistics? What are the opinions of experts? Are there similar situations?), identification of causes of the problem (Why are conditions as they are? Which are symptoms and which are causes?), and consideration of the relative impact of each cause. This opening phase of problem analysis is usually guided by the chairman. He calls attention to the problem, reviews or asks members to review its background, and generally encourages a full discussion of the nature of the problem.

The second step in problem-solving is the establishment of criteria which the solution must satisfy. No one proposes answers or solutions without a frame of reference (a set of criteria) in mind. Sometimes the criteria are too irrelevant and too few in number to be of value in problem-solving, but every person has something in mind when he suggests solutions, as foggy and poor as that "something" may be. The point is that the group cannot function effectively in solving the problem if each member operates with his own set of criteria so that five, six, or seven sets of criteria are being used. Nor can the group operate efficiently if the criteria or standards for the solution are poor in quality or are not clearly understood by the group. It is important, therefore, that the group give some attention to the establishment of relevant and important criteria which solutions must satisfy.

The third step in problem-solving is the discovery of possible solutions. This phase should be the most permissive, free, and uncritical period of the discussion. One of the biggest mistakes in group discussion is evaluating, criticizing, and judging each solution as soon as it is offered—often before it has been adequately explained, and certainly before all other solutions have been identified. Brainstorming is often highly productive in this step of problem-solving.

Step four is evaluating and testing each solution. Evaluation is done in terms of the criteria established and in terms of other decisions that may now be made such as, should the present system be modified? Should the present system be discarded and an entirely new approach taken? and Are there one, two, or three criteria of such high priority that satisfying them is more important that satisfying *all criteria*? Evaluating the proposed solutions generally and a few specifically leads naturally to the next step, the selection and testing of one specific solution. Arriving at the *best solution* is tantamount to reaching a decision. During these steps of problem-solving, evaluating, judging, and debating (in the best sense of these terms) occurs. The focusing on one solution is a *critical step* in problem-solving and should be done as carefully and with as much agreement as possible. The advantages, disadvantages, cost, ease of implementation, and chances of success for the accepted solution should be carefully considered.

The final step in solving any problem is "taking action"—doing something. The best solution to the problem is doomed to failure if it is *not* properly implemented. Too many groups make decisions and then drop the matter there, leaving it to no one to carry out the solution. Decisions that are carefully made require too much effort to be dropped just because a chairman and the group do not perceive that implementation of the solution is a necessary part of problem-solving.

It should be understood that simply listing a series of steps for solving problems is no guarantee that the problem will be solved, nor do groups move mechanically and rigidly through the steps. Sometimes groups jump from one point to another point. They discover in evaluating solutions that an important criterion was overlooked earlier and must be added; or they discover that the "perfect solution" is not among their list of possible solutions and so they decide to modify the criteria they will use. In general, however, the best problem-solving follows a logical plan of attack. Some things are naturally antecedent to other things—i.e., establishment of criteria before evaluating any solution in terms of meeting criteria. Even in creative problem-solving (creativity) the sequence of steps or activities have been found to parallel closely those steps identified in this chapter section. Problem-solving is not magical. It requires the best of interpersonal communication skills and the best of thinking skills. A group's understanding of the rational approach to problem-solving is an important element in small group discussion.

GROUP SIZE—A final problem which affects group proficiency is group size. Throughout this chapter the phrase small group has been used because it is the small group that is most efficient in terms of solving problems. Four to seven members is the optimum range in number of participation for a problem-solving group, with five being the personally most satisfying number.[7] The group needs to be small enough to allow its members to speak directly to each other. Groups larger than seven, or ten at most, almost always tend to develop subgroups. It is more difficult for the group to retain its unity, and the role each member can play is diminished. Group interaction is extremely important to group productivity and the small group best facilitates adequate interaction.

Functions of Group Leaders

There are functions that must be performed by the chairman or members of the group who assume leadership. It should be noted that the functions are not always carried out by the chairman. To keep the group functioning as a unit, some of these functions are handled by other group members.

Group leaders are not considered effective unless they facilitate the

---

7. Bernard Berelson and Gary A. Steiner, *Human Behavior: An Inventory of Scientific Findings* (New York: Harcourt, Brace & World, Inc., 1964), p. 360.

group in reaching its goals. Effective leaders work at solving group task problems as well as solving interpersonal problems of the group. An effective leader maintains a high morale and increases cohesion in the group, facilitates the development of liking and involvement, and carries out specific task functions.

He often introduces new ideas and calls attention to problems; he assists the group in clarifying and defining goals; and he opens the meeting and starts the discussion. The leader's main obligations during the meeting are: (1) to adhere to the agenda, (2) to aid in structuring procedures or in adhering to procedures that facilitate the group's orderly functioning, (3) to create or develop the atmosphere of the group by discouraging attacks on personalities, polarization, and hostility; and encouraging respect, openness, liking, and task involvement, and (4) to be aware of the group's progress and to keep the group aware of its progress and problems. When necessary, the leader summarizes progress, makes transitions from one step to another or from one agenda item to another, and focuses the group's attention on special group problems. Although there are other responsibilities and duties of leaders that vary with the types of groups or the objectives of the group, those identified above are the most important general functions.

Functions of Participants

You will undoubtedly be a participant in dozens of conferences, committees, and other small groups for every one in which you are the leader. It is easy to take participant responsibilities for granted—not only to fail to prepare for participation, but also to develop an attitude of indifference toward your responsibility to the group. A committee member can be productive only when he takes sufficient time in advance to read and to prepare adequately for the subject or problem on the agenda. It is unfair to impose on the time of other members of the group if one is not prepared to contribute constructively. Preparation on the topic, then, is one of the duties of the productive participant. Other duties or characteristics, as identified by experts on discussion, include:

1. an attitude of respect and open-mindedness toward others
2. a favorable attitude toward flexible, permissive interaction
3. an awareness of communication barriers
4. an understanding of group processes
5. an ability and willingness to speak to the point
6. an ability to listen effectively

7. an ability to think logically and analytically
8. a desire to cooperate and to conciliate in order to reach group goals[8]

Several of these skills or characteristics have been or will be treated in other chapters in this text. Chapters 2 and 3 dealt specifically with thinking logically, attitudes of flexibility, respect, openmindedness, and with intrapersonal communication breakdowns. Chapters 5 and 6 investigated interpersonal communication factors that are related to communication successes and failures. Chapter 12 focuses on listening skills. Thus, the traits identified by experts as most important for participants in small group discussion are, for the most part, those traits necessary for effective intrapersonal and interpersonal communication generally.

In addition to these skills and to being knowledgeable on the topic, let us consider two other matters—when to participate and how much to participate.

Studies show that members of a group who contribute early in the group's deliberation tend to gain the initial respect of the group and will be looked to for influence as the group progresses. The person who sits back and says nothing until late in the conference or meeting may find it difficult to gain the attention and respect of the group.

Some persons, unfortunately, believe that the answer to the question, When should one speak? is, All the time or as much as possible. The verbosity of some members can, and often does, overpower other members of the group so that they decide to let him have the whole show. Some group members utilize a "chain method" of speaking, i.e., they put out a continuous flow of talk adding one subject to another, to another, and to another so that it is virtually impossible for others to contribute except to break in or interrupt. Conferences and committees need good listeners, and their verbose members, especially, need to become better listeners. One government official is reported to have stated: "The 1000 hours a year I spend in conference could be cut down materially if members would come prepared to listen as well as to talk. Perhaps it should be remembered that it is as valuable to absorb the other man's point of view as it is to expand on your own."[9]

As to when and how much to participate, there can be no exact formula. The best advice is that each participant should be able to listen while others speak, to understand others, and to speak when he has something worthwhile to say. Each member of the group should be

---

8. Major Herman Farwell, "An Evaluation of a Televised Method of Teaching Group Process," (MA thesis, University Park: Pennsylvania State University, 1964).
9. Harold P. Zelko and Frank E. X. Dance, *Business and Professional Speech Communication* (New York: Holt, Rinehart and Winston, Inc., 1965), p. 180.

aware of how much he is talking in relation to others, and he should not dominate the discussion. Neither should a person talk for a long period of time on one point or even on several points. It is better to keep each remark limited to one point and, if he has more to say, he should say it at different times. None of these suggestions should be taken to mean that a good participant speaks only rarely. In fact the opposite is true. Studies indicate that *quality of participation is positively correlated with quantity of participation.*

Summary

This chapter has presented a brief description of small group communication. The nature, characteristics, and definition of the small group has been considered. We have noted that not every assemblage of people constitutes a group. We have identified the major types of small groups —primary groups, educational groups, casual groups, therapeutic groups, and problem-solving groups. Major problems related both to the individual and to the groups were discussed. In addition, the duties of the group leader and of the group participants were identified.

Most of the business of society is carried on in small groups. In committee meetings and conferences in the churches, school, governments, and business organizations of our nation, decisions are made and problems are solved that permit men to integrate and live cooperatively—this creates our social structure. No responsible individual can escape from or ignore small group participation; and no group, if it is to be productive, can operate satisfactorily if its members are ignorant or unskilled in interpersonal communication in the small group. Each of us is challenged to continue to increase our understanding of the process and to improve our skills as participants in the process of small group problem-solving.

For Further Reading

1. Dewey, John. *Logic: The Theory of Inquiry*. New York: Holt, Rinehart and Winston, 1938.

2. Haiman, Franklyn S. *Group Leadership and Democratic Action*. Boston: Houghton Mifflin Company, 1957.

3. Harnack, R. Victor, and Fest, Thorrel B. *Group Discussion: Theory and Technique*. New York: Appleton-Century-Crofts, 1964.

4. Homans, George C. *The Human Group*. New York: Harcourt, Brace & World, 1950.

5. McGrath, Joseph E., and Altman Irwin. *Small Group Research*. New York: Holt, Rinehart and Winston, Inc., 1966.

6. Olmstead, Michael. *The Small Group*. New York: Random House, 1959.

7. Phillips, Gerald M. *Communication and the Small Group*. Indianapolis: The Bobbs-Merrill Co., Inc., 1966.

8. Tannenbaum, Robert; Weschler, Irving R.; and Massarik, Fred. *Leadership and Organization*. New York: McGraw-Hill Book Co., 1961.

Part III

Public Communication

Chapter 9

Speaker-Related Variables

Part 3 of this book focuses on public communication. Public communication, like interpersonal communication, is essentially a transaction between communicator and receiver. Although public communication is dynamic, on-going, and therefore difficult to describe with finality we will in this section of the book examine the various elements, or variables, of which it is constituted. By looking at one major element at a time as though it were a discrete and isolated element, the public communication process will tend to appear static. If we bear in mind that we are studying parts of the total process in isolation for purposes of analysis, however, we can keep distortion to a minimum and at the same time enhance our total understanding of the process.

This chapter examines the role of the speaker in public communication, Chapter 10 focuses on the message, and Chapter 11 deals with the audience. Listening behavior is treated in Chapter 12, and Chapters 13 and 14 are concerned with protests, demonstrations, and violence and with mass communication as special forms of public communication.

Students of communication have long noted that *who* says something is as important as *what* is said in terms of communication effectiveness. Common sense and experience also tell us that the perceived character of the speaker is one of the factors which affects an auditor's response to a verbal message. The vividness of the speaker's personality, his sincerity, power, status, and expertise, the fear, awe, admiration, trust, and affection the audience holds for him—these and other factors are important speaker-related variables in the public communication situation.

Since the time of Aristotle, speech scholars and social scientists have attempted to discover the specific characteristics which enhance the speaker's communication effectiveness. Students of communication and practitioners of the art have observed carefully and have suggested several behaviors—vocal, physical, and logical (i.e., decisions the speaker makes and reveals to the audience)—that are believed to be related to this general factor, *the influence of the speaker.* During the past few years, speech scholars who are trained as social scientists have continued the quest by attempting to describe the public communication process scientifically and by experimentally testing certain hypothesized relationships.

The general factor (influence of the speaker) has many labels including ethos, prestige, status, image, and source credibility. Source credibility is probably the most used term currently, but whatever the label, it is apparent that the impact of a message depends on who the sender is. Consciously, subconsciously, or unconsciously, listeners react personally to the speaker. In this day of communication saturation and overload, audiences—both student and non-student—demand that speakers be worth listening to. They expect a speaker to know his subject, to accept responsibility for what he is saying, and to be sincere and trustworthy. In short, audiences today, perhaps more than ever before, stand ready to confer or deny credibility to the speakers claiming their attention.

The Components of Source Credibility

For thousands of years source credibility has been considered an important factor in public address. Aristotle listed ethos (source credibility) as one of the three major means of artistic persuasion in speaking. He said of the speaker, "we might almost affirm that character is the most potent of all the means to persuasion."[1] In recent years, various studies in psychology, sociology, and communication have provided empirical confirmation of Aristotle's observation; but as late as 1963 there was no confident answer as to what, specifically, a speaker could do to achieve high credibility. Anderson and Clevenger, in their excellent summary of experimental research in ethos, stated that the findings were not sufficiently sophisticated to enable one to draw definite conclusions about the operation of ethos.[2] In fact, nearly all the findings of the first thirty-five years of empirical research in this area can be summarized in the single low-level generalization that high credible sources are

1. Aristotle, *Rhetoric,* trans. Lane Cooper (New York: Appleton Century-Crofts, 1932), p. 9.
2. Kenneth Anderson and Theodore Clevenger, Jr., "A Summary of Experimental Research in Ethos," *Speech Monographs* 30 (1963): 59-98.

more effective than low credible sources. As stated by Anderson and Clevenger, the conclusion was:

The finding is almost universal that the ethos of the source is related in some way to the impact of the message. This generalization applies not only to political, social, religious, and economic issues but also to matters of aesthetic judgment and personal taste.[3]

The fact that thousands of years of study and more than thirty-five years of empirical research have brought little improvement to our understanding of the basis of source influence was due in part to a false assumption that source credibility is an inherent property of the speaker. If the speaker has it, he has it for everyone. The one-way influence model was used as the base for all early quantitative studies. The common practice in early empirical studies on source credibility was to introduce a tape-recorded speaker as a Senator (high credible source) and as a high school student (low credible source), or as a college professor and then as a Communist Party spokesman. Experimenters rarely attempted to find out how the members of the audience perceived these sources. We know now that *credibility is given to the speaker by the listener* and not by an experimenter. It is how the speaker is perceived by the listener that determines source credibility.

A second false assumption about source credibility was the belief in its unidimensionality. Aristotle, having observed public communication closely, had suggested that ethos was composed of at least three dimensions, but early empiricists ignored it.

The assumption that source credibility was a static attribute also proved false. In the early quantitative studies source credibility was manipulated by varying the pre-experimental conditions, i.e., by describing the speaker in an introduction. It was assumed that a person of this description, this *who,* was held in the minds of all audiences as a static, non-changing thing. Little attention was given to areas such as the possible modifying effects of the message, the audience's values and beliefs, or the context of the communication situation. It was assumed that a speaker's credibility remained the same for any topic, for any situation, for any audience, and for any speaking condition. We know now that:

1.   Source credibility is not totally inherent in the speaker; it is in the perceptions of the audience
2.   Source credibility is composed of several relatively independent dimensions
3.   Source credibility can be modified by events in the communi-

3. Ibid., p. 77.

cation situation—by decisions revealed in the speech, by who the listeners are, and by numerous other happenings in the situation.

These assumptions are nothing more than restatements that communication is complex, dynamic, and transactional.

As the old, one-way influence model was discarded for a better model, empirical studies began to offer hope for a better understanding of the functioning of source credibility, of its antecedents and its behavioral consequences. Within the last few years, for example, a number of researchers have attempted to determine empirically the specific dimensions of source credibility. These investigations, while independently conducted, have generally shown similar results. The findings suggest that receivers judge three relatively independent dimensions of source credibility which determine the influence potential of any given speaker for a given audience on a stated topic at a stipulated time. Specifically, these studies indicate that audience members evaluate a message source along three lines: (1) his "safety" or "trustworthiness" (good-will, intentions, predictability, honesty, integrity, etc.), (2) his "expertise" or "competence" (qualifications, intelligence, judgment, experience, first-hand knowledge, etc.), and (3) his "dynamism" (energy, liveliness, likeability, attractiveness, etc.).

These results emphasize the multi-dimensionality of source credibility and verify the assumption that credibility must be defined in terms of the perceptions of the receiver. But what can a speaker do or say that will cause the audience to perceive him as trustworthy, competent, and dynamic? Indeed, if each receiver determines whether the speaker is of high or low credibility, can the speaker do anything? This problem will be discussed in more detail in Chapter 11, but we can observe here that there are likenesses among people that permit us to make generalizations. These likenesses make possible language, although each individual has his own meaning for every word; these likenesses make possible societies and cultures, although no individual is an exact duplicate of another; and these likenesses do produce common general values, interests, desires, and beliefs. The important thing to remember is that the audience does determine source credibility, and that generalizations upon which one operates must always be held as tentative and subject to modification. The suggestions made in the remainder of this chapter, then, are generalizations of a lower level of confidence than those which related to the dimensions of source credibility, and of a lower level than the generalization that source credibility operates to determine communication effectiveness. Nevertheless, to the extent that we discover specific instrumental acts, verbal and nonverbal, that produce source credibility for us from one listener, or from one audience or type of audience, we improve our ability to influence our environment and we improve our repertoire of purposeful behavior.

Delivery

How important is the manner of speaking (delivery) in determining the outcome of the speech event? What are the elements of delivery and the standards of excellence and effectiveness? Each variable or characteristic will be considered in isolation, but we must keep in mind that they never exist alone. Delivery is a multifaceted aspect of the speech act, and it never occurs outside the context created by the speaker, audience, occasion, place, and topic of the speech. Because context influences the manner in which delivery variables are received as well as the effect they have, our discussion of delivery is over-simplified. Although our discussion will isolate several characteristics, it is the specific speech situation that dictates which delivery variables are important on a given speaking occasion.

DELIVERY: VOCAL—The voice, which reflects the speaker's attitudes, feelings, and inner states, can be controlled and developed to reinforce verbal messages. Some of the major elements in vocal delivery are loudness, pitch, articulation, quality, rate and rhythm, dialect, and conversational style.

The primary function of the voice in delivery is to help the speaker communicate effectively. The speaker must be *heard, understood,* and he must be *pleasing*—three objectives which relate to the seven elements identified above.

Loudness. Little communication occurs if the audience cannot hear the speaker. The receiver should not have to strain, turn his head, or cup his hand behind his ear in order to hear. Nothing is more distressing to a listener than to have to strain to catch a few words now and then. The weak, mumbling speaker greatly impairs his own communication effectiveness. To be heard requires adequate and sustained vocal loudness and projection. The speaker must adjust his volume to the size of the room, and he should always project to the last row in which members of the audience are seated. Some speakers are careless about adjusting their voices to the particular speaking situation. They may be speaking too loudly or too softly for the size of the room or for the "atmosphere" of the situation.

Loudness is conditioned by psychological state. Excitement, depression, fear, and other attitudes or emotions can decrease the speaker's sensitivity to his vocal delivery. He may talk too loudly or too

softly and inhibitedly without realizing it. The effective speaker, therefore, learns to be aware of his own psychological state and to compensate accordingly in his vocal delivery. In an intense communication
situation a speaker will, if he is not careful, increase his volume to match
the intensity of the situation. Indeed, increased volume can be used
effectively to call attention to the idea or to emphasize the idea, but
undue loudness born of intense emotion may detract from the message
and become irritating to the listeners. We do not communicate well
when we shout at each other. The sheer loudness may cause the listener
to focus on the volume and lose the message. Many of us tend to increase the loudness of our voices as the validity and strength of our
argument decreases, unaware that a message that did not get through
when sent in an adequate conversational tone will do no better when
it is shouted.

On the other hand, some persons speak too softly. They seem to
have no feeling, emotions, or awareness that anyone is seated in the
audience beyond the first row. They go on and on at a low-level of
intensity. Is it any wonder that they are not granted high credibility?

Pitch. Pitch refers to the location of a tone on a musical scale and
is determined by the frequency of sound vibrations per second. A
speaker who uses only one pitch speaks in a monotone voice. Although few of us speak in a monotone voice, many persons—especially in the public speaking situation—tend to restrict their range
of pitches so that their voices are monotonous. The effective
speaker constantly uses a variety of pitches in order to reinforce
meaning and to add color to his speech.

Pitch is our interpretation of the frequency of the sound. If the
vibratory pattern is slow, the pitch of the sound is lower; hence, the
higher the frequency of vibrations, the higher the pitch. People normally have a pitch range (distance between highest pitched and lowest
pitched tones) of one and one-half to two octaves. Although a speaker
may use a wide variety of pitches, there is a habitual basic pitch level
which is characteristic of much of his speaking. It is the basic pitch level
to which one refers when he says of a person: "He has a high pitched
voice," or "Her voice is unusually low pitched." The male voice is
usually about an octave lower than the female voice with the average
habitual pitch of the male voice at about 250 cycles per second, or very
close to Middle C.

An inappropriately high-pitched speaking voice may result from
imitation or habit. It may also result from tension caused by fatigue,
stage-fright, anger, or frustration. It is possible, although sometimes
quite difficult, to change the habitual basic pitch level of one's voice.

Pitch is important in the effective transmission of speech. Through pitch the speaker adds color and meaningful reinforcement to the words of his message. Appropriate use of pitch can clarify meaning, secure and hold attention, and help to build imagery and interest in the speech.

Rate and rhythm. Both are significant elements in vocal delivery. A rapid delivery can suggest to the audience that the speaker is rushing to get through rather than calmly seeking to send a message.

When we say that speech is "too fast," we are not referring so much to the rate of pronouncing the words as we are to the rapidity of the ideas and points, although it is possible for a speaker to pronounce words so rapidly that he also becomes careless in diction and articulation, making the words unidentifiable. The brain can process identifiable words at three or four times the speed at which they are spoken. The problem occurs when new or difficult ideas, meanings, or content require that the listener take time to let the message "soak in." It is not unusual that the public speech especially, with new information and new ideas put together compactly, demands that the speaker talk slowly enough to allow the listeners to absorb the message. Most college students have had the unfortunate experience of listening to a rapid-fire, jet-speed, fifty-minute lecture by a professor who has to cover all the material today.

Research evidence on speaking rate indicates that when the material is of average difficulty or is easily understood, the normal speaker need not worry about speaking too fast; but when the speech is composed of material that is difficult to understand, the speaking rate must be reduced. Many students have experienced in mathematics classes the problem of a "too rapid" delivery. The professor did not pronounce the words rapidly, but he moved from one step in the formula to the next and then to the next before the students had time to *understand* what he had said.

One can also speak too slowly, and once listeners become bored with too little information they may decide to tune the speaker out and let him plod along by himself. Studies show that changes in rate of speaking and in rhythm are associated with attitudes and emotional states. Faster rates, shorter comments, and more frequent pauses are associated with anger or fear, while slower rates and drawn-out speech are associated with grief and depression.[4] Duration, the temporal length of sounds and silences in speech, is also related to the mood of the speaker.[5] This special factor in rate is used to create the drawl of

4. Dean C. Barnlund, *Interpersonal Communication: Survey and Studies* (Boston: Houghton Mifflin Company, 1968), p. 529.
5. Grant Fairbanks and LeMar W. Hoaglin, "An Experimental Study of the Durational Characteristics of the Voice During the Expression of Emotion," *Speech Monographs* 8 (1941): 85–90.

the sterotyped cowboy. In order to project clearly and accurately, a speaker usually increases the duration of sounds as well as the intensity or volume.

Quality. Quality is an element in vocal delivery that is difficult to define. By way of analogy, when you hear the same note on a musical scale played with the same degree of loudness on a trumpet and on a violin, the difference you hear between the two is in the quality of the two tones. Just as we recognize the tones of a violin as different in quality from the same tones of a trumpet, so we recognize an individual voice as distinctive from other voices because of its quality. Quality refers to the subtle blending of elements into a unique voice; and we speak of voices as being clear, husky, harsh, nasal, guttural, falsetto, sonorous, hard, soft, shrill, warm, twangy, penetrating, syrupy, and honeyed.

Quality is determined, in part, by the size, shape, flexibility, and condition of the vocal folds, resonators, and the entire vocal mechanism. It is also affected by the speaker's emotional and physical states. A voice of clarity, richness, resonance, and strength depends on a certain favorable physical and emotional state of the speaker—that he is able to breathe properly and to use the nasal and mouth cavities for maximum resonance, and that he avoids unnatural tensions in the speaking mechanism. As noted in the chapter on nonverbal communication, the voice is a mirror of the inner person. If confidence, hostility, openness and affection are related to source credibility, as studies have shown them to be, then voice quality is an important element working for or against the public speaker.

Articulation and pronunciation. Precision in articulation and accuracy in pronunciation are important factors in being understood. The organs most essential to clear diction are tongue, teeth, lips, jaw, and velum, all of which are used in varying degrees to help us speak clearly and distinctly. The process of articulation by which man modifies vocalization to create individual sounds in almost unending combination is the unique step that makes possible intelligible speech. Without articulation and pronunciation, man could not produce intelligible speech. He could only vocalize. With an energy source, a vibrator, and resonance, sounds could be created, but man could not create and communicate with the code he uses today.

Articulation refers to the formation of individual speech sounds, and pronunciation refers to the fitting together of these sounds into words. Articulatory problems are of four types: sound substitutions, sound distortions, sound omissions, and sound additions. Young children often substitute one easy-to-make sound for a more difficult sound.

Rabbit sometimes becomes "wabbit," and run becomes "wun." One of our children substituted the "y" sound for "l" for a period of a few months; once, when he saw the Christmas lights spanning the main street at each intersection in the little town of Lakin, he excitedly exclaimed, "Yook at the Yights in Yakin!" Although such substitutions may be understandable and expected in a four-year old child, when an adult persists in substituting "th" for "s" or "w" for "r" it is unexpected and it becomes a handicap to his communication effectiveness. Similarly, sound distortions adversely affect one's ability to present an effective message.

Problems of omission and addition of sounds are even more common in adult speech than are distortions or substitutions. These problems relate directly to pronunciation and are often embedded in one's speaking as a habit. An extremely rapid rate of speaking sometimes causes omissions; in many cases it is sheer carelessness that ingrains the habit. Sloppy diction is often the result of habitual omissions (probly, cuz, libary, doin', goin', sord) and habitual sound additions (elum for elm and filum for film and stastistics for statistics). Some articulatory problems may be due to physical causes. These as well as other-caused articulatory problems are best handled by trained speech therapists; but when habit, imitation of a poor model, or carelessness cause the problem, *you* can do something about it.

Correct pronunciation is that which closely matches a standard of pronunciation, but there are various standards which may be used. Heinberg has identified them as: the majority standard (used by the majority of the people of the country), the regional standard (acceptable in a given region), and the audience standard (pronunciation used by one's audience); an authoritarian standard (imposed by some officially sanctioned group), and the cultured speaker standard (pronunciation used by those persons of prestige who engage frequently in public communication).[6] This fifth standard is probably the best for use in a college speech class, as expressed by the editors of the Merriam-Webster Dictionary: "At present all cultivated types, when well spoken, are easily intelligible to any speaker of English, and there is a very large percentage of practical identity in the speech sounds used."[7] The function of most dictionaries is to present the pronunciations currently prevailing in the best usage and not to attempt to dictate what that usage should be. Suggested pronunciations in dictionaries are periodically revised to reflect the observed changes in pronunciations.

6. Paul Heinberg, *Voice Training for Speaking and Reading Aloud* (New York: 1964), pp. 256–59.
7. Webster's New International Dictionary, 2d ed., s.v. "Preface."

Poor articulation and pronunciation can reduce the speaker's credibility. For this reason, you should check your articulation and pronunciation and, if need be, embark on an improvement program.

Fluency and conversational style. The purpose of public communication, to transfer a message as effectively as possible, can best be accomplished through a fluent, conversational style of delivery. Rather than delivering the message in dramatic, oratorical, or any other odd or unique style, the message should be delivered in a style that harmonizes articulation, pronunciation, quality, pitch, rate, rhythm, and all other voice elements into a warm, personal style as might be found in the best of informal conversations. The aim is for each listener to feel that you are *talking with him*—not performing for him, lecturing to him, or demonstrating your beautiful oral communication skills, but communicating with him. Your interest, enthusiasm, concern with the listener, and sincerity must show in your vocal delivery. Superficiality is never an adequate substitute for sincerity. Oratorical vocal gymnastics cannot satisfactorily replace a live, melodious, well-projected vocal delivery.

Conversational delivery is appropriate in almost any kind of speaking situation, from an intimate, dyadic interchange to a formal lecture or televised address. Effective speakers learn to use a conversational style in public speaking. Occasionally, someone will have an image of public speaking in which physical and vocal delivery is characterized by trite and rigid behaviors ranging from shouting, to whispering dramatically, to lowering the pitch and speaking in pear-shaped tones. Such delivery interferes with the message rather than aiding it, and the usual result is either a jerky, bombastic, exploding delivery or another essentially non-fluent style.

"Conversational style" does not mean an unrehearsed, rough, rambling manner of speaking. "Rambling" is *not* a characteristic of effective and enjoyable conversation. A rambling, bumbling delivery can be as disastrous in a public speech as is the glib mechanistic or the bombastic delivery. Rambling, too, is a barrier to communication. The public speaker who wanders from his message into detours, who verbalizes notions that fleet through his mind, and who gets lost in his own message will soon lose his audience. The outcome of his efforts will not be rewarding to him. Rambling and mumbling are not characteristics of an effective conversational style of delivery. The fluent, conversational speaker makes listening easier and more enjoyable than it might otherwise be. The speaker who advances his ideas smoothly, confidently, clearly, and positively stands a better chance of getting the desired audience response than does the speaker who is hesitant, jerky, and rambling. Effective vocal delivery enhances public communication effectiveness.

DELIVERY: USING THE BODY—Not only does the speaker send auditory cues, but he also sends visual signals through physical activity. The body is used as a communication transmitter in at least four ways: eye-contact, facial expression, gestures, and movement.

Eye-contact is essential for effective public speaking. When the speaker avoids the audience by *not* establishing eye-contact, the audience feels uneasy, embarrassed, suspicious, and generally negative toward the speaker, whether in the social conversation, the small group, the interview, or in the televised lecture. If the speaker looks at the floor, out of the window, at the ceiling, or past the listener, it will be difficult for the listener to maintain the kinds of attitudes that enhance receptivity. When the speaker establishes eye-contact with the listener, however, he not only communicates more directly, but he is also watching the reactions of the auditors so as to be sensitive and alert to feedback. He can pick up the signs of doubt, misunderstanding, and acceptance.

Facial expression is extremely important as a conveyor of attitudes and emotions, as you will recall from the chapter on non-verbal communication. Through facial expression a speaker can show his interest and enthusiasm in his message: he can scarcely expect listeners to be interested in a subject which does not interest him. A beginning or inexperienced speaker sometimes allows fear, anger, or stage fright to force him into an expressionless, stone face, so hiding his positive personality and attitudes behind a lifeless mask and conveying negative, inhibited attitudes that betray the message being sent.

Gestures are used to reinforce the verbal message, and the speaker who acquires the ability to use them freely, naturally, and effectively enhances his communicativeness as a public speaker. Gestures can be used to punctuate thought and emphasize meaning, to help create clear pictures, to reflect attitudes, to identify and delineate ideas, to break up stiffness and awkwardness with physical animation that releases the warmth and humanness of the speaker, and to relax the mind from the tensions produced by physical rigidity. Gestures that seem natural, spontaneous, and suitable to the speaker are an important asset to the public speech.

Movements of the body are also used to reinforce verbal messages or to contradict them. The slumped speaker conveys dejection, the lax, sloppily postured speaker conveys indifference, the tense speaker conveys fear—all of these postures and body messages are received by the listeners and act to negate the verbal message. Again, as shown in the non-verbal communication chapter, body movement is important in communication, especially in the public speaking situation. As with gestures, effective body movement not only reinforces the verbal message but also helps the speaker to achieve poise and freedom of expression through the physical activity that releases the pent-up energy.

For several years, speakers were instructed precisely on how to stand, how to gesture, and what facial expression to use. The positions of the hands for expressing various emotions were illustrated; the placement of the feet to convey resistance, etc. was carefully described. All such instructions were stated in rules. Today, we believe that such standardization is undesirable, since no two speakers nor receivers are identical. Each person must develop his own skills in bodily communication, to meet his own specific personality characteristics. Rather than memorizing artifical positions of the feet or hands for the expression of a given emotion, each speaker must allow his bodily communication to spring from his inner feelings associated with his message. In addition, each speaker should embark on a self-improvement program aimed at discovering and eliminating frantic, distracting movements, gestures, and postures that contradict and intrude on his message. Shifting of the feet, repetitive and meaningless facial movements, arms folded across the chest, rocking to and fro, leaning on the podium, and other distracting bodily communication should be replaced by comfortable, positive physical communication.

Bodily communication is an important and inescapable part of public speaking. Before any speaker utters a word, the audience is sizing him up, forming opinions about him by the way he looks, walks, is dressed, and stands. Listeners score points for or against the speaker on the basis of his posture, poise, and physical appearance—are attracted to him or not attracted to him; they see him as warm or cold, as sincere or insincere, as intelligent or unintelligent. These perceptions and evaluations are derived, in part, from what each listener sees— from reception of the nonverbal messages sent by the speaker. It is important to recall, at this time, the detailed nonverbal cues that were discussed in Chapter 6. The principles identified in that chapter are quite applicable to the public speaking situation.

Effects of Delivery

Thus far in this chapter we have observed that the speaker is a significant factor in the process of public communication. We have noted the three major dimensions of the effect the speaker exerts, and we have discussed delivery of the speech as one important avenue through which source credibility is established. Now, we will consider the effect of delivery on credibility; in addition, we want specifically to consider two additional effects delivery can have on the public communication outcome.

EFFECT ON CREDIBILITY—In many public speaking situations, you as a listener may have only limited knowledge about the speaker and his background, having received sketchy information only at the speech event, i.e., in the introduction of the speaker and in observing and listening to him. In other public speaking situations, you may have ample information about the speaker through newspaper stories, from acquaintances, and from knowing the speaker's background (connections and associations)—the organizations to which he belongs, and the agencies he represents—so that you bring to the speaking situation an image of the speaker. In either case, you also receive information during the speech, information from what the speaker says and from his delivery of the speech. The sources or references he uses, the experiences he reveals, the similarity of attitudes, values, and beliefs to those of the auditor are all revealed in the content of the speech and they constitute information the listener can use in determining his image of the speaker and the credibility he bestows on the speaker. In addition, throughout the speech the listener also receives information about the speaker by listening to his vocal delivery and observing his bodily communication. This effect of delivery (influence on credibility) is the most significant of all effects. Delivery also affects information gain and emotional arousal (the two other effects that will be discussed in this chapter), but small differences in delivery, which might have no effect upon information gain or upon emotional arousal, may have a significant effect upon the image projected by the speaker. Moreover, the effect may operate not only upon the outcome of the present speech, but upon all future speeches this speaker may give before this audience. For that reason, delivery is an extremely important consideration in public speaking.

As we noted in the earlier chapter on non-verbal communication, various vocal characteristics are used by listeners to form their impression or image of the speaker. The use of "ih" rather than "eh" in such words as pen, when, and again distinguishes low-status from high-status persons in many communities.[8] Using these and other cues, listeners estimate the social status of a speaker.[9] Certain characteristics of delivery produce typical impressions in a wide range of listeners. Rate of speaking is associated with vitality, energy and dynamism. Slow speakers are viewed as slow thinkers, as conservative and lethargic.[10] Pitch

8. Huber W. Ellingsworth and Theodore Clevenger, Jr., *Speech and Social Action* (Englewood Cliffs, N.J.: Prentice-Hall, Inc., 1967), p. 174.
9. L. Stanley Harms, "Listener Judgments of Status Cues in Speech," *Quarterly Journal of Speech* 47 (1961): 164-70.
10. Ellingsworth and Clevenger, *Speech and Social Action*, p. 175.

and loudness are associated with strength, and inflectional variety is seen as indicative of liveliness, interest, and enthusiasm, while a monotonous voice indicates a lifeless, dull, unhappy, and uninterested speaker. The listener's categorization of the personality traits of a speaker on the basis of vocal, physical appearance, and bodily action cues is a well established fact; and such a determination of personality traits is directly related to ethos or source credibility. The inferences made by listeners relative to who the speaker is may be valid or invalid, but the important point is that, on the basis of delivery characteristics, inferences are made nevertheless. Moreover, these inferences are often made by the listener outside his awareness threshold and, though he may be unable to identify the basis of his opinion about the speaker, the listener nevertheless does perceive him as dull, slow, and uninterested or as bright, alert, and dynamic, or as having other characteristics— characteristics that constitute a speaker's credibility.

EFFECT ON INFORMATION GAIN—Information is gained when the listener understands something a speaker has said. We infer that information has been gained when the listener can recall statements or points made by the speaker, or when he can answer correctly questions about the information content of the speech. As a student in college you are quite interested in information gain as an effect of communication, but how does delivery relate to information gain? What is its effect on information gain?

Virtually any one of the vocal or bodily characteristics of delivery can, under certain circumstances, have significant effects upon information gain; under other circumstances, faulty delivery in any single aspect might have no effect whatsoever upon information gain; in still other circumstances, while no single aspect of delivery affects information gain, the combination of several negative factors in delivery produces an adverse effect. Although the relationship between delivery and information gain is highly complex, we do have some knowledge and understanding of this relationship.

A rather obvious fact in this regard is that speech sounds must reach the listener's ear for information to be transmitted. To that extent, one must speak loudly enough and project well enough; but beyond that, there are unusual situations (such as extreme fatigue of the listeners or poorly motivated listeners) when the degree of loudness and projection of voice correlate positively with information gain. If, for example, the speech is very long and motivation is extraordinarily low, a weak voice will impair the transmission of information. Noise, like fatigue and low motivation, can have similar effects upon information gain as related to loudness of voice.

Another factor in delivery, rate of speaking, is known to affect information gain. As noted earlier in the chapter, the difficulty level of material is inversely related to rate of speaking; i.e., the more difficult the material, the slower the rate of speaking should be. To speak too slowly with easy material or too rapidly with difficult material can adversely affect information gain.

Rate of speaking and loudness are known to affect information gain under certain conditions, but all available research suggests that factors of delivery usually have but slight affect upon information gain. Variety in pitch, for example, has not been found to be related to information gain.[11] Similarly, voice quality, in one study, was found to have no effect upon the transmission of information.[12] Although these delivery factors, when studied individually, have no adverse effects on information gain when other factors in the speaking situation are reasonably normal, the presence of marginal or weak delivery variables may establish conditions in which the operation of other variables is more pronounced.[13]

In combination, several weaknesses in delivery may impair the transmission of information; and when extraneous factors such as fatigue, low motivation, or noise are present, any single delivery factor or combination may be important to the transmission of information.

EFFECT ON AUDIENCE'S EMOTIONAL RESPONSE—The audience's emotional response is often an important element of the speaker's success in achieving his goal. Sometimes the audience's emotional response is the primary goal of the speaker. Emotional response is usually associated with the content of the speech (the ideas and language which evoke images in the mind of the listener), but emotional response is also related to delivery variables. If you recall the discussion of nonverbal communication, you will remember that emotion is communicated easily in the nonverbal channels of voice, facial expression, posture, and movement—in other words, in delivery. The fact that delivery, regardless of content, is capable of eliciting emotional response from an audience is demonstrated by the well known story of Helena Modjiska, the Polish actress who moved an American audience to tears by simply reading numbers from a telephone book in Polish. In most speaking situations, however, delivery factors and speech content work together in an interactive way to produce emotional response in the listener. In fact, a change in one (emotionality of the content of the speech, for example) is usually accompanied by corresponding changes in the other

11. Charles F. Diehl, Richard C. White, and Paul H. Satz, "Pitch Change and Comprehension," *Speech Monographs* 28 (1961): 65–68.
12. Charles F. Diehl and Eugene T. McDonald, "Effect of Voice Quality on Communication," *Journal of Speech and Hearing Disorders* 21 (1956): 233–37.
13. Ellingsworth and Clevenger, *Speech and Social Action,* p. 164.

(visceral expressions of emotion in delivery). This means that a public speaker who wants to elicit a specified emotional response from an audience will be most successful if he has the "inner feeling" of that emotion freely expressed in his ideas, language, and nonverbal behavior. The attempt to convey to the audience an emotional state the speaker does not himself experience to some degree runs a high risk of failing. On the other hand, some speakers may experience the emotion, but their inhibitions do not permit them to express their emotion in free, appropriate, and yet controlled nonverbal behavior. Sometimes the negative emotions related to the speaking situation override the emotions related to the ideas of the speech. Nevertheless, for ill or good, it seems clear that delivery is related to the emotional response of the audience in the public speaking situation.

The Speaker Revealed Through Speech Content

We have discussed how the speaker, through his delivery, can affect cognitive and affective outcomes of the speech; we have discussed how the speaker, through his delivery, exerts an influence on the credibility accorded him by the audience; and we have noted that source credibility is also influenced by what the audience knows about the speaker before he comes to the speaking situation and by what he says about himself through his decisions relative to the content of the speech.

What a speaker knows, believes, likes, and dislikes is revealed by the things he says. Who he perceives himself to be as well as his perception of who the audience is may be revealed in what he says. Whether he handles ideas carefully and accurately or "muddles through" is evident in the arguments or discourse he uses. His prejudices may "leak out" in remarks he makes. Indeed, through the content of speech, the listener receives a picture of the speaker. The speaker's attitudes are revealed through the evaluations he voices. It is practically impossible to talk about anything without baring one's preferences, values, attitudes, judgments, and general view of the world. One's intelligence is judged by what he says—by his level of understanding revealed in his ability to comprehend difficult and subtle relations among concepts and by the superficiality with which he handles concepts.

As all these traits are revealed (attitudes, values, integrity, training, experience, intelligence, etc.) the listener constructs an image of the speaker. How he defines the speaker (likable, honest, competent, like or unlike me) determines the credibility that will be accorded the speaker. This source of information and influence on source credibility should not be overlooked by the student of public speaking.

Summary

This chapter has focused on the speaker as an important influence on public communication outcomes. Although we know that the speaker is but one element in the dynamic public speaking situation, and even though we know the speech and the audience influence him, yet the speaker can, by his own behavior, exert an influence toward the objective of shaping or controlling the outcomes of the communication situation. It has been noted that *who* the speaker is, as perceived by the audience, is a powerful variable in public communication. Further, we have identified the major dimensions used by listeners to define the speaker—trustworthiness, competence, and dynamism. Finally, we investigated the relationship between delivery and the speaker's ability to influence the communication outcome. We have clearly shown that delivery is directly related to credibility, information gain, and emotional response of the audience. To the extent that a speaker can utilize delivery effectively, he can increase his influence over communication outcomes.

For Further Reading

1. Anderson, Kenneth, and Clevenger, Theodore, Jr. "A Summary of Experimental Research in Ethos." *Speech Monographs* 30 (1963): 63–67.

2. Harms, L. Stanley, "Listener Judgments of Status Cues in Speech." *Quarterly Journal of Speech* 47 (1961): 164–70.

Chapter 10

Message Variables

One of the key elements in public communication, along with the speaker and the audience, is the message. Of these three elements, it is the message that has received the most attention and study throughout man's historical attempt to understand public communication. This chapter will not attempt a detailed description of all the elements in a spoken message; it will instead summarize in a general way the major elements of public messages.

Although we will consider individual elements—purpose, organization, language, reasoning pattern, types of supporting materials and evidence, and psychological-emotional appeals—we must remember that these elements are not perceived by the receiver as discrete units. Rather, spoken messages are perceived as one unit: various elements may interact to produce the impact on the auditor. The public speech, if it is to be most effective, must have a structure that unifies the individual elements we shall discuss.

Messages of all types have an internal structure. Paintings, musical compositions, computer programs, plays, and speeches too have an internal structure, which means that they can be analyzed or broken into parts—there is an arrangement of elements into specific relationships. Speeches, like musical compositions, are highly structured with the basic elements combined to produce an effective public speech. The major elements comprising a public speech are purpose, organization, language, reasoning pattern, types of supporting materials and evidence, and psychological-emotional appeals.

Purposes of Public Speeches

The purpose of communication is to win a response. Unless the speaker knows the response he wishes to elicit, he is almost certain to wander along in a disorganized manner, aimlessly talking about irrelevant details. It is therefore necessary for the speaker to have a *general purpose* for his speech.

Responses sought from public speeches are not identical. The after-dinner speech at a banquet, the classroom lecture, the political campaign speech all seek different responses. Each speech has a different purpose. Writers on public speaking have identified three general speech purposes—to inform, to persuade, and to entertain. The speech to inform seeks a response of comprehension or understanding, the speech to persuade seeks a response of attitude change and change in behavior or action, and the speech to entertain seeks a response of enjoyment.

Speeches to inform can be further classified as speeches *to impart knowledge* and speeches *to augment knowledge.* Every year thousands of conferences are held on university campuses, at convention centers, and elsewhere in which speaking to impart knowledge plays a major role. Men translate technical and research information into usable directives. Experiences and events are described. At such conferences there may also be speeches to augment knowledge—to probe for definitive meanings and to interpret things and events so as to point out their implications.

Speeches to persuade can be further classified as speeches that affirm propositions of fact, propositions of value, and propositions of policy. Propositions of fact offer the truth of an existence, legality, or causality. In such a speech the speaker seeks to prove that the proposition of fact he espouses is, in reality, true. His purpose goes beyond helping his audience to understand an event, process, or concept; he seeks approval and acceptance of the "fact" he presents. Attorneys in courts of law attempt to win acceptance of propositions of fact. With any proposition of fact, the speaker asks the audience to accept his assessment of reality. In order to accomplish this, the speaker must present knowledge about the fact to be accepted or rejected, identify appropriate standards to be used in making the judgment, and apply the standards to the data.

Propositions of fact may deal with past fact (Did John Doe commit this act?), present fact (Persons are now in training to become professional arsonists.), and future fact or propositions of prediction (that college enrollment will decrease next year).

A second kind of persuasive speech focuses on propositions of value. Values shape the goals of collective human action and guide personal thought and behavior. Hence, there are times when a speaker wishes to persuade his audience that a proposition of value has merit. Sometimes such speeches are referred to as speeches of inspiration. Often, the speaker attempts to reinforce values already held by the audience. Most commencement speeches are of this type, as are many sermons; but there are also other occasions, political and non-political, when the speaker seeks to change values, intensify commitment to a value, or formulate a value. In all such speeches, the proposition of value is concerned with rightness or wrongness, goodness or badness, justice or injustice, or with wisdom or foolishness. It does not seek to establish the existence or reality of some act, event, or object as does the proposition of fact; instead, it seeks to pronounce a judgment as to the *worth* of the act, event, or object.

The third type of persuasive speech deals with a proposition of policy. A proposition of policy is concerned with a proposed course of action. When a public speech is given urging the listeners to vote to approve a school bond, it is a proposition of policy. When the abolition of capital punishment is proposed, a proposition of policy is being urged.

Regardless of the nature of the proposition or the type of informative speech, there must be one—and only one—general purpose of the speech. Within the speech, however, one may entertain and inform as a *means* to persuasion. Nevertheless, one guiding general purpose should undergird the entire speech.

Beyond the general purpose, one must define a *specific purpose* of the speech. The specific purpose is the general purpose stated in terms of the subject for the specific audience to which it is directed. The specific purpose identifies the *precise response* desired from the audience by the speaker. It is usually a single, concise, clear statement that delineates precisely what the speaker wants the audience to do, feel, believe, understand, learn, or enjoy. The following examples illustrate general and specific purposes.

Subject: The salesman's use of nonverbal communication
General Purpose: To inform
Specific Purpose: To explain to the audience the salesman's use of nonverbal cues to derive useful information about the customer

Subject: Abortion
General Purpose: To persuade

Specific Purpose: To get the members of the audience to write to
their representatives in Congress urging ap-
proval of proposed legislation liberalizing abortion

The specific purpose must be selected in terms of audience analysis, speaker's objective, available time, and the occasion. It is the focal
point toward which all comments, arguments, and supporting materials
are directed.

Organization

Organization is integral to most of the experiences of the normal individual. From architecture to feelings and thoughts, the average person tends toward the acceptance of form and the rejection of the
formless, toward the acceptance of harmony and the rejection of dissonance. Man is organized in his eating, sleeping, working and playing.
In fact, he reacts to material presented in a disorganized manner by
rejecting it or organizing it according to his own system—to his own
prejudices. No phenomenon of life, animate or inanimate, appears to
the normal individual as completely devoid of order. Such form or
structure is equally a part of the public speech—from the most basic
form of introduction, body, and conclusion to the more sophisticated
forms of sequence of ideas. In life, when one's plans follow his habitual
organized patterns, he is more satisfied, more receptive, and freer from
frustration. So it is in the public speech. Effective organization can
reduce frustration for both the receivers and the sender. When the
speech is unorganized, listeners tend to lose interest, to become confused, and to become resentful of the imposition upon their time. Quintilian stated:

... speech, if deficient in that quality arrangement, must necessarily be confused, and float like a ship without a helm; it can have no coherence; it must
exhibit many repetitions, and many omissions; and, like a traveler wandering
by night in unknown regions, must, as having no stated course or object, be
guided by chance rather than design. ... just as it is not sufficient for those who
are erecting a building merely to collect stone and timber and other building
materials, but skilled masons are required to arrange and place them, so in
speaking, however abundant the matter may be, it will merely form a confused
heap unless arrangement be employed to reduce it to order and to give it
connexion and firmness of structure ...[1]

1. H. E. Butler, trans., *The Institutio Oratoria of Quintilian* (Harvard University Press,
1950), vol. 3, bk. 7: 2–3.

Organization seems to be an extremely important and pervasive phenomenon in man's existence. Edward Sapir has written that even such highly personal activities as breathing fall into categories of polite and impolite and, therefore, become *organized physiological responses*.[2]

Learning is another area in which order and organized patterns play a strong role. Learning involves the perception of patterns, and authorities in learning psychology are giving increasing emphasis to the importance of this organizing function of the mind. Research indicates that learning is painfully slow when organization is not present. Inasmuch as a public speech is a learning situation, organization is imperative.

Organization is helpful to the speaker for it enables him to clarify his ideas and to develop the speech into a meaningful cohesive unit. It aids the receiver because it permits him to more easily understand the message. Wheeler and Perkins report the following findings as a result of their studies investigating the relationship between learning and organization: (1) the more easily recognized the plan of arrangement, the more quickly learning takes place; (2) the longer the content to be learned, the more necessary becomes orderly arrangement; (3) when orderly arrangement is expected but fails to appear, it causes confusion; and (4) learning is most effective when the orderly arrangement is as explicit as possible and is deliberately explained to the learner at the beginning.[3] Later studies, Darnell's for example, have shown that manipulating organization even at the level of a sentence, makes a difference in comprehension.[4] Clearly, organizaion is an important variable in the public speech.

THE THREE MAJOR PARTS OF A SPEECH—The simplest level of analysis of a speech, as to organization, reveals that an effective speech has an introduction, a body, and a conclusion. The introduction is an important part of the speech, for as we have noted in other chapters in this text, first impressions, first perceptions, and first judgments exert an unusual amount of influence on subsequent behavior. There is, therefore, much to be accomplished in the opening remarks of a speech. The speaker must get the attention of his listeners. He will, hopefully, establish rapport with his audience so that they will accept him as a person to whom they will listen on this topic. He must arouse interest in what he

2. Edward Sapir, "The Unconscious Patterning of Behavior in Society," in *Selected Writings of Edward Sapir in Language, Culture, and Personality* (Berkeley, Calif: University of California Press, 1951), p. 545.

3. Raymond H. Wheeler and Francis T. Perkins, *Principles of Mental Development* (New York: Thomas Y. Crowell Company, 1932), pp. 292–96.

4. Donald K. Darnell, "The Relation Between Sentence Order and Comprehension," *Speech Monographs* 30 (1963): 97–100.

is going to say, and the audience must be given some indication of the subject for the speech.

Three studies of introductions and conclusions of public speeches indicate that the average length of introductions was 0.80 percent, 8.55 percent, and 9.00 percent of the total length of the speech.[5] On the basis of these descriptive studies, introductions appear to occupy about 9 percent of the total length of the speech. From these same studies, eleven frequently used kinds of introductions were identified, as follow: reference to subject, reference to audience, reference to occasion, quotation, reference to current events, historical reference, anecdote, startling statement, question, humor, and personal reference.

Some of the objectives of the speech introduction may be accomplished through the remarks made by the person introducing the speaker. This person may aid greatly in polarizing the audience so that its attention is on the speaker and his speech. Effective introduction of a speaker enhances his credibility, reveals the nature of the topic, and creates in the audience an expectancy and readiness for the speaker. To accomplish these objectives it is often necessary for the introducer to relate to the audience the speaker's experience, background interests, and qualifications to speak on the topic at hand. Further, the introducer may need to increase the audience's interest in the subject by showing why the topic is of particular interest and how it is related to their needs and wishes.

The second major part of the speech is the body or substantive part of the speech, with which the remainder of this chapter deals.

The third basic part of the speech is the conclusion. Having developed and supported an idea, the conclusion should serve the purposes of summarizing and stimulating the audience to make the response sought by the speech. The studies by Miller, Hayworth, and Runion show that conclusions averaged 5.40 percent, 5.10 percent, and 9.12 percent of the total length of the speech.[6] The most frequently used conclusions are: the challenge, the quotation, the summary, visualizing the future, the appeal, the inspirational, advice, the proposal of a solution, the question, and reference to the audience.[7]

---

5. See: Edd Miller, "Speech Introductions and Conclusions," *Quarterly Journal of Speech* (April 1946): 181–83; Donald Hayworth, "An Analysis of Speeches in Presidential Campaigns from 1884 to 1929," *Quarterly Journal of Speech* 16 (1930): 35–42; and Howard L. Runion, "An Objective Study of the Speech Style of Woodrow Wilson," *Speech Monographs* 3 (1936): 75–94.
6. Miller, "Speech Introductions and Conclusions"; Hayworth, "Speeches in Presidential Campaigns"; and Runion, "Speech Style of Woodrow Wilson."
7. Miller, "Speech Introductions and Conclusions."

PATTERNS OF ARRANGEMENT—There are several ways to arrange the major points of the body of the speech so as to give the ideas and materials a structure, pattern, or pleasing relationship. Insofar as research findings are concerned, many different patterns may be equally satisfactory. To help you learn to use various patterns of organization, the following patterns are presented. Some are probably more suited to a particular speaker, to particular listeners, and to specific purposes than are others; but the effective public speaker must be acquainted with all these patterns in order to select the most appropriate one.

Time sequence or chronological pattern. One method of organization is to begin at a certain point in time, then move forward chronologically. All human experience can be organized in terms of time. From accounts of travels, the day's events, to recipes, information can be organized according to a time sequence. Children who have never considered "organization" find it easy to recount the events of a party chronologically with a series of "and then" transitions.

When time order patterns are used, one may move forward from a chosen point in time (or backwards in some rare instances), but if one jumps haphazardly from date to date disregarding the natural sequence, the receivers are confronted with an unclear and confusing picture.

Space sequence. A second method of organizing material is on the basis of a spatial pattern. Speech topics such as geography, flood control, football strategy, and plans for developing an area of a city in an urban renewal program often necessitate the use of a spatial pattern of organization. In the space sequence, material is arranged in terms of physical location, moving from east to west, north to south, from the center to the outside, clockwise, etc. Space is the element that relates each point to all other main points.

Topical pattern. Some subjects fall into topics or categories that are parts making up the whole. Neither space nor time unifies these main points, but the fact that they are each and all members of the same family—parts that are related inasmuch as they do combine to make the whole, serves to unify them. For example, financial reports may be given in terms of assets and liabilities or income and expenses. A talk about the national government may be divided into three main areas —the legislative, executive, and judicial branches of government. The topical arrangement is one of the most widely used forms of organization. In fact, some speakers make the mistake of relying entirely on this one pattern, and they use this pattern even when it is less effective than another pattern would be.

Logical patterns. The patterns of arrangement identified as logical patterns include: problem-solution, cause-effect, analogy, inductive, and deductive. Actually, all patterns of arrangement are "logical" (otherwise they are not *patterns*), but those listed immediately above are generally thought of as being related to argument, debate, and rational persuasion.

The problem-solution pattern has two major points—the problem and the proposed solution or solutions. Similarly, the cause-effect method of organizing a speech has two main points—a description of factors that are the *cause* and a prediction or identification of the subsequent *effect*. Speeches on farm surpluses, the rising cost of living, cancer, etc. lend themselves to a cause-effect or problem-solution pattern of organization.

The inductive and deductive patterns of arrangement are also logical methods of organizing material. Although every pattern of arrangement can be classified as either inductive or deductive, we shall treat these patterns separately as logical patterns of organization.

The inductive pattern of organization moves from specific examples or instances to the conclusion which the examples dictate. It is reasoning from the specific to the general, from examples to the generalization that can be appropriately drawn. One learns early to use the inductive pattern in reasoning and probably uses it daily throughout his lifetime.

Following is a hypothetical example of the inductive pattern:

Example 1: Program A required thirty cents of each dollar for administrative costs while a similar program in State Z required twelve cents of each dollar for administrative costs.

Example 2: Program B required thirty-six cents of each dollar for administrative costs, while similar programs in States W, X, and Y cost fourteen, twelve, and sixteen cents of each dollar for administrative costs.

Conclusion or inference drawn: Therefore, it is evident that Federal Programs are more costly than similar State Programs.

This particular conclusion may or may not be warranted in this argument, but at this point we are concerned only with illustrating the inductive pattern.

It should be noted that the number of examples used—one or many —depends upon the quality of the example and the nature of the item about which we are generalizing. If we are attempting to make a generalization about the effect that jumping off a ten-story building would have on a person, one example may be quite enough to warrant a conclusion. Generally, however, more than one example is required in order to win belief or acceptance of the conclusion from the audience.

A second method of organizing ideas, the deductive pattern, is opposite to the inductive pattern in that the reasoning moves from the generalization to the specific instance. The generalization is already accepted by the listener, and so the deductive pattern involves showing that the specific instance or example at issue is a member of the family of the larger generalization. Hence, if the specific instance is included in the generalization in all essential ways and the generalization is already accepted as true, then the specific instance may also be accepted as true. This method of argument often labels, classifies or categorizes the specific example or situation at issue. Following is a hypothetical example of the deductive pattern:

Conclusion (Relative to the statement at issue): This specific animal is a dog.

Accepted Generalization: Dogs are animals having characteristics A, B, C, D, E, and F.

Application of the tests to see if this specific animal fits into and only into the generalization: This animal does have the characteristics A, B, C, D, E, and F.

Conclusion: This animal is a dog.

Not uncommonly in a public speech, one wants to relate a specific problem to a commonly accepted generalization. The important requirement is to discover the essential tests that must be satisfied in order to make the specific instance "like those in the generalization."

Inductive and deductive patterns of organization of the types just described are often used by attorneys in legal summations, by senators or congressmen in legislative speeches, and by research scholars in talks before scientific groups who demand rigorous logical procedures. These patterns may be poorly suited to audiences of lower educational level; the pattern may seem somewhat difficult to follow.

Another logical pattern, the analogy, consists of comparing two similar examples in which the audience knows what is true of one example and must accept it as being true of a second example *if* the second example is exactly like the first in all essential aspects. This "truth" about the second example is the point at issue—the conclusion that one wants the audience to accept. The known and accepted truth of the first example and the essential aspects of the two examples that are supposedly alike constitute the main points of this pattern of organization.

Whatever pattern of organization is used, that pattern and *only* that pattern must be used for that level of breakdown or analysis. For example, if the topic is transportation and ones uses four main points,

all four points must be related according to a *single principle* governing
that pattern of relationship.

Subject: Transporation

Correct Topical Pattern	Incorrect Mixed Pattern Topical and Spatial
I. Automobiles	I. Automobiles
II. Planes	II. Planes
III. Ships	III. Transportation in Alaska
IV. Trains	IV. Transportation in Nigeria

At the secondary level, or when another *unit* or *whole* is broken into parts, another pattern of arrangement may be used. For example, although the first-order breakdown of the body of the speech on transportation above uses a topical pattern, one might use a time order pattern
to discuss automobiles.

I. Automobiles
    A. 1890 - 1919: Age of Discovery
    B. 1920 - 1935: Age of Competition
    C. 1936 - 1965: Age of Power and Speed
    D. 1966 - ? : Age of Ecological Adaptation

A second important fact related to organization is that, after determining the best pattern to follow in organizing the speech, one must
give special attention to the transitions. Transitions provide the link-
ages which enable the audience to see the pattern being used, to move
with the speaker from one main point to another, from one sub-point
or supporting point to another, and from the introduction into the
speech. It is always good practice to plan transitions from point to point
and include them in the outline.

PHRASING MAIN POINTS—The main points of the speech should be
carefully worded so as to give the speech emphasis and clarity. Various
supporting materials, discussed next in this chapter, constitute the bulk
of the speech; but the major thrust of the message is conveyed by the
main points—the foundation or framework upon which details are
fitted. Effective public speakers phrase main points carefully so that
they are clearly understood and more easily remembered. Four characteristics should be evident in the phrasing of main points—vividness,
conciseness, immediacy, and parallelism.

Main points stated in vivid, attention-getting words and phrases stand out clearly and can be remembered easily. Similarly, main points that are concise rather than rambling and cumbersome increase the clarity of the speech. Third, main points that appeal directly to the immediate concerns of the receivers enhance the effectiveness of the speech; and finally, whenever possible, a uniform type of sentence structure and similar phraseology should be used.

Types of Supporting Materials

After one has selected the subject, determined the purpose, researched the topic, and selected, arranged, and phrased the main points, he can then select subordinate points and supporting materials to give form and substance to the speech.

Supporting materials include: explanation, comparisons, figurative and literal analogies, hypothetical illustrations, factual illustrations, specific instances, statistics, testimony, restatement, and visual aids. Sometimes two or more of these types of supporting materials best serve certain purposes. Figurative analogies, comparisons, and hypothetical illustrations are especially useful to make ideas clear and understandable; specific instances, statistics, and testimony are more useful as evidence to gain belief, e.g., to persuade; and literal analogies, factual illustrations, and restatement serve both purposes.

Explanations are expository statements clarifying the meaning of a term or setting forth the relationship between parts—seldom adequate when used alone. It is better to follow the explanation with comparisons or illustrations. One should also remember to keep explanations simple, short, and accurate.

Analogies are comparisons of two things similar in certain essential characteristics and, therefore, judged to be similar on other characteristics. Analogies are of two kinds—figurative and literal. Figurative analogies compare things in different classes, e.g., the eye with a camera or a thermostat with communication feedback. Literal analogies, on the other hand, compare things of the same class, e.g., Cadillacs with Lincolns, Indianapolis with Wichita, or Purdue with Ohio State. Literal analogies are used as evidence to prove points, but figurative analogies are primarily used to clarify points.

Illustrations are detailed examples or instances. If the example is not explained or detailed, but merely referred to or pointed to, then the example is a *specific* instance and its usefulness is primarily that of establishing proof. If, however, the example is explained through the revelation of details, then it is an illustration. Illustrations may be real (factual) or they may be hypothetical. Factual illustrations may serve to establish proof, while hypothetical illustrations are useful to clarify meaning.

Statistics are figures which summarize *many instances* and indicate relationships among phenomena. They enable one to summarize a large amount of data quickly and to interpret a mass of specific occurrences or instances. Hence, they are useful as evidence in persuasive argument.

Statistics may sometimes be difficult for audiences to comprehend; therefore, the relationship or comparison represented in the statistics should be clearly identified and explained. Also, statistics should be translated into immediately understandable terms. Large numbers can be stated in round numbers, comparisons can be used. Pie or bar graphs can be quite helpful in making statistics understandable.

Testimony is the verbatim reporting of a person's opinion or conclusion. First-hand testimony is one of the primary forms of evidence (supporting material) used in courts of law. In speeches, the testimony of authorities is quoted by the speaker. Testimony can be used both for clarity and for evidence to establish proof. It must meet two essential tests: (1) The person who made the statement must be qualified to make such a statement. Is he an authority by virtue of skills, training, recognition, and reputation? and (2) The testimony must be acceptable and believable to the audience.

Restatement is reiteration of an idea in different words. Repetition is the process of reiterating an idea in the same words previously used. Restatement and repetition do not constitute evidence, but they often have a persuasive effect not unlike the piling up of evidence. The utility of reiteration and repetition is amply demonstrated by the profits resulting from these persuasive tactics when they are used in advertising. Reiteration and repetition in public speeches serve the purpose of clarifying and recalling patterns of arrangement and patterns of development. Initial summaries, during-the-speech summaries, and end-of-speech summaries are examples of useful repetition and reiteration to enhance understanding through constant clarification.

A final form of supporting material is visual aids. Visual aids include charts, diagrams, maps, pictures, simulated models, and real objects. Demonstration speeches rely upon the use of visual aids, but other kinds of speeches may also profit from their use. It is important that one consider carefully the *purpose* of the visual support when choosing visual aids. Sometimes a simple diagram better fulfills the purpose of clarifying than would the real object. If one wanted to explain the parts of the heart, for example, a simple diagram, or a large walk-through model, might be preferable to a real heart. Actual equipment and objects are not necessarily better than other types of visual aids, although in some instances only the real object is capable of adequately fulfilling the objective in mind.

When a speaker uses visual aids, he should remember three important rules: (1) do not stand between your listeners and the visual aid; (2) use only visual aids that are *relevant* since complex and irrelevant detail will function as noise and counteract the positive effect of the visual aid; and (3) be sure the visual aid is of a size and in a position clearly visible to the entire audience.

Language and Style

Another variable in the public speech is language. Effective use of language, the words selected, the arrangement of these words, and the development of specialized functions of the various arrangements all contribute to the force of the message and even more to clarity. Language can contribute to message clarity or to confusion, to a forceful message or a weak message.

The use of one type of language throughout the speech results in monotony and destroys the listener's interest. Long and involved sentence structure becomes fatiguing to the listener. A "written style" rather than an oral style in public speaking is artificial to the listener, and excessive use of slang is tiresome and deadly. The best use of language in a public speech points as directly as possible to the idea or feeling being expressed. One starts with the basic element in language: words.

The effective public speaker works continually for a better understanding and appreciation of the words available to him in the vocabulary of his society. The English-speaking societies have more than one-half million words available to them; and the average individual has a vocabulary of about ten thousand, about two thousand of which are used in his habitual patterns of conversation. The average college student recognizes sixty thousand words and can use approximately twenty thousand. Robert Browning, considered by many persons to have had the most extensive usable vocabulary of all English writers, used some thirty-five thousand different words in his writings. The task for the effective public speaker is to expand his vocabulary (conversational and general) and to acquire new understandings about *how best to use* the vocabulary he has, i.e., how to *select words,* and how to *arrange words in terms of effective sentences.*

To become aware of the many word availabilities from which the most forceful or effective word can be chosen, the student of public speaking must be a student of dictionaries and of the practices of others in using words. Dictionaries attempt to record all the words used in speech, but they do not create or prescribe words. They only record how a word has been used in the past. While the use of some words is so narrow that only one definition is required, other words may have several meanings and may require numerous definitions in the dictionary.

As everyone has two sets of manners, informal and formal, so there are two levels of language, informal and formal. Informal language style abounds on television and radio, as well as in the movies. So persuasive is this influence that a *mass language* has evolved in the U.S.A. This level of language sacrifices *precision* in word usage to cliches, jargon, euphemisms, and worn out metaphors, all of which have one common characteristic—impression. The effective public speaker, when he speaks to an audience, must *not* fall into the patterns of mass language style unless he wishes to sound like the television-game emcee or like the soap, underclothes, or toothpaste salesman. Wonderful, awful, heap of trouble, etc. are examples of cliches, words or phrases robbed of their effectiveness and meaning through overuse.

In addition to vague words and cliches, ineffective speaking is sometimes characterized by the use of jargon—the technical language of a profession. The lawyer who uses many "whereases" and "therefores" in a public speech is using jargon. These terms may be necessary in his contracts to provide for contingencies he cannot foresee, but they are deadly to an audience. Similarly, the college professor who uses "it would seem," "it is not unreasonable to say," or "it might be considered helpful," in a public speech will be considered affected by the audience. His language may be appropriate for the scientific journal, but it is jargon in the public speech and may create suspicion and rejection in the minds of the audience.

Another way to look at words is in terms of their concreteness and abstractness. Concrete words refer to specific things which can be seen, felt, smelled, or experienced, while abstract words are signs or symbols for ideas, concepts, or relations that are not "sensed" directly Everyday language is a mixture of both, and although both types of words are essential to communication, too many abstract words in the public speech can cause problems. Inexperienced public speakers tend to avoid using concrete words, not realizing that concrete words increase attention and clarity.

Words are also classified as popular and learned, i.e., simple and monosyllabic as compared to more vague and polysyllabic. The common reference to this classification system is: "He uses big words" or "You can understand what he says; he doesn't use those big words." Following are some examples of popular words and their learned counterparts:

Popular		Learned
round	———	circular
thin	———	emaciated
fat	———	corpulent
brave	———	valorous
king	———	sovereign
book	———	volume

A style that uses popular words tends to be clearer and more direct than a style containing learned words.

Concrete and abstract words are *not* synonymous with popular and learned words. Concrete and abstract words are classified according to criteria different from those used to classify popular and learned words. The concrete-abstract classification is based on the referents of words while the popular-learned classification is based upon the level of usage. In deciding which words to use, one must be guided by the need for clarity, the tone desired in the speech, and the expectations of the audience. Although one should generally use popular, concrete, and simple words, there are situations when the nature of the topic and the audience demand a higher level of language usage. In studies conducted by Brooks and Emmert, Brooks and Adrian, and Adrian, it was found that the effect of congruency of language usage between speaker and listener (upon source credibility, for example) varied according to the perceived role-relationships and expectations of the audience.[8] Students accorded *higher credibility* to professors whose public speaking language usage was moderately congruent with the students' language usage than they did to professors whose public speaking language usage was highly congruent with the students' language usage. Students *expected* professors to use language a little differently than did the students. The use of learned words by professors did not decrease the source credibility of those professors. A positive relationship between language usage congruency and retention was found in the studies.[9]

As the studies cited show, it is difficult to make hard, absolute rules about using language, but George Orwell has suggested six rules which generally will serve to improve one's public speaking, especially if rule six is kept in mind:

8. William D. Brooks and Philip Emmert, "The Effect of Language Usage Congruency Upon Source Credibility, Attitude Change, and Retention" (Paper delivered at the National Convention of the Speech Association of America, Los Angeles, December 28, 1967); William D. Brooks and Paula J. Adrian, "Language Usage Congruency and Academic Achievement," (ms., The University of Kansas, 1966); and Paula J. Adrian, "A Study of the Relationship Between Language Usage Congruency and Perceived Ethos" (M.A. thesis, The University of Kansas, 1967).
9. Ibid.

1. Never use a metaphor, simile, or other figure which you are used to seeing in print.
2. Never use a long word where a short one will do.
3. If it is possible to cut a word out, always cut it out.
4. Never use a passive phrase where you can use an active one.
5. Never use a foreign phrase, a scientific word, or a jargon word if you can think of an everyday English equivalent.
6. Break any of these rules sooner than say anything outright barbarous.[10]

In addition to these suggestions related to language as a variable in the public speech, one should recall and apply those understandings gained from chapter 3 on using language in communication. The public speaker must remember that it is people, not words, that mean; that it cannot be assumed that everyone else "speaks my language"; that it is a dynamic, complex world that we are abstracting from and representing with a limited vocabulary; that language is always a calculated risk; and that feedback should be used to check on the message received and to guide further messages.

Not only must the speaker pay attention to the words he selects, but he must also organize and arrange them in a way most likely to convey his intended meaning, feeling, or attitude to the audience. A large vocabulary permits the speaker to be specific, vivid, affective, and accurate if he can also put words together into effective phrases, clauses, and sentences. Although oral style permits more latitude in structuring sentences and in expressing ideas than does the standard written style, the speaker who makes grammatical errors such as incorrect verb tense or disagreement between subject and verb must recognize that many audiences will hold him accountable and will not accord him the credibility he desires.

Psychological Validity of the Speech

In addition to logical appeal produced by proper organization, accurate and sufficient evidence, and compelling interpretations and conclusions, another persuasive element is the psychological appeal. It should be recognized that logical appeals may and often do have a strong psychological appeal as well, and in some instances a strong appeal to a listener may exist without any clear or compelling formal logical elements in the speech or that part of the speech producing the appeal. Hence, for the sake of clarity we will treat psychological appeals sepa-

10. George Orwell, "Politics and the English Language," in *Shooting an Elephant and Other Essays* (New York: Harcourt, Brace & World, Inc., 1960).

rately from logical appeals knowing full well that such a separation may be an artificial one.

Strong appeals to certain emotions or psychological states can be made through language and supporting materials. The following three pairs of emotions, or six psychological states, are offered as examples of psychological and emotional appeals that can be observed in public speeches. Understanding these appeals is advantageous not only to the public speaker, but also to the receiver of public communication. It may well be that the major value of understanding the phenomena of psychological appeals lies in the fact that the "consumer" of public speaking is able to *participate* in the transaction in a more rational or intelligent manner. The following theoretical explanation of emotional appeals and how they may be used via language and supporting materials is based, in part, upon material presented in lectures given by Paul Brandes.[11]

Emotions often come in pairs that can be represented as being at opposite ends of a continuum. Pride and pity, affection (or love) and anger (or hate), and fear and the absence of fear (security) are examples of some pairs of emotions. Let us consider the effects these appeals may have and some ways by which the appeals may be made in public communication.

Pride and pity. An appeal to pride results in the creation of a feeling of high esteem. In the public speech one normally appeals to the pride of the audience, i.e., to the audience's self-esteem. The primary technique used in public communication to appeal to the listener's pride is the compliment which may be used directly or indirectly. An audience may be directly complimented in terms of its intelligence, sophistication, educational level, social position, possession of power or wealth, and potential abilities and skills. Probably no technique has a longer history of use in man's attempt to influence others through emotional appeal than the pat on the back—the soft-soaping, sweet-talking, complimenting behavior. Untold millions of dollars worth of products are sold by telling the receiver directly how great he or she is with this product.

There is some evidence to indicate that "accidental" or unintentional appeals are more effective in persuading the receiver than are recognized, purposeful attempts. Consistent with this position, is the explanation that *indirect compliments* to an individual or audience are even more effective in appealing to pride than are direct compliments.

11. Paul D. Brandes, Professor of English and Chairman of the Speech Division at the University of North Carolina at Chapel Hill, gave a series of classroom lectures in 1964 at Ohio University which set forth this theoretical framework concerning emotional appeals in public speaking.

For example, the public speaker who shows accurate familiarity with the problems of an audience, indirectly compliments that audience. He has taken the trouble to learn about them. Similarly, knowing persons by their name and referring to them by name, rather than by "hey you" or "you folks," is an indirect compliment. Association of the speaker with persons the audience knows and holds in high esteem is an indirect compliment and appeal to the esteem of the audience. Allowing the audience to participate through humor, a question-answer process, or acknowledgment of feedback constitutes an indirect compliment. Finally, humility on the part of the speaker is an indirect compliment which recognizes the corresponding worth and esteem of the audience. Studies of the public speaking of President Lyndon B. Johnson indicate the rather extensive use of humility.

An appeal to pity, the counterpart of pride, produces sympathy in the audience. It may be self-pity, i.e., the speaker pities himself and creates sympathy in the audience for himself. "Old soldiers never die. They just fade away" is an example of self-pity. A speaker may appeal for pity for the theme or topic of the speech, or he may appeal to pity for the audience and the terrible condition and mistreatment they have experienced. Some cues by which the emotional appeal to pity may be identified include reference to: poor financial position ("I'm a poor person, I don't have the money to buy this election."), unfortunate physical appearance, lack of educational opportunity, the failure of people to appreciate, being misunderstood, being mistreated or unfairly treated, being denied rights, falling from greatness, and martyrdom. Such "poor mouthing" is an appeal to pity.

Affection (or love) and anger (or hate). Appeals to affection result in adoration, identification, and sharing. Such appeals come from family relationships, "overcoming" accomplishments, shared struggle or tragedy, and reminiscing. When one hears a speaker making reference to his wonderful wife, his children, home, and kids he plays baseball with, it can be identified as an appeal to affection, whether it be intentional or unintentional. Similarly, the political candidate who appears publicly with his wife, family, or a group of children appeals to affection. Reference to shared tragedies or struggles is an appeal to affection. Some very tender and affectionate moments between a losing political candidate and his loyal workers have been witnessed on television following announcements of defeat, i.e., of congratulations to the winner. Reminiscing, whether in dyadic communication or public speaking, has the effect of appealing to affection.

Anger and hate grow out of injustice (which refers to past events), and to disappointment and frustration (which refer to a continuing future situation). The common techniques include name calling, appeals to prejudice (especially using a scapegoat), and direct reference to injustice and frustrating or hopeless situations.

Fear and security. The only emotional appeal to be extensively investigated by behavioral research scholars in speech communication is fear. Theoretically, the three major fears among adults are threat to survival (food, shelter, health), lack of fulfillment (freedom, development of talents, experiencing a full life), and ignorance. Most fear appeal research has focused directly on threats to survival, but ignorance and lack of fulfillment are also fear-producing.

The cues by which one identifies appeals to fear are: (1) making the audience aware of any problem related to survival, fulfillment, or ignorance, (2) advocating any change, (3) talking about the success of others (the child or student who listens to his dad or teacher talk about the achievement and success of his brother or classmate may experience fear), and (4) talking about money and costs.

A number of studies have been conducted and several articles have been published in speech journals and other journals on fear appeals, and there is some evidence that mild fear appeals are more effective than are strong fear appeals for some persons on some topics. Despite the extensive research in fear appeals, however, many questions are still unanswered. Nevertheless, fear is a commonly used emotional appeal in public speaking.

Besides emotional appeals of the types just discussed, there are other psychological factors that can profitably be taken into consideration when one prepares a public speech. These include cognitive dissonance, Maslow's hierarchy of needs, and ego-involvement.

COGNITIVE CONSISTENCY AND COGNITIVE DISSONANCE—Psychological structure—the organized set of cognitions a person has about himself, others, and the world—is also an important element to consider in persuasive speaking. The principle of cognitive consistency suggests that a person's psychological structure is composed of an integrated and organized set of cognitions relative to the person, object, or event with which one is concerned. If new information (cognitions that are inconsistent with cognitions presently held) enters the person's awareness, he will experience *cognitive dissonance,* the disruption of his organized cognitive and psychological structure and the subsequent production of disequilibrium. The theory suggests that the person who experiences such dissonance feels compelled to make an adjustment between his ongoing cognitive structure and the new information so that equilibrium and harmonious integration of all his cognitions can be reestablished. People are continually striving for consistency, for congruous, harmonious, fitting relationships among the thoughts, beliefs, values, and behaviors that make up their world. When inconsistency occurs and the person becomes aware of it, psychological tension is produced in the individual and he is thereby motivated to change his actions, attitudes, values, or beliefs. Osgood, Festinger, Heider, Tannenbaum and others have conducted research and have written about cognitive dissonance, balance theory, the principle of congruity and their relationship to persuasion.[12] The implication for persuasive speaking is that persuasion is more likely to occur when dissonance is experienced by the one being persuaded; and since dissonance results from an awareness of discrepant, contradictory, or inconsistent cognitions, the task of the persuader is to present information that makes the one being induced aware of contradictory cognitions he already holds, or to create dissonance by giving him new information that is inconsistent with the cognitive structure he holds. Any number of previously discussed patterns of organization might be used in presenting information aimed at creating cognitive dissonance.

The creation of cognitive dissonance does *not* necessarily mean that the one being persuaded will accept the solution proposed by the persuader. A person experiencing psychological tension produced by cognitive dissonance will seek to restore equilibrium in his cognitive structure, and accepting the persuader's proposed change is only one way of doing so. The subject may choose to not believe the persuader; to rationalize by saying, "It applies, but not to me"; to become angry at the persuader and repress the information; or to accept some change other than that proposed by the persuader. To help the person change in the direction advocated, one might want to consider the relative strength or importance of each of the inconsistent cognitions and attempt to argue for a change that is more salient to the individual than is the cognition he must reject. One way of doing this is to consider the hierarchy of man's needs.

Maslow's Hierarchy of Needs—Maslow has classified the basic needs of man into five broad categories: (1) physiological needs, (2) safety needs, (3) love needs, (4) esteem needs, and (5) the need for self-actualization.[13] The hierarchy is arranged with the most basic and demanding of needs (physiological) at the bottom and the least basic and demanding (self-actualization) at the top, as shown in Figure 12.

12. See: A. R. Cohen, "Communication Discrepancy and Attitude Change: A Dissonance Theory Approach," *Journal of Personality* 27, 386–96; Leon Festinger, *A Theory of Cognitive Dissonance* (Evanston, Ill,: Row Peterson, 1957); Fritz Heider, *The Psychology of Interpersonal Relations* (New York: John Wiley & Sons, Inc. 1958); C. E. Osgood, "Cognitive Dynamics in the Conduct of Human Affairs," *Public Opinion Quarterly* 24, 341–65; and P. H. Tannenbaum, "Attitudes Toward Source and Concept as Factors in Attitude Change Through Communications" (Ph.D. diss., University of Illinois, 1953).
13. A. H. Maslow, *Motivation and Personality* (New York: Harper and Row, Publishers, 1954), pp. 80–92.

Figure 12

Physiological needs are necessary for physical survival. They include the need for food, drink, shelter, sex; avoidance of injury, pain, discomfort, disease, or fatigue; and the need for sensory stimulation. In America, the physiological needs are generally satisfied routinely so that most men are seldom preoccupied with them. Physiological needs, consequently, do not motivate people in America as strongly as do needs higher in the hierarchy, even though the higher needs are weaker. *If physiological needs are not satisfied, they are stronger in their motivation than any higher needs.* Persons with empty stomachs do not care about esteem or self-actualization.

Safety needs focus on the creation of order and predictableness in one's environment. They include preference for orderliness and routine over disorder, preference for the familiar over the unfamiliar, desire for tenure, for savings accounts, insurance, police and fire departments, welfare plans, social security and armed forces. When one's safety is threatened, love, esteem, and self-actualization needs lose their motivating power.

Love needs are of two types: love and affection between husband and wife, parents and children and close friends; and the need for belonging—for identifying with larger groups (church, club, work organization, etc.). When these needs are not met, feelings of rejection and isolation result with subsequent feelings of mistrust and suspicion toward others.

Esteem needs refer to the desire for reputation, prestige, recognition, attention, achievement, and confidence. Some sociologists believe that esteem needs are powerful motivators in America. Packard's book, *The Status Seekers,* illustrates how Americans are preoccupied with status.[14]

The highest of man's needs is self-actualization—the fulfillment of one's capabilities and potentialities. An example of such motivation is the pianist who desires to be as great a pianist as it is possible for him

14. Vance Packard, *The Status Seekers* (New York: David McKay, 1959).

to be. Self-actualization needs take on strong motivating power only when other more basic needs have been fulfilled.

In persuasion, the greater the congruence between the belief or action advocated and the felt need of the person to be persuaded, the higher the probability that persuasion will occur.

EGO-INVOLVEMENT—A third psychological element to consider in speeches to persuade is ego-involvement. As Sherif, Sherif, and Nebergall state: "It is one thing to change a person's . . . preference for one brand of candy over another. It is another thing to try to change the person's commitment to the value of the family, to his religion, to his politics, to his stand on the virtue of his way of life. The latter commitments and stands are ingredients of his self-picture—intimately felt and cherished in his own eyes. As such, the latter are among his ego-involved attitudes. The term involvement in our approach refers to the arousal of such attitudes."[15] Ego-involved attitudes are derived from values. Information which is inconsistent with an ego-involved attitude will, of course, create more tension or dissonance than will information inconsistent with a peripheral or non-ego-involved attitude. For this reason, ego-involvement is an important element to consider along with cognitive-dissonance in persuasive public communication.

Emotional appeals, cognitive dissonance, basic needs, and ego-involvement are factors that operate to give the speech psychological validity to the listener. Attention to these elements can be highly beneficial to the speaker as well as to the auditor.

Summary

In this chapter we have considered the major variables in the speech —purpose, organization, supporting materials, language and style, and psychological appeals. Once again, let us be reminded that these elements in the speech are not isolated from the total public speaking process; they are an integrated part of the dynamic and complex total phenomenon of public communication. The speech, the speaker, and the audience exert influences upon each other and upon the total process. The effective public speaker is aware of the fact that all elements interact to affect each other. He is therefore concerned with and alert to the many forces involved; and although he is careful to plan as intelligently and accurately as possible, he remains flexible and open to feedback and correction.

15. Carolyn W. Sherif, Musafer Sherif, and Roger E. Nebergall, *Attitude and Attitude Change* (Philadelphia: W. B. Saunders Co., 1965), p. vi.

For Further Reading

1. Maslow, A. H. *Motivation and Personality*. New York: Harper and Row, 1954.

2. Miller, Gerald R., and Nilsen, Thomas R., eds. *Perspectives on Argumentation*. Chicago: Scott, Foresman and Co., 1966.

3. Packard, Vance. *The Hidden Persuaders*. New York: David McKay Co., 1957.

4. Rokeach, Milton. *Beliefs, Attitudes, and Values*. San Francisco: Jossey-Bass, 1968.

5. Rosnow, Ralph L., and Robinson, Edward J. *Experiments in Persuasion*. New York: Academic Press, 1967.

6. Sherif, Carolyn W., Sherif, Musafer and Nebergall Roger E. *Attitude and Attitudinal Change*. Philadelphia: W. B. Saunders Co., 1965.

Chapter 11

The Audience as a Variable

What is the role of the audience in the communication process? Is it one of passive acceptance in which the communicator presumably has power and does something to the audience with or without its consent? Such a concept is commonly held by the general public and is thought to be the model commonly used by those in advertising and public relations, and particularly by those engaged in propaganda. This concept of the audience emphasizes man's exploitation of man. To view the audience in this way, as a passive mass of individuals waiting to be told what to think and what to do is to view the communication process as a one-way street. This linear concept of the communication process suggests that the speaker need only to push certain verbal buttons to gain the desired response. The idea of the powerful communicator being able to change either the attitudes or the behavior of the respondents at will lacks convincing support from research. Some situations, however, appear to create the kinds of circumstances which do successfully result in the exploitation of audiences. These situations are mainly created and controlled by the communicator and require more time, energy, ingenuity and resources than are ordinarily available for almost any legitimate communication situation. Such "communication circumstances" raise serious moral questions and are not the primary concern of this book.

Communication research seems to support a far different view of the role of the audience than that of recipients in a one-way or linear communication process. Recent research views communication as a two-way transaction between communicator and audience in which each party is actively engaged, and in which both communicator and audience give and get something in return. The role of the audience in the communication process is not a passive one. The audience actively engages in the speech act by reacting to the speaker and the speech, often affecting the speaker's message from moment to moment. This transactional concept of the role of the audience suggests that the audience and speaker mutually influence each other. The fact that the audience exerts influence on the speaker and the speech is evidence of the importance of the audience as a variable in the communication process. The transaction between the speaker and his audience is dynamic and complex and presents every speaker with the challenging responsibility of knowing and understanding his audience.

The primary responsibility of any speaker wishing to communicate his ideas to others is to discover the nature of those to whom the message is directed. Discovering the nature of an audience, their wants and needs, their attitudes and beliefs, in short, all there is to know about them, is essential to effective and successful communication. In speech communication, this discovery process is referred to as audience analysis.

More than two thousand years ago, Aristotle recognized the importance of audience analysis when he observed that a speech was composed, or grew out of, the interaction of three elements: the speaker, the subject, and the persons addressed. He added that of these elements it is the persons addressed, the audience, that determines the speech's end or object. Aristotle's pronouncement still holds true today. When all is said and done, the end result of the speech, its success or failure, is determined primarily by the audience, although, as we have seen in chapters 9 and 10, the speaker and the speech may also exert an influence. But, if there is any one element more important than the other two elements, it is the audience, for they grant or deny the speaker's request. This clearly suggests that if the speaker wishes to be effective, he must: (1) analyze his audience, and (2) adjust and adapt both himself and his ideas to the audience. The audience, then, is the single most important element for the speaker to consider in the public speaking process.

What is an Audience?

Social psychologist Kimball Young states that the chief features of the formal audience are: (1) It has a specific purpose, (2) it meets at a predetermined time and place, and (3) it has a standard form of polarization and interaction.[1] The specific purpose, of course, is to attend to the message of a speaker. In the more common forms of public address, the President's State of the Union Message, political rallies, Sunday

1. Kimball Young, *Social Psychology*, 3d ed. (New York: Appleton-Century-Crofts, 1956), p. 286.

sermons, and lectures, the audience is aware of the time and place the speech will occur. Perhaps the most unique qualities of the audience are polarization and interaction. Polarization is what makes a group of persons into an audience; it introduces direction and purpose into an otherwise unorganized group. Polarization occurs when the individual members of a group direct their attention to a common object—the speaker—rather than to each other. When the members of an audience consciously accept their roles as listeners and the role of the speaker as speaker, the audience is polarized. Without polarization, there is merely a group of individuals devoid of structure. The people in a subway terminal at rush hour, hurrying to various trains, or those in an airport, waiting the arrival or departure of flights, lack polarization; hence, they are not audiences.

In the audience situation, there are two significant forms of interaction present at all times (but at varying levels): (1) that among individual members of the audience, and (2) that between the audience and the speaker. The interaction among the individual members of an audience is manifested most overtly during those moments just prior to and after a speech. There is a great amount of concerted social activity present during these pre- and post-speech periods. Open greetings, handshakes and pats on the back are common during these periods. We should hasten to point out that, depending on the nature of the audience, the speaker, and the occasion, hostilities as well as pleasantries may well occur. The speaker who has carefully analyzed his audience can rather accurately predict the kind of social interaction which will take place within the audience. Careful observation of the audience during this prespeech period can provide the observant speaker with invaluable information about his audience. Such analysis may allow the speaker to adjust to the immediate mood of the audience and the occasion. The interaction of audience members during the actual speech is often more subtle. The intensity of interaction during the actual speech depends primarily on the degree of homogeneity or group feeling which exists within an audience. Audiences of high homogeneity tend to reinforce and intensify their feelings and responses towards the speaker and the speech. The higher the degree of audience homogeneity, the more predictable is the interaction and response of the audience.

The speaker who addresses an audience of high level homogeneity can anticipate reasonably unified behavior from the individual members during the speech. This is to say that audiences who share a "common ground" or sense of togetherness, tend to react in the same manner to the message. On the other hand, the speaker who addresses an audience of low homogeneity (possessing little common ground or sense of togetherness) is likely to find the behavior of that audience unpredictable. The lower the degree of homogeneity, the more uncertain we are as to how the audience will interact or what their response to the message will be. It is this behavior, however, which is the basis of interaction between the speaker and his audience. The way in which the audience is reacting to the speaker and his message is the only key for determining the immediate success or failure of public communication.

The audience, by virtue of its behavior, exerts considerable control over the speaker's message, from moment to moment throughout the speech. This process of interaction between the speaker and his audience is a continuous one. The speaker who is insensitive to his audience will discover that he has failed in having his ideas understood and accepted by his audience. On the other hand, the speaker who is aware of and adjustive to his audience enhances greatly his chances of effective communication.

The beginning speaker is primarily concerned with analyzing the audience in a formal speech setting; a setting in which the individual members of the audience have willingly chosen to attend the speech. Such a setting suggests that the speaker will be able to determine the general nature of his audience by virtue of their interest in the subject, the occasion, and/or the speaker himself. From this point of view, we can define the audience as an assembled group of individuals who typically meet at a predetermined time and place for the specific purpose of seeing a speaker and hearing his message.

Types of Audiences

Unfortunately, not all audiences have the same degree of purpose and direction toward the speaker and his message as does the formal audience. Hollingworth gives a useful classification of audiences based on the degree of their organization or orientation toward the speech situation.[2]

The audience which has the least amount of unified attention is the *casual* audience, sometimes referred to as "pedestrian." Shoppers who stop momentarily to watch and listen to a demonstration on the use of floor wax—sightseers wandering about a museum, occasionally listening to an explanation of some ancient relic—are illustrations of this type of audience. Such audiences display little or no homogeneity and have little speaker-listener orientation or polarization. In fact, they are hardly audiences and, hence, the speaker's first task is to gain attention—to set up a speaker-audience situation.

2. H. L. Hollingworth, *The Psychology of the Audience* (New York: American Book Company, 1935), pp. 19–32.

Distinguished from the casual or pedestrian audience is a second type which Hollingworth refers to as *passive* or partially oriented. This type is most frequently composed of captive listeners. Partially oriented audiences are found in many college classrooms, social organizations, and perhaps, most typically, the after-dinner audience. The speaker's first task with the passive audience is to establish interest.

A third type of audience is the *selected* audience. It is composed of individuals who have gathered for some common and known purpose. Usually the individuals in this audience have been especially invited to attend this closed or semiclosed meeting because they are known to have previous interest in the subject to be considered. The speaker normally has the attention and interest of the selected audience. His first task then, is to make an impression on them.

Fourth is the *concerted* audience, which has an active purpose, with sympathetic interest in a mutual enterprise, but with no clear division of labor or rigid organization of authority. The concerted audience has a high degree of orientation toward the speaker and his purpose. Graduate seminars, specialized training groups and some political meetings are examples of concerted audiences. The primary task of the speaker is to persuade these audiences and to direct action.

A fifth and final type is the *organized* audience, typified by military units and athletic teams. The members of these groups are completely oriented toward the speaker. In such an audience the labor is fixed and the lines of authority clearly demarcated. The speaker enjoys considerable control of the organized audience. His main task is simply to direct the specific action to be taken.

The speaker's responsibilities at the various levels of audience orientation are summarized by Hollingworth as follows.[3]

Speaker's Responsibilities for Various Audience Levels				
Pedestrian Audience	**Passive Audience**	**Selected Audience**	**Concerted Audience**	**Organized Audience**
Attention	. . . . .	. . . . .	. . . . .	. . . . .
Interest	Interest	. . . . .	. . . . .	. . . . .
Impression	Impression	Impression	. . . . .	. . . . .
Conviction	Conviction	Conviction	Conviction	. . . . .
Direction	Direction	Direction	Direction	Direction

Figure 13

3. Hollingworth, *Psychology of the Audience*, p. 25.

Hollingworth's classification of audiences into types is a practical and careful guide in the identification, study and analysis of the audience. The five major types of audiences identified by Hollingworth however, should not be considered mutually exclusive. Such a classification system is based on the *degree* of organization or orientation of the audience toward the speech situation. As the degree of audience organization or orientation changes then the labels used to identify and "type" that audience must also change. For example the pedestrian or casual audience wandering from room to room enjoying an art exhibit may suddenly discover that they have inadvertently wandered into a lecture on modern art thus becoming a captive or *passive* audience. A *selected* audience may be so moved by the speaker that they are readily persuaded and willing to undertake some form of action, in which case such an audience would be more accurately "typed" as being *concerted*.

Only through careful audience analysis will the speaker be able to determine the predisposition of the audience toward the subject, occasion, and speaker. Audience analysis is a continuous process and is essential to the preparation, delivery, and evaluation of the effectiveness of the speaker and his message. Audience analysis then must take place three times—before the speech, during the speech, and after the speech. Let us consider pre-speech audience analysis.

Pre-Speech Audience Analysis

Pre-speech audience analysis is the essence of speech preparation. No facet of message preparation, whether it be conducting research, structuring the speech or practicing the delivery, should be considered independently from the audience to which the speech will be given. As the opening chapters have stressed, communication consists of evoking a response from a receiver. As a speaker prepares a speech he must have a constant mental image of the audience he will speak to. Audience analysis consists of asking oneself (1) what do I know about the group of people who will listen to this speech? and (2) how can I use that knowledge to increase the probability of achieving my goals?

APPROACHES TO AUDIENCE ANALYSIS—Theodore Clevenger classifies the two traditional approaches to audience analysis as the *demographic approach* and the *purposive approach*.[4] Demographic audience analysis consists of gathering as much information as possible about the demographic characteristics of the audience such as age, sex, political

4. Theodore Clevenger, Jr., *Audience Analysis* (Indianapolis: The Bobbs-Merrill Co., Inc., 1966), pp. 43–51.

preference, socio-economic status, religion, and the like. Purposive audience analysis is concerned with the strategies a speaker uses to achieve his goal with a certain audience. It is evident that demographic data in itself is of little use to a speaker. The value of collecting information about the age, sex, and socio-economic status of an audience is limited to the speaker's ability to draw inferences from that information about the values and attitudes which will affect the outcome of the communication. If a speaker's goal were to convince a city council of the need to spend funds for a mass transit system, he would probably have little use for a detailed analysis of the religious affiliations of his audience. Knowledge of the occupations and economic status of the audience, however, might be very helpful in predicting their predispositions toward his topic. For another speaker, whose speech purpose was to win support for liberalized abortion laws, knowing the religious beliefs of his audience might be more helpful than any other demographic data he could collect. Thus, Clevenger wisely suggests that the speaker combine the two forms of audience analysis. Within the context of his particular speech purpose the speaker should consider relevant demographic data.

Once a speaker has decided what information he would ideally like to have about his audience, practical considerations govern how much information he can collect and what methods he will use. Occasionally a communicator has sufficient time, money and cooperation from listeners to conduct a very thorough audience analysis. Some political candidates, for instance, contract public relations firms to survey the attitudes and opinions of the voters. Through extensive interviews and questionnaires advertisers are able to collect data on the audiences to which they will try to sell their products. Broadcasters gather information on the composition and characteristics of the television audience on different days of the week and at different hours of the day. Producers of individual television shows often obtain quite specific data on the audience for their first shows, so they can adapt programming for subsequent shows to the characteristics of their viewers.

The availability of such detailed statistical data upon which to base an audience analysis is extremely rare, however. More often a speaker must draw inferences about his audience on the basis of informal observations. Direct personal experience with an audience is surely the best source of an informal analysis. The minister who speaks to the same congregation every week knows most members of his audience personally and can make many intelligent generalizations about their attitudes, values and predispositions. Classroom teachers are often heard to label certain classes as liberal or skeptical or fun-loving. These inferences are based on several hours of direct interaction and are probably sound examples of audience analysis. When a person is a long-time member of a group his audience analysis is almost intuitive. He knows from direct experience what "goes over" with that audience. As he prepares a speech he can be fairly certain what kinds of jokes they will laugh at, what would bore them, what arguments would seem logical to them and what appeals would move them emotionally.

When a speaker does not have such direct personal experience he should try to find out as much as he can about the audience. Any outside speaker will have some sort of contact with the audience, usually a representative, such as the program chairman who invited him to speak. A speaker who questions this person about the audience should not be apologetic, for his questions will show his interest and seriousness about the speech he is planning. One thing a speaker should always try to ascertain is how much knowledge the audience has on his particular topic. A college professor invited to speak to a woman's club on water pollution might well assume that they were uninformed. He might prepare a very general speech in oversimplified layman's terms only to arrive at the meeting and discover that his speech was part of a series on the environment and that his audience had been hearing speeches, reading books and holding discussions on his topic for months. A speaker should also ask questions about the format of the program on which he will appear. What is the time limit? (He should adhere to it strictly.) Is a question and answer period following the speech desired? Will the audience be finishing a large meal? Is his speech the main event of the program or will he speak between a glee club performance and the annual election of officers?

Sometimes a speaker may have questions about the physical setting in which he will be speaking. He should feel free to ask if the audience will be seated at tables or in rows of chairs. He should certainly ask for an estimate of the size of the audience. He may want to check on the availability of a lectern, a microphone, a blackboard or equipment for showing slides or films. Some speakers are very adaptable and have no trouble speaking from an upside down wastebasket in a third grade classroom when they had expected a large lecture hall. However, if there are some aspects of the physical setting that a speaker knows do affect his speaking, he owes it to himself and his audience to check on these factors in advance.

There is another aspect of general information about the speech situation that a speaker ought to consider but which may require more subtle means of information gathering. The speaker should have some idea of what image the audience has of him. Is he viewed as an expert? Do they have any misleading ideas about his qualifications? Do they view him as a "curiosity" of some sort? Or do they consider him as a sort of villain that they would like to argue with rather than listen to? Often a speaker can get cues about his image from talking to one or more members of the audience. Certainly knowledge of this expected image can be an important factor in preparing a speech. If the image that the audience has is approximately correct, the speaker should probably adjust to audience expectations. Audiences have some ideas about what a foreign exchange student or a doctor or a school principal is like. Audiences also expect certain behavior from women speakers or from younger speakers. As long as image reflects general cultural standards the speaker is wise to adjust to his image. On the other hand, no speaker should try to project a misleading image. A cardinal rule of communication effectiveness is Be Yourself. Speakers who try to borrow images that work for others usually meet with disastrous results. Perhaps you have heard a fifteen year old girl in an oratory contest try to adopt the image of the late Everett Dirksen. She usually loses to someone sincere enough to sound like a fifteen year old girl. Another example of borrowing images is the sad situation of a speaker trying to borrow jokes or humorous remarks that do not really fit *his* sense of humor.

DEMOGRAPHIC DATA—In addition to this general information about audience knowledge, format, physical setting and expected image, the speaker will often ask questions or otherwise seek information about demographic characteristics of his audience. In this section a few of these demographic factors are considered.

Age. It is a good idea for a speaker to try to find out the average age and the age range of his audience. While the generation gap is often exaggerated, there is no doubt that communication among different age groups or to an audience composed of different age groups is very difficult and complex. Disraeli is credited with the statement, "If a man's not a little liberal when he's twenty, there's something wrong with his heart. If he's not a little conservative when he's fifty, there's something wrong with his head." Although we can all think of many exceptions, the generalization that younger men are more liberal and older men are more conservative is basically valid. The generalization is more applicable if we use the terms liberal and conservative to represent basic world views rather than specific political ideologies. Younger people are frequently more idealistic, more impatient and more optimistic than older people who tend to be more pragmatic, cautious and pessimistic. Most middle aged and elderly people have a substantial stake in the institutions of society. They are understandably reluctant to change those institutions, often at the expense of property, status and difficult personal adjustments, unless they are sure that the changes are definite improvements. Teenagers and young adults, also understandably, are outraged at corruption, injustice and imperfections in institutions and are eager to try various reforms. They are discouraged by the response of their elders who say, "We've tried that before."

The group differences that exist among age levels are not innate to the biological process of aging but reflect different experiences. Today's college students accuse their parents of being materialistic. Many of these students have never known real economic deprivation, therefore they cannot really understand the sense of security that a well-furnished home, two cars and a savings account might mean to their parents who may have literally existed from day to day during the depression. The older generation accuses youth of being disrespectful and ungrateful in their attitudes toward higher education. Yet these older people have had no direct experience with the permissive philosophy of education under which their children were trained for twelve years to think for themselves, to be creative, to ask questions.

As a general rule, it is suggested that a young audience will respond well to challenges and exciting new ideas while an older audience will respond more favorably to appeals to tradition and to moderate reforms with extensive practical justification. However, the speaker who plans to speak often to age groups other than his own will need more than this general rule. Young speakers should talk to older people and try to envision the days of high unemployment, the surge of patriotism of World War II days, rationing and the nature of social and educational life only a generation ago. Mature adults who will frequently speak to youthful audiences should try to understand the frame of reference of an affluent generation, committed to an expressive life style, who have learned to "live for today" in a nuclear age and to analyze international affairs according to the subtleties of a Cold War and wars of national liberation. Once the basic contact has been made, the two generations are often surprised. Middle-aged members of the Establishment learn that not every youth with long hair lives in a commune, uses hard drugs and advocates the violent destruction of all social institutions. Students discover that their parents and grandparents had unlikely fads and social customs and also had social consciences and dreams for a perfect world.

In addition to adjusting speech content to the age level of the audience a speaker must make certain adjustments in his style of presentation. A study by Kausler and Lair showed that younger people can gain information from a faster rate of presentation than older people can.[5] It seems that in general older people also prefer a slower, more deliberate style of speaking and younger people prefer a faster, livelier

5. Donald H. Kausler and Charles V. Lair, "Information Feedback Conditions and Verbal-Discrimination Learning in Elderly Subjects," *Psychonomic Science*, 1968, pp. 193–94.

pace. Marshall McLuhan would attribute this difference to the fact that the current younger generation has grown up in a television culture where all the senses have been simultaneously excited. The pretelevision generations received most of their information through the visual media of the printed page where ideas were presented one at a time in linear fashion. Regardless of the cause of the difference, it is clear that a speaker with a predominantly older audience should use a leisurely rate of delivery and a clear, step by step development of his points. With a more youthful audience the speaker should have a faster rate of delivery (although of course he must be intelligible) and should feel free to adopt an imaginative or varied pattern of organization, as long as there is a coherent progression of ideas.

Sex. Many psychological studies have demonstrated that men and women are different in more than the obvious ways. The Women's Liberation Movement has refocused attention on the nature of these differences. Its protagonists argue that the psychological differences are not innate but that society has taught women that as part of their cultural role they ought to display certain attitudes, such as being emotional, submissive and home-oriented. Margaret Mead's anthropological study *Male and Female* provides excellent evidence that in other cultures the traits and functions which the Western world ascribes to the sexes are reversed.[6] Still, every culture does seem to differentiate certain roles and activities along sexual lines.

The American culture is certainly undergoing many changes in its sexual stereotypes and any generalization should be regarded with caution. Moreover, certain subcultures (perhaps, for example, many groups of artists; or highly eduated people; or urban dwellers; or hippie groups) may make fewer sex role distinctions than the general culture does. Despite these trends and the need for contemporary research, it is safe to say that knowing the sex of the average American would enable one to predict many characteristics of that person with well above chance success. Of particular interest for audience analysis is the general tendency of studies to find that women are more easily persuaded than are men.[7] There is also some evidence to suggest that men reason more logically than women and retain more information about a message.[8]

Some of the personality variables that appear to be sex-linked may

6. Margaret Mead, *Male and Female A Study of the Sexes in a Changing World*, (New York: William Morrow and Company, 1949).
7. Thomas M. Scheidel, "Sex and Persuasibility," *Speech Monographs* 30 (1963): 353–58.
8. A. I. Gates, "Experiment on the Relative Efficiency of Men and Women In Memory and Reasoning," *Psychological Review* 24 (1927): 139–46; O. L. Pence and T. M. Scheidel, "The Effects of Critical Thinking Ability and Certain Other Variables on Persuasibility" (Paper presented at the Speech Association of America Convention, Chicago, December, 1956).

suggest ways that a speaker can adapt his message to his audience. In the American culture men generally play instrumental roles and women play expressive roles.[9] Men build things, manufacture things and handle financial transactions. Women manage homes, raise children or tend to select careers like teaching, nursing or artistic endeavors. Another way of explaining this difference is to say that women tend to be more people-centered. One study showed that men are less accurate in estimating interpersonal relations than are women.[10] This is probably related to Jourard's description of women's expressive role where his research showed that women give and receive more self-disclosing statements than do men. Another study indicates that men have a tendency to attribute difficulties to external factors while women are more self-critical, turning blame for their dissatisfaction inward.[11] Perhaps these findings confirm the old maxim:

A woman thinks about her faults until they seem like double. A man, he just forgives himself, and saves the Lord the trouble.

The speaker should consider these sex differences if he speaks to an audience exclusively or predominantly composed of one sex. He should also remember that the differences are culturally linked, so that while women in general are very home oriented, an audience of sociologists with Ph.D.'s, who happen to be women, may not be very responsive to a speech loaded with references oriented to women in general. Finally, it need hardly be mentioned that a speaker should remember certain customs of our society regarding sex—especially that certain risque humor and certain colorful expressions are considered taboo in mixed audiences.

Socio-economic Status. The United States does not have a rigid class system based on birth and family background. However, occupation, income, education and family history combine to form a characteristic labeled socio-economic status. Many studies have examined differences among socio-economic groups. According to one major finding, cultural deprivation of lower socio-economic groups is especially great in the area of language development. In fact, what appeared to be evidence of lesser intelligence in the lower socio-economic groups has been related to the inability of those groups to cope with intelli-

9. Sidney Jourard, *The Transparent Self* (Princeton, N.J.: D. Van Nostrand Co., Inc., 1964).
10. R. V. Exline, "Group Climate as a Factor in the Relevance and Accuracy of Social Perception," *Journal of Abnormal and Social Psychology* 55 (1957): 382–88.
11. Phillip W. Jackson and Jacob W. Getzels, "Psychological Health and Classroom Functioning," in *Studies in Educational Psychology* (Waltham, Mass.: Blaisdell Publishing Company, 1968), pp. 150–58.

gence tests which tended to be culturally weighted toward the experiences and vocabularies of the middle class. There is no need to cite
research to prove that members of culturally deprived classes are often
frustrated and angry. They are bitter and suspicious toward members
of higher socio-economic groups who appear to have blocked their
progress.

When a speaker addresses an audience of a lower socio-economic
status he must remember that they are probably not inferior to him in
intelligence although they may be deficient in middle class vocabulary
and language. The speaker should omit words and phrases that are
unusual or that sound erudite or impressive. He should *not* change his
whole style of speaking—attempting, for instance, to inject "ghetto
talk" through the use of slang expressions he has heard and read. As
explained in the previous discussion of image, this would be unnatural
and insincere; however well-intentioned, it would be obvious. At best,
it would be ludicrous. At worst, it would be interpreted as trickery and
condescension. When in doubt, it is better with any audience to talk a
bit above them, as long as one seems concerned and sincere, than to
appear to talk down to them. Remember that the late Robert Kennedy
quoted a line of poetry by Aeschylus in an Indianapolis ghetto on the
night of Martin Luther King's assassination. He did not say the quotation in Greek, nor did he refer to "that well-known phrase of Aeschylus'." Consequently, the audience did not see a rich politician trying
to impress them with his education. They heard a concerned man who
wanted to share a thought that was meaningful to him.

Religion. At earlier points in American history knowledge of the
religion of an audience might have been the most valuable information
a speaker could have. One could say with some certainty that Baptists
did not drink alcoholic beverages or that Catholics were opposed to
artificial methods of birth control. Today, religion, at least institutionalized religion, seems to have less direct influence on the specific attitudes of individuals. Each denomination seems to accept more diversity
of belief and behavior and the ecumenical movement is breaking down
rigid doctrinal differences among denominations. The trend is toward
a more personal set of religious beliefs which one may or may not
practice within the context of a given church.

There have been many studies of the traits, attitudes and values of
Catholics, Protestants and Jews. These studies have served to break
down some stereotypes. (For instance, the scale of economic values set
by Jews are no greater than those set by the other two groups.) However, such generalizations seem only to apply to doctrinaire and active
members of those denominations. Hence, it is not very helpful for a
speaker to know that his audience is ninety percent Catholic unless he

has some further information about what "being Catholic" means to those people.

It is important to remember the point made earlier that demographic data about an audience is helpful only if it can be used by a speaker to help achieve his speech objective. Facts about age, sex, socio-economic status and religion might help to draw inferences about *some* audiences in terms of their predispositions on *some* topics. These predispositions, classified as audience values and audience attitudes, are discussed in the following sections.

AUDIENCE VALUES—An evaluative predisposition which deals with institutions, broad philosophical concepts or styles of behavior is called a value. To say "Family life is good" expresses a value, but so does a negative statement such as "Cheating is bad," because both statements are evaluative. When an evaluative predisposition is directed toward a specific issue it is called an attitude. "Capital punishment should be abolished in the United States" is an attitude which might reflect the value "It is wrong to take a human life under any circumstances."

Some generalizations about an audience can be made on the basis of the values of the society in which the audience lives. An extensive study by Steele and Redding classified the values of Americans into core categories and secondary categories.[12] Core categories of American values:

1. *Puritan and pioneer morality*: the tendency to view the world in moral terms as good or bad, ethical or unethical.
2. *Value of the individual:* the primacy of individual welfare in governmental and interpersonal relationships.
3. *Achievement and success:* the primary desirability of material wealth and success; the secondary desirability of success and achievement in vocations, professions, social service, etc.
4. *Change and progress:* the widespread belief that society is progressing and developing toward better things and in change as an index of progress.
5. *Ethical equality:* the ideal of spiritual equality for all in the eyes of God; closely related to equality of opportunity promised in part by free public education.
6. *Effort and optimism:* obsession with the importance of work. Hopeful, optimistic effort will cause all obstacles to yield.
7. *Efficiency, practicality and pragmatism:* higher regard for practical thinkers and doers than for artists or intellectuals.

Secondary categories of American values: rejection of authority (freedom from restraints by government or society); science and secular rationality; sociality (getting along, making contacts); material comfort; quantification (tendency to

12. Edward Steele and W. Charles Redding, "The American Value System: Premises for Persuasion," *Western Speech* 26 (1962): 83–91.

equate value with size or numbers); external conformity (adherence to group patterns); humor; generosity and considerateness; patriotism.

The reader will probably agree that the majority of Americans do hold at least most of these values. Yet it is evident that a common set of values does not lead to agreement among all members of a society. The reason is that values are such general statements that they often cause conflict when applied to specific issues. For instance, the values of the individual and the values of practicality and progress may conflict as when one considers an issue such as whether the government should be allowed to tear down family homes so a new highway can be built. Because of the many natural contradictions among values, it is usually not very helpful to have a listing of an audience's values unless one also has some estimate of the hierarchy on which the values would be ranked if they came into conflict. Rokeach's scheme for the ranking of beliefs can be applied to show the different levels of values.[13]

Figure 14

Core values are those so central to a person's belief system that to change one of those values would amount to a basic alteration of his self concept. *Authority values* are based on the reference groups and the individuals that influence a person. *Peripheral values* are the more or less incidental beliefs of an individual that can be easily changed.

Whenever two values come into conflict, the one closer to the core is most likely to determine an auditor's response. Therefore a speaker should try to draw intelligent inferences about his audience's core values and stress those in his speech. Suppose a speaker has an educational innovation he would like a school to adopt. In speaking to the school board he might stress the values of practicality, efficiency and local control of education. In speaking to the teachers he might stress more idealistic values of progress in education. It is important to note that the speaker is not assuming that teachers are impractical or that school board members do not care about educational progress. No doubt ev-

13. Milton Rokeach, "Images of the Consumer's Mind On and Off Madison Avenue," in *Speech Communication*, ed. Howard Martin and Kenneth Anderson (Boston: Allyn and Bacon, Inc., 1968), pp. 256–62.

eryone in both audiences values all the concepts mentioned here. In a limited speech the speaker has made the decision to stress those values that are probably closer to the core in each audience.

There is a second way that the speaker can use values in analyzing an audience. He can try to forge new links between issues and values and strengthen or weaken existing links. Perhaps an audience has linked the issue of spending money on the space program to the values of patriotism, scientific progress, quantification and achievement. All of these links are perfectly logical. However, a speaker who wishes to cut back spending on the space program can try to link the issue to other values such as economy, humanitarian values (in terms of other priorities), and the value of human life (stressing danger to astronauts). These links can also be defended logically. All of the new values introduced are common ones and perhaps some members of the audiences hold them as core values. If the speaker convinces his audience that these new issue-value links exist, they may change their opinions or at least lean more toward the speaker's position.

Audience Attitudes. Probably the most valuable information for any speaker is a knowledge of the attitudes his audience has toward his topic. If the central idea of the speech were stated as a single declarative sentence, it would be possible to have each member of the audience indicate his initial position along a continuum like the following.

| strongly disagree | disagree | no opinion | agree | strongly agree |

Figure 15

If either through a formal survey or through inferences based on other audience data a speaker is able to decide where the majority of his audience would be placed on such a continuum, he can categorize the audience as neutral, hostile or favorable.

The Neutral Audience. An audience may indicate lack of opinion on a topic for one of three reasons. (1) It may be *indifferent.* A ladies' church group might be neutral on whether turbine powered engines should be allowed in the Indianapolis 500 simply because they don't care enough about the issue to form an opinion. (2) It may be *uninformed.* A certain audience might be highly concerned about medical standards but still have no opinion about the adequacy of osteopaths' training, because they have no background or information on the topic. (3) It may be *undecided.* An audience of doctors might be very well informed and very much concerned about the effects of oral contraceptives, but believing that the pro and con evidence balances out, they may state that they have no opinion on the safety of "the pill." Such an audience is often called a committed neutral audience. It is evident that a speaker's strategies would vary considerably among the three types of neutral audiences.

Attention is the speaker's prime concern with the indifferent neutral audience. The great danger is that the audience will "tune out" as soon as they hear the topic. As explained in Chapter 3, each person has an elaborate filtering system that leads him to attend to those stimuli that he sees as related to his own self concept. When an auditor seems to be saying "So what?" he is really saying "What's it to me?" The speaker with an indifferent neutral audience should use vivid examples, humor, novelty, suspense and all the other techniques that are designed to gain attention, but the use of personal references is his most valuable aid. His speech should make liberal use of the pronoun "you." The major goal is to show the audience that they are directly involved in the speaker's topic.

With the uninformed neutral audience the speaker takes on the role of educator to a great extent. An error frequently made in speaking to this kind of audience is the use of technical terminology which the group doesn't understand. While a speaker should not overestimate the specific knowledge of such an audience, neither should he underestimate its general intelligence. Any audience resents a speaker who seems to talk down to it. The speech to an uninformed audience must be didactic in effect but not pedantic in tone.

The undecided neutral audience is treated much like the hostile audience which will be discussed next. To win agreement from this kind of audience the speaker must tip the balance so that the arguments on his side of the issue outweigh those against him. A study by Sears and Freedman suggests a promising strategy for influencing an undecided audience. They found that people who thought they were hearing new arguments on an issue were more likely to change their opinion toward those arguments than people who heard the same arguments but were told that they were hearing a summary of points they had heard earlier in the experiment.[14] This shift in opinion was especially marked among those who had indicated uncertainty about their original position. This study would seem to suggest that the speaker with an undecided audience would be successful if he could present new evidence or arguments on a topic or if he could appear to be presenting arguments that the audience had not heard before.

The Hostile Audience. The speaker facing an unfavorable audi-

14. D. O. Sears and J. L. Freedman, "Effects of Expected Familiarity with Arguments upon Opinion Change and Selective Exposure," *Journal of Personality and Social Psychology* 2 (1965): 420–26.

ence must be extremely sensitive and diplomatic in his approach. Too zealous an attempt to win over this audience completely to the speaker's viewpoint can work against the purpose of the speech. First, as with the indifferent audience, there is the risk that the hostile group will tune the speaker out. The discussion of selective perception in an earlier chapter explained that people perceive what they want to perceive. Thus Democrats may refuse to really listen to the arguments of a Republican candidate, or a group of angry workers may be convinced that nothing management has to say is worthy of their attention. The second danger is that a hostile audience *will* listen to a speech and that something in the content or presentation will make them even more hostile toward the speaker's position—a phenomenon known as *boomerang effect.* To minimize either of these dangers a speaker must make adjustments in his immediate goals, his speech content, and his presentation.

Recognizing that on any important topic the process of attitude change is a slow one, the speaker should be reasonable in the goals that he sets for any one message to a hostile audience. If a person strongly disagrees with the position that gun control legislation should be strengthened, it is very unrealistic to expect that he will strongly agree with that position as the result of a speech. It is far more realistic to hope that he will disagree less strongly or perhaps adopt a neutral position. If a speaker takes this more realistic approach, he will avoid asking the members of his audience to commit themselves to a specific course of action. If they cannot accept the speaker's specific solution they will tend to reject his entire message. With a hostile audience one should offer several options for consideration. Rather than urging auditors to join an alien cause or donate money to the campaign of a candidate they are known to oppose, it would be better to ask them to think about the points raised in the speech and suggest sources for more information. An excellent example of setting realistic goals for a hostile audience is the campaign promoting half-way measures for smokers. Many smokers who would reject a message urging them to stop smoking will consider smoking fewer cigarettes or a smaller portion of each cigarette.

Once the speaker has restricted his speech purpose to a manageable task for a single speech, he can begin to structure his speech content in a way that will win acceptance from the hostile audience. The most useful technique in such circumstances is known as *the common ground approach.* The speaker should stress the issues on which he and the audience agree and the values that they hold in common. Often a speaker and a hostile audience will agree on ends but not on means. For instance, a speaker who advocates the busing of school children to an audience of parents who oppose busing would be wise to stress at the outset of his speech: "All of us are interested in providing a quality education for all children of this community." The hostile audience is psychologically set to disagree and argue with the speaker. The most important thing he can do is to break down this set and present some material that the audience must agree with.

With all hostile audiences speakers should rely heavily on logical proof and complete evidence. If possible, quotations should be used from authorities with which the audience identifies itself. A speaker must be very cautious in his use of emotional appeals with a hostile audience. Such an audience tends to see any obvious effort to arouse emotions as a trick by the speaker to cover up for the lack of a sound logical case.

By far the greatest challenge for the speaker with a hostile audience is to establish personal credibility. Because the audience rejects his position, there is a great tendency for them to reject him as a person. If the speaker can win some level of personal acceptance and respect there is a good chance that the audience will at least consider his position. All of the techniques mentioned so far can help to build a speaker's credibility. Taking a realistic stand on the topic makes him seem like a reasonable person. Building common ground helps the audience to identify with him as "one of us." Relying on logical proof and solid evidence makes him seem intelligent, thorough and knowledgeable. In addition, the speaker must be cognizant of any aspect of his appearance, dress or language that might be offensive to his audience. The general tone of his delivery should be sincere, direct and conciliatory. If the speaker uses humor he might try to direct it toward himself or his cause. It is often a good idea for a speaker to dissociate himself from the more extreme and objectionable proponents of his viewpoints by stating directly what he is *not* in favor of. For instance, a student arguing for more student participation in the governing of universities might tell a hostile audience, "I am not in favor of students determining faculty promotions or granting their own degrees. I do not want to do away with all administrators." Then as the speaker goes on to talk about the additional sources of student input and student power that he does want, the audience may be listening to him as an individual distinct from its stereotypes of "those campus radicals." As is evident, the speaker, the speech, and the audience are variables that interact—that become intertwined into one process. The speaker who can integrate his knowledge and skill relative to himself as a speaker, to the speech, and the particular audience can more easily accomplish his purpose. The late Norman Thomas, four times the Socialist party's presidential candidate, spent most of his career addressing audiences who were hostile to his cause. An authoritative summary of the strategies for coping with hostile audiences is offered in Thomas's observation:

> Some things you do not do unless you are intent on failing. You don't insult your audience, but you may kid it; you don't patronize it or talk down to it; you don't apologize to it for your convictions; you don't whine about being "misunderstood"; you don't beg for favor. You assume and may occasionally appeal to an audience's spirit of fair play, its sporting instinct, its desire to know what you think. You seek a point of contact—sometimes by sharp challenge to arouse attention, sometimes by beginning with partial agreement with what you assume is majority sentiment and then on that basis developing your divergence in thinking. You try—but not too often or too hard—to appeal to your audience's sense of humor even in divergence of opinion. If the facts warrant it, and you have led up to it, you may denounce specifically and vigorously ideas and actions with which large sections of your audience have been in accord. But be sure of your facts and be very sparing in imputing to your opponents base motives. In the minds of some men, honest, well supported denunciation may stick and bring forth later fruit.[15]

The Favorable Audience. A speaker is indeed fortunate if he discovers that the majority of his audience is favorably predisposed toward his topic. Such an audience is not without challenges, though, for the speaker who wishes to have optimal influence on his audience. The main goal of the speaker with a favorable audience is to reinforce and intensify the positive attitudes that they hold and to try to move those who agree with him to a point where they will *act* on their beliefs. In trying to make positive attitudes more vivid and intense the speaker can rely heavily on emotional proof. The favorable audience is likely to respond to moving examples, strong value appeals and emotion-laden language. Unlike the hostile audience who sees a speaker's use of emotion as a substitute for logic and evidence, the favorable audience tends to accept emotional appeal as the legitimate extension of logical arguments they have already agreed to. It is equally evident that a favorable audience will not challenge a speaker's credibility as much as a hostile audience will. The favorable audience seems to reason, "If he's on our side, he must be a nice guy." Consequently, this kind of audience is likely to be much more tolerant of idiosyncracies and imperfections in the speaker's presentation. This is not to suggest that a speaker can be totally indifferent toward the personal impression that he makes. He must guard against the reaction we have all experienced upon hearing a personally offensive individual whose ideas we agree with. We often remark, "With friends like that, who needs enemies?"—a reaction that could mark the beginning of a corrosion of our favorable attitude.

15. Norman Thomas, *Mr. Chairman Ladies and Gentlemen . . .* (New York: Hermitage House, 1955), p. 116.

While logical argument need not play as central a role with a favorable audience as it does with the neutral and especially the hostile audience, a solid rational structure should be the basis for all speeches. There are two uses of reasoning and evidence that are uniquely suited for a favorable audience. In both cases the speaker assumes the role of "coach." First he must try to move the audience from passive agreement to overt action. In direct contrast to the vague and varied solutions offered the hostile audience, the favorable audience requires specific direction. They should be told what organizations they can join, what public leaders to write to, what projects they can volunteer to help with, where they can send money. Often people strongly agree with a proposition and leave a speech hoping that "the scientists will do something about the environment" or "the President will straighten out our foreign policy" or "Congress will help the poor people." With complex problems and a society where sources of power seem farther and farther removed from the individual, it is a real challenge for a speaker to make a favorably disposed audience aware of their own power to bring about change. Suggesting alternatives for specific action calls for creativity and knowledge on the part of the speaker. He should be as specific as possible to the extent of giving addresses and phone numbers and passing around sign-up sheets.

The second "coaching" job of a speaker with a favorable audience is not unlike the role of a speech teacher. He should train the members of his audience to persuade others. It will be explained in a later chapter that much opinion change takes place through informal *opinion leaders* who gain their information from a speech or the mass media and pass it on to personal acquaintances. The speaker should assume that some members of his audience are opinion leaders. He should use dramatic examples and graphic statistics that are likely to be remembered and quoted to others. He should directly urge members of his audience to talk about the issues to other people. Ministers often ask committed members of their congregations to bring a friend to church next Sunday. Speakers at political rallies try to extend their influence by asking partisans to talk to their friends and neighbors.

In summary of pre-speech audience analysis we can say that a speaker should gather his data directly and indirectly. He should consider his prior image as a speaker, the physical setting of the speech and the format of the program. Demographic data offers much useful information for planning a speech. However, this data is useful only insofar as the speaker can relate it to his speech purpose. Knowledge of an audience's general values and specific attitudes is directly helpful in adjusting speech content so that a speaker has a high probability of meeting his goals.

Audience Analysis and Speaker's Adaptation During The Speech

Through pre-speech audience analysis, the speaker carefully constructs his message to insure maximum attention, interest, comprehension, and acceptance by his listeners. As he approaches the audience and prepares to begin his speech, he is concerned with two questions: (1) what effect will his speech actually have on the audience, and (2) what effect will the audience have on him? Will he be successful in his attempts to gain the listeners' attention, maintain their interest, insure understanding, and gain acceptance of his ideas? No amount of preparation or pre-planning can assure absolutely how a particular audience will react to a speaker or to his speech, or, for that matter, how the speaker will react to or be affected by the audience. The speaker must, throughout the entire speech, be constantly analyzing the behavior of his audience and adjusting or adapting his own behavior to that of his listeners. If the speaker wishes to intensify or modify the behavior of his audience, then he must intensify or modify his own behavior. This transactional process is carried on by the exchanging of messages between the speaker and the audience. Feedback, a concept discussed in Chapter 5, is an important part of the transactional process.

As you will recall, the concept of feedback is used to describe a kind of reciprocal interaction between two or more events, in which one activity generates a secondary action, which in turn redirects the primary action. In applying feedback to the speaker-audience communication process, the following elements may be seen: the speaker generates the initial activity, the speech; the secondary action is the reaction by the audience to the speaker and the speech. The redirection of the primary action, the speech, takes place as the speaker adjusts and adapts to the reaction of the audience. This process is a dynamic and continuous one. The speaker, in front of an audience, generates a course of action, visually and verbally, then modifies or intensifies his communication behavior in terms of the audience feedback that he receives. Feedback is used to describe the effect on the speaker of the responses of his hearers, the consequent reinforcement or modification of his own communicative behavior, and its subsequent effect upon the hearers.

The concept of feedback in public speaking asserts that a speaker, in order to be a successful communicator, must adapt and adjust during the actual presentation of the speech to the responses of his audience. The obvious questions then are, how does a speaker determine when an audience is responding? what kinds of responses are there? what do they mean? and how does a speaker reinforce or modify his behavior accordingly? Let us examine some characteristics or cues (audience responses) which can be measured and/or observed in an audience and make some practical suggestions as to how the speaker might interpret and react or adjust to them.

We can place audience behavior into two basic categories: (1) behavior which can be measured, (2) behavior which can be observed, even though not easily measured.

The prerequisites for accepting a speaker's ideas are attention, interest, and comprehension. These, then, are the variables of audience behavior we are most interested in measuring and/or observing. These during the speech responses fall into three categories: physiological processes measured by electronic devices, the listener's continuous self-reporting of his responses by using electrical or mechanical switches or other devices, and the listeners' behavior during the speech which the speaker can observe. The third type of during the speech response is, obviously, the most important in the typical public speaking situation, but let us also consider the other two categories of responses. They are especially useful research areas in public communication.

Measures of an audience's physiological reactions to the visual and verbal stimuli of the communication process have received new impetus in the last few years. Until recently, the measuring of physiological behaviors suffered from methodological problems of confounding instruments and devices that could be used only in a laboratory situation. The laboratory situation, of course, allowed the audience to know that they were being measured. With the advent of transistorized "mini-circuits," and other equally sophisticated electronic devices, physiological behaviors can be monitored more easily.

What these electronic devices attempt to measure are the physiological changes (rate of heartbeat, rate of breathing, blood pressure, brain activity, skin temperature, psychogalvanic skin response, palmar sweat response, muscular tension and capillary dilation) which take place in auditors as a result of the communication stimuli. Among the devices used in measuring physiological responses are: the electrocardiogram (EKG), for measuring the rate and strength of heartbeats; pneumograph, used for measuring respiration; baumanometer, for measuring blood pressure; electroencephalogram (EEG), for measuring brain activity; thermector or electronic thermometer, for measuring skin temperature; graphic level recorder, for measuring psychogalvanic skin responses; electronic humidity sensor for measuring palmar sweat, small electrodes on the skin which monitor and record the electrical currents in the muscles (muscle tension) and electroplethysmographs which measure capillary dilation—the amount of light passed through the skin from a source of known standard intensity. We know that individuals react physiologically at varying levels to any number of stimuli. From these measures, inferences are drawn which can be helpful in interpreting an audience's responses to communication stimuli.

A problem inherent with the use of physiological measuring devices derives from the fact that the information acquired from such measures is not available for immediate application by the speaker. In most instances, meaningful inferences can only be made after careful interpretation of the data. The value of immediate feedback, which enables the speaker to modify his communicative behavior, is thus lost. Those measures in which interpretation and inference occur simultaneously with the stimulus response appear to be of no practical value to the speaker. The results of the measures, though of little immediate practical value to the speaker can be utilized as post-speech audience analysis data. The examination of the data from physiological measures may well enable the speaker to determine the degree of attention and interest inherent in his message and might well suggest various strengths and weaknesses in his appeals and approach to the subject. Such information could be utilized in preparing for future speech performances.

"Audience analyzers" are a second way of measuring audience responses, interest, comprehension, and acceptance as related to the speaker and the speech. The individual members of an audience are provided with a means (normally electronic) by which they can, from moment to moment, throughout the speech, respond to the variables the speaker (or experimenter) wishes to examine. For example, a speaker wanting to test the interest level of a message will provide each of his listeners with an electronic pushbutton machine, connected to some central "scoring" center, with the instructions to push the button whenever the speech becomes uninteresting. The "uninteresting sequels" can be simultaneously recorded and projected on a screen in full view of the speaker, allowing him to make instantaneous adjustments in his presentation. Any number of communication variables can be tested in this way by simply providing the audience with a more elaborate response mechanism.

Audience behavior which can be observed, is of the most practical value to the speaker as far as his speech analysis made during the course of the speech is concerned. It is this observable behavior, in the form of overt physical movement which provides the speaker with cues from which he infers the audience's response to his message. On the basis of this information, the speaker adjusts and adapts his own communication behavior in an attempt to modify or intensify the behavior of his auditors. Such analysis is based on the assumption that, within a particular culture, fairly uniform connections exist between the physiological, mental, and emotional states of an individual. For example, an auditor who is fidgety in his chair or one searching through her purse, is thought to be paying little if any attention. The auditor "slouched" down in his chair with his eyes closed, is looked upon as being totally uninterested. The auditor who sits, apparently paralyzed, staring out the window, is considered to be off in his own little world. A look of puzzlement, accompanied by the shrugging of the shoulders, we take to mean total lack of comprehension. Icy glares and the biting of lips we assume to be anger. Of course, not all obserable behavior is negative. The speaker is generally rewarded by approving nods of heads, warm smiles and applause, all of which he interprets as positive reinforcement toward him and his message. The auditor who follows every move of the speaker and "hangs on his every word" is naturally thought to be deeply interested in what is being said. The list of inferences, predicting internal states by their external manifestations, is virtually endless. The hypotheses would appear to be that auditors will manifest their internal states in observable physical behavior and that that behavior is a reasonably accurate index of their true internal states. In earlier chapters in this text, and especially in Chapter 6 on nonverbal communication, we have noted numerous studies that have indicated strong relationships between observable behavior and inner states.

The speaker should be cautioned that sometimes his inferences can be wrong, especially if they are based on one specific act of one or two auditors. The auditor who appears to be off in his "own little world" may indeed be concentrating deeply about the speaker's message. The slouching auditor may be in deep concentration. The smiling face which was taken for positive reinforcement may have been reflecting pleasure that had nothing to do with the speech content or the speaker. The reading of audience response behavior with accuracy will improve as the speaker gains experience in facing audiences and as he learns to rely on *several* cues from *several* auditors. Regardless of the hazards, which do exist, observable audience behavior remains the most sound, practical, and immediate basis which a speaker can use for determining, from moment to moment, the impact of his message, and so adjust and adapt his own behavior accordingly.

The speaker should remember that he must adjust and adapt his behavior in order to modify or intensify the behavior of his listeners. If the audience "appears" to be inattentive or uninterested as exemplified by their behavior (falling asleep, staring out the window, talking, fidgeting, etc.), the speaker will certainly wish to modify their behavior. There are numerous ways during the speech in which a speaker may accomplish this goal. Perhaps the most effective technique is to become more aggressive in delivery. The speaker can assert himself physically. It is difficult to listen for any length of time to a speaker who is "buried" behind the podium, who is inanimate—in short, who exhibits poor delivery as was discussed in Chapter 9. Effective delivery, incorporating physical movement and appropriate gestures may well be the stimuli needed to envoke attention and interest from the audience. When the audience appears to be straining to hear, the problem can be corrected by simply raising the volume of the voice. If the speaker perceives, through audience cues, that his listeners do not comprehend the message, he should not continue to lead them through a maze of perplexing facts and figures, but stop, check his rate, and perhaps, slow down. More often, however, the audience is simply unable to grasp the meaning of the ideas. If this is the case, the speaker must "re-explain," or reiterate the ideas. The use of internal summaries (periodic summations of information) will add greatly to the clarity of a speech. The perceptive speaker will prepare these internal summaries in advance and, based on audience cues, will use them as needed.

The reinforcing responses are just as important as the negative cues. An audience may nod in agreement and smile happily, and the speaker will be reinforced and proceed with greater confidence than before. The importance of perceiving observable behavior and accurately reading the audience cues cannot be overemphasized. The success or failure of the public communication act may well depend on the speaker's ability to interpret audience behavior and adjust and adapt his own accordingly. The adage "practice makes perfect" is perhaps nowhere in communication more applicable than in the speaker's ability to accurately interpret an audience's observable behavior. The beginning speaker who maintains an attitude of awareness toward his audience will improve his ability to read audience cues with each succeeding speech.

Environmental Factors Affecting The Audience

Operating in every public communication situation are environmental factors which tend to affect audience attention, interest, and comprehension. These environmental factors can be placed into three main categories: (1) physical setting (2) competing stimuli, and (3) audience size and proximity. As pointed out earlier in this chapter, one aspect of careful, pre-speech analysis is to determine the physical setting in which the speech is to take place. Discovering how the audience will be seated, the anticipated size of the audience, and available facilities (i.e., chalkboard, audio-visual equipment, microphone, lectern, etc.) will minimize the problems a speaker might face. Regardless of how carefully one analyzes the physical setting for his presentation, certain problems are bound to occur during the speech which simply could not be foreseen. Characteristic of these unforeseen problems are power breakdowns causing the microphone to go dead, the motion picture or slide projector to quit and the air conditioning or heat to shut off, all of which can be extremely unpleasant and distracting to an audience. The speaker who "panics" only adds to the distraction. A simple acknowledgment of the problems (not a lengthy apology) will serve to ease the tension for both the audience and the speaker. The capable speaker will simply adjust to the problem and carry on. Amazingly, the audience will soon forget their discomfort, too.

Competing stimuli, such as the screaming of a police or ambulance siren, noisy traffic, lawnmowers, the roar of a passing jet, or the slapping of window blinds, present the speaker with a series of frustrating problems. Such stimuli are bound to distract even the most intent listeners. A general rule to follow is, if the competing stimuli is only momentary, adjust to it by increasing your volume so that you can continue to be heard above the temporary disturbance. In the event that you are completely "drowned out," it would be futile to continue. Again, don't panic, simply acknowledge the interruption and begin again as soon as possible. It is even possible to make such competing stimuli work in your favor as in the case of the individual who was delivering a highly controversial speech to a rather hostile audience. Midway through the speech he was interrupted by the screaming of a number of police sirens passing by just outside the auditorium where the speech was taking place. Noting that the audience was completely distracted by the sirens, he commented, "I knew this talk was going to be controversial, but I had no idea it would be this controversial." The audience laughed in appreciation of his ability to adjust to the interruption and perhaps became even less hostile, at least toward the speaker.

The size of an audience and the physical proximity of its members has a definite affect upon the individual auditor. Communication research indicates that as the size of the audience increases, the intellectual functioning of its members decreases.[16] The larger the audience, the more apt auditors are to be distracted.

The size of an audience will determine, in part, the mode of presentation. With smaller audiences, presentation of a speech will be informal. As the size of the audiences increases, the formality of the presentation will increase. With large audiences, the elevation of the speaker above the floor level favors his prestige and often gives added

16. M. Deutsch, "An Experimental Study of the Effects of Cooperation and Competition Upon Group Process," *Human Relations* 2 (1949): 199–231.

influence to his ideas. Dispensing with the platform for smaller audiences induces a stronger rapport between speaker and audience, which is conducive to more effective communication.

The proximity of the speaker to the audience is an important consideration in public speaking. As the distance between the speaker and the audience increases, the interaction between the two decreases. Speaker-audience rapport is lessened as the distance between them is lengthened. Generally, the closer the speaker to his audience, the more personalized his message appears to be.

Placement of individual auditors, their proximity to one another, provides additional concern for the speaker. The closer the auditors are to one another, the stronger the interaction among them. Close physical proximity tends to cause the members of the audience to conform to acceptable standards of behavior—and seems to produce a feeling of togetherness. Dissension among individual auditors is decreased as they come physically closer together.

Communication research does not strongly support any one arrangement as being the ideal public speaking situation. Having the audience close to the front, close together and the speaker close to the audience does, however, possess some face validity.

The speaker must be aware of the environmental factors operating during the speech and the effects they are having on his audience. The ability to cope with and adjust to the unexpected are necessary prerequisites for a successful speaker. The beginning speaker should remember that at all times he must be in command of the situation. Once he has lost the command, his ideas have lost their power. This means the successful speaker must be able to adjust and adapt both himself and his message from moment to moment throughout the speech.

Post-Speech Audience Analysis

The most common and informal means of post-speech analysis is based on immediate, overt audience response. Applause, questions, compliments and criticism from audience members all help the speaker gauge his effectiveness. Attitude questionnaires, interviews with some audience members and followup studies are excellent sources of data for such an analysis but are impractical in a great many speech situations. Direct observation of audience behavior is another indicator of speech effectiveness. If the speaker asked them to sign up for a project, how many actually signed up? If he asked them to investigate a topic further, how many read books, talked to other people or listened to more speeches on the topic? Like the previously mentioned techniques, this behavioral analysis presents several practical problems. Moreover, the speaker must be cautious in attributing changes in audience behavior directly to his speech. If, however, his audience adopts a course of action substantially different from similar groups who were not exposed to his speech, it is reasonable to assume that his message played some role in influencing their behavior.

Post-speech audience analysis may take a number of different forms. Plays, movies, night club acts, advertisements and some speeches are often field-tested on selected audiences. Post-speech data is analyzed to revise the messages for their final presentation. The nonprofessional speaker can make use of a similar technique by trying out a speech on friends, roommates, families and others to see how an audience actually reacts.

When a speaker regularly addresses the same audience his post-speech analysis serves a different function. Teachers and ministers are able to plan long-range strategies. They seek regular feedback on their audiences' comprehension and acceptance of message content and try as well to assess their own personal appeals as speakers. Through this process they are able to clarify or reiterate concepts and adapt future presentations with greater effectiveness. The student who is assigned several speeches in a class should seek similar feedback since he will face the same audience frequently.

The speaker addressing an audience only once might tend to assume that post-speech analysis is not important for him. On the contrary, such analysis does provide him with the only means of determining what effect, if any, he had on his audience. While he may never speak again to that audience on that topic, any information he can gain about the strategies he has used or his strengths and weaknesses as a speaker is helpful. Every speech experience, if evaluated, adds to the speaker's repertoire of skills and his understanding of audiences, thus forming a basis for more sophisticated and sensitive audience analysis in the future.

Summary

In summary, the audience is the single most important variable in communication because ultimately it determines the success or failure of the speaker and his message. Audience has been defined as an assembled group of individuals who typically meet at a predetermined time and place for the specific purpose of seeing a speaker and hearing his message. Audience analysis is the process of collecting information about an audience and using that information to draw inferences about the best way to achieve one's speech purpose. Before the speech the speaker should try to determine the relevant demographic characteristics of his audience, their general cultural values and their specific attitudes toward him and his topic. During the speech he should be sensitive to feedback, especially that manifested in observable behavior. Following the speech he should seek some measure of the effectiveness of his speech. At each of these "check-points" the speaker should use the information to adapt both himself and his message to his audience.

For Further Reading

1. Clevenger, Jr., Theodore. *Audience Analysis.* Indianapolis: The Bobbs-Merrill Co., Inc., 1966.

2. Hollingworth, H. L. *The Psychology of the Audience.* New York: American Book Company, 1935.

3. Monroe, A. H. *Principles and Types of Speech.* 5th ed. Chicago: Scott, Foresman and Co., 1962.

4. Thomas, Norman. *Mr. Chairman, Ladies and Gentlemen* ... New York: Hermitage House, 1955.

Chapter 12

Improving Auditing Skills

It has been said that as much as 98 percent of speech training emphasizes *sending skills* while less than 2 percent focuses on *receiving skills*. Yet what the listener brings to the communication situation is of prime importance to effective speaking. The listener needs to be aware of what he has at stake in the public speaking situation, and the speaker needs to understand the listening process and the listener if he is to achieve the response he desires. Unfortunately, listening behavior is often overlooked or ignored in the speech communication classroom.

Rankin found that adults spend about 70 percent of their waking hours engaged in communication activities with 9 percent of this communication time spent in writing, 16 percent in reading, 30 percent in talking, and 45 percent in listening.[1] Hence, 75 percent—and later studies show up to 90 percent—of all human communication is carried on by speaking and listening. The extensive use of the telephone, movies, radio, television, and public address system have amplified the importance of listening. Our democratic form of government is based upon a well-informed public; modern entertainment depends upon a variety of good listening habits; many jobs and positions depend quite heavily upon effective listening; and learning in school relies upon listening ability. In the classroom and in everyday life, effective listening helps one to get along and to learn.

The evidence is overwhelming that without specific training we do not develop listening skills that are adequate to meet the needs of modern life. The data indicate that most of us are poor listeners. We can

---

1. Paul T. Rankin, "Listening Ability," *Proceedings of the Ohio State Educational Conference, 1929* (Columbus, Ohio: Ohio State University), pp. 172–83.

accurately recall only 50 percent of the information we hear immediately after hearing it.

Confusion, misinformation, and misunderstanding are the products of poor listening. Effective listening can make the difference between knowledge and ignorance, information and misinformation, involvement and apathy, and enjoyment and boredom.

I. The Listening Process

At the outset it seems desirable to define listening. In a sense it is a combination of what we hear, what we understand, and what we remember. Hearing, the first element, is the detection or perception of sound. It is the response of the nervous system of the human body to the stimulation of a sound wave. A listener does not receive a word or message instantly, rather he accumulates sounds, receiving a word after a brief but measurable interval of time. The listener accumulates sounds bit by bit, identifies short sound sequences as words, and then translates these words and groups of words into meaning. It may be helpful to think of the act of listening as comprising three stages: hearing, identifying and recognizing, and auding. The diagram following illustrates these three states.

Hearing refers to the process by which speech sounds in the form of sound waves are received by the ear. The second stage is one in which patterns and familiar relationships are recognized and assimilated. Through auditory analysis, mental reorganization, and association the sounds and sound sequences are recognized as words. The third stage, auding, is the translation of the flow of words into meaning. Auding involves one or more avenues of thought—indexing, comparing, noting sequence, forming sensory impressions, and appreciating.

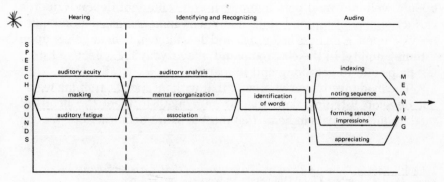

Figure 16

As identified in Figure 16, one of the first factors to affect the hearing of sound is auditory acuity, the ability of the ear to respond to various frequencies (tones) at various intensities (levels of loudness). Human speech frequencies range from 125 to 8,000 cycles per second, although most words fall between 1,000 and 2,500 cycles per second—the critical range of auditory acuity.

The loudness of sound is measured in decibels, and ranges for speech from 55 decibels (soft talking) to 85 decibels (loud conversation). A person is said to have a hearing loss when he requires more than the normal amount of intensity (volume) in order to hear sounds of certain frequencies. A 15 to 20 decibel requirement over normal would be considered a significant hearing loss. Any loss of this amount in the critical range of 1,000 to 2,500 frequencies is especially serious since it affects the intelligibility of speech.

Another factor influencing hearing is masking. When background noise, especially competing conversation, enters the ear in the same frequency range as the speech one is intending to receive, the extraneous noise is said to mask the intended oral message. When the extraneous sound is composed of all frequencies it is called white noise. White noise is sometimes produced when a large number of persons (a roomful) talk in loud voices—all at the same time.

Auditory fatigue is yet another factor that can affect hearing. Continuous exposure to sounds of certain frequencies can have the effect of causing a temporary hearing loss. A monotonous tone or a droning voice can have the effect of creating auditory fatigue. Studies today are showing that hearing losses, some of an enduring nature, are resulting from prolonged exposure to noise in urban communities. Some researchers have suggested also that music played at high volume levels for prolonged periods can cause a hearing loss.

The second stage in listening can be affected by the quality of auditory analysis, mental reorganization, and association. Auditory analysis refers to the process of comparing the incoming sounds with sounds that are already familiar to the individual. Sounds are recognized in terms of their likenesses and differences.

A second part of the process is mental reorganization. In mental reorganization the listener applies some system that will aid retention and structure the incoming sounds. He may syllabify a word, for example, as he pronounces it to himself. If it is a series of numbers, he may place them in groups of three; or he may repeat the series to himself several times. Whether he groups, recodes, or rehearses, he is engaged in mental reorganization.

Finally, sounds are associated with prior experiences with sounds. Words used in speech may be entirely strange to the listener—e.g., a foreign language—or they may have become associated with subjective meanings quite different than those the sender had in mind. In any event, there is a process for identifying words in which the listener's experience, background, and memory are used to create associations in regard to the incoming sounds.

The third major stage of listening is auding, the process of assimilating the continuous flow of words and responding with understanding or feeling. Again, the listener's experiential background is brought into play along with various skills in thinking to make sense of the stream of words he is receiving. The listener may index, make comparisons, note sequence, react by forming sensory impressions or appreciating what is heard.

Indexing, as it is used in auding, refers to the outlining or ranking of information according to importance. It is the searching for main ideas and supporting or secondary ideas; it is the separating of the relevant from the irrelevant; and it is the structuring of bits and pieces into more meaningful wholes. Some persons who are exceptionally skilled in indexing apparently have an unusual ability to visualize an outline of incoming information.

Another aid to the assignment of meaning is arranging the material according to time, space, position, or some other relationship; i.e., by noting sequence. All these functions aid the listener in creating a layer or framework into which information can be placed and related. Material is also easier to remember when the order of events, placement of parts, etc. are noted.

Sometimes the listener reacts with his senses to incoming information. Probably the sensory response most frequently used in association with incoming information is sight—the ability to add a visual dimension to the information. Some persons are apparently highly skilled in forming sensory impressions so that they taste tastes, smell smells, and generally translate words into sensory images, thus adding to the meaningfulness of the verbal message.

A final function that may be engaged in during the auding stage is appreciating, i.e., responding to the esthetic nature of the message. Appreciation can play an important role in listening to public speeches that are ceremonial in nature, as well as in the reception of messages that are intended to activate the feelings and emotions of the listener.

All these elements and more are used in dynamic relationships to carry out the process of listening—the process by which information is assimilated, ideas are received and reacted to, and interpretations, judgments, and applications are made to derive meaning from the messages received.

Ⅱ. Purposes of Listening

The development of good listening ability involves recognizing that there are specific purposes in listening, each with defined requirements and skills. The three most important purposes are: (1) listening for information, (2) listening for enjoyment, and (3) listening in order to evaluate critically. One may listen, of course, with all three purposes in mind. One may enjoy while he also learns, but the most effective listening appears to occur when one knows what he is listening for and listens with that specific purpose in mind rather than listening in a vague general way.

LISTENING FOR ENJOYMENT—Appreciative listening can increase our enjoyment of life, enlarge our experience, expand the range of what we enjoy, and decrease the tension of daily life. Much of the daily conversation in which each of us engages serves a social purpose—a therapeutic and enjoyable function of sharing feelings and responses to build and maintain positive, supporting relationships. In addition, we engage in listening to satisfy our desire for appreciating and experiencing esthetics. In the adult world listening for enjoyment is composed of listening to music, listening to stories or drama on television, engaging in social conversation, and, for some persons, listening to live drama, oral interpretation, or literature read aloud.

Many people cheat themselves out of pleasant and beneficial listening experiences because they have a limited, narrow experience in appreciative listening. When one denies himself the pleasure of esthetic listening, he is always the loser. The person who believes he has to get practical information from all the material he listens to condemns himself to a poverty of cultural experience. Similarly, the person who does not attempt to expand his experiences in appreciative listening short-changes himself. To limit one's self to a diet of "soap opera" for appreciative listening is to miss the opportunity to live more richly, deeply, and pleasantly through expanded esthetic appreciations.

LISTENING FOR INFORMATION—Another purpose for listening is to receive information—to acquire an answer to a definite problem or question, to listen for direction, to listen to the news of current interest, and to acquire the opinions and views of others. We have noted previously in this chapter the important contribution that listening makes to learning in general, the important relationship between listening ability and the acquisition of a viable picture of the world and ourselves. Further, as a student in college, you are keenly aware of the central role listening plays in the acquisition of information and understanding.

LISTENING IN ORDER TO MAKE CRITICAL EVALUATIONS—The word "critical" can be a source of confusion. We use the term to refer to careful evaluation rather than to negativism, aggressive attack, or to the constant challenging of statements. The antagonistic, challenging aspect of being critical can be the antithesis of effective listening as we shall note later when we discuss special problems in listening. Even critical listening in the positive sense of the term (to carefully evaluate) can have dire consequences if the listening objective of receiving information accurately is interfered with by inappropriate timing of the evaluative process. If one attempts to examine carefully each sentence and idea during a speech meant to transmit information, the efficiency of listening for information will be seriously decreased; and if an antagonistic, criticizing process is engaged in as one listens to the speech meant to inform, the results are disastrous: faulty analysis, snap judgments, distortion, and impeded learning. Once again, it should be stressed that the purpose for which one listens must be considered if one is to listen effectively. We need to have evaluative assimilation in informational listening, but the careful evaluative assimilation should be *withheld* until one has fully comprehended the entire message. We are usually well repaid for postponing evaluation.

On the other hand, if the purpose of our listening is to make a decision, a judgment, then we profit by adopting an evaluative attitude more immediately. We profit by evaluating the strength of each main point advanced by carefully testing the reasoning used and the quality of the evidence used in supporting the point. Such weighing and evaluating is most effectively done point by point rather than by waiting until the end of the speech. Critical listening makes us aware of prejudices in ourselves and in others. It forces us to judge on the basis of facts and information, rather than on emotions and falsehoods. It calls for patience, objectivity, and the testing of thinking and reasoning.

The important point to keep in mind at this time is that one may have various purposes in mind when he listens, but the specific purpose for which he listens ought to determine the skills he calls into play. The major concern of any listener is to discover the purpose and nature of the performance of the message involved and to make his own adjustment to it.

III Misconceptions and Problems in Listening

Poor listening can occur as the result of false assumptions about listening, poor listening habits, and ignorance about good listening techniques. We will consider first four unfounded—but widely held—assumptions about listening. These misconceptions, and recent evidence suggesting how badly we have been misled by them, are deserving of our attention.

MISCONCEPTIONS—*Listening ability is largely a matter of intelligence.* The relationship between listening ability and intelligence is not nearly as close as many have assumed. Of course, intelligence has something to do with listening just as it has something to do with many behaviors—especially with all intellectual activities—but we listen with more than intelligence. We listen also with our experience and with our emotional and psychological capacities.

Many reports of the relationship between listening and intelligence have tended to disprove a close relationship. One study shows that males with a lower mean intelligence than females are better listeners than females by a critical ratio of two to one, and that the offspring of farmers demonstrated much higher listening ability than could possibly have been predicted through comparing their average intelligence score with that of the offspring of other occupational groups.[2] Another study, in which very careful comparative measures of listening ability and intelligence were reported, showed the correlation to be only .36 when a group type intelligence test was used and only .22 when the language factor was controlled.[3]

Daily use of listening eliminates the need for special training. Another naive assumption is that training in listening is unnecessary because, like learning to walk, one just learns to listen as a part of the process of growing up. The truth is that no amount of practice and use of listening will insure improvement in listening if the practice is not accompanied by intelligent monitoring and guidance. Evidence tends to show that the kind of practice most people get, if limited by the process of growing up, merely develops and reinforces listening faults rather than skills.

Improving reading ability also improves listening ability. Educational research has shown this assumption to be false. The best way to improve listening skill is to receive direct training in that skill. Improvement in reading does not transfer to listening ability.

Listening is easy. A fourth serious assumption that interferes with improving listening is the assumption that listening is easy, that it is a passive sport in which one relaxes and receives information. This misconception suggests that the listening process is one in which the listener is not actively involved. Nothing could be further from the truth. Listening—especially critical and informational listening—is difficult and fatiguing because it requires continuous, active mental effort. It is true that in some communication situations listening is voluntary; yet when a person listens only when he wants to or is tempted to, he hears

2. Ralph H. Nichols, "Factors in Listening Comprehension," *Speech Monographs* 15 (1948): 154-63.
3. "Brown-Carlsen Listening Comprehension Test Manual," *Evaluation and Adjustment Series* (New York: World Book Co., 1953), p. 11.

only what he wants to hear and only what captures his fleeting attention. He is afflicted with nonlistening habits. Effective listening requires skills and behaviors characteristic of emotional and mental maturity. Productive listening is work. It requires effort and purposeful activity.

PROBLEMS IN LISTENING—Another cause of poor listening is the development of bad habits in listening. Eight of the most common problems in listening follow.

Premature dismissal of a subject as uninteresting. One rationalization for not listening is that the subject is uninteresting. When one decides that a subject is uninteresting, listening is greatly impaired; in fact, it is entirely turned off. But uninteresting subjects are not necessarily without value. To equate interestingness with valuableness is a mistake. It reveals an underlying attitude of "Interest me and entertain me! If you succeed, then this information is valuable for me." This attitude is a denial of the role the listener plays in the communication situation. Knowing that communication is transactional, we can easily predict the effect on the speaker that is produced by the nonverbal communication of such an attitude by the listener. Further, some messages lacking in interestingness may contain highly important and relevant information, but if the listener has prematurely decided not to listen, he will not receive that information. Undoubtedly, some students do not learn because they do not listen. When the responsibility is placed entirely on the speaker, little communication can occur. To stop listening prematurely because you think a subject is uninteresting is a bad habit that can be broken by a planned effort of listening to all kinds of subjects.

Avoiding difficult listening. A second bad listening habit is that of avoiding difficult material. Too many of us listen only as long as it is easy, comfortable, and entertaining. If the material becomes difficult, we just decide to not listen. That habit, of course, deprives the individual of most of his opportunities to learn and to acquire new insights and understandings. Many students who fail in college do so because they have acquired the habit of not listening to anything difficult. Throughout life they have seldom been subjected to any oral discourse that was difficult to understand. In college they find themselves listening to lectures in which new and sometimes complex concepts are presented. When a student lacks experience in listening to things that require mental exertion, or when he has developed the habit of avoiding or ignoring the difficult, he will find that he handicaps himself. If you are afflicted with this bad listening habit, the only solution is to make a planned effort to listen to difficult material. Try to include news commentary, panel discussions, and lectures in the scope of your listening.

Criticizing delivery and physical appearance. A third common problem in listening is that of focusing on the external aspects of the speaker and listening only if the speaker's appearance and delivery are attractive. If the appearance is not to the listener's liking, or if the delivery is either vocally or physically distracting, some persons become so busily engaged in criticizing the delivery or appearance that they fail to listen to the message.

A junior in college, a prospective student teacher, was recently interviewed by me and another person. It was apparent from observing the other person during the interview that he was not hearing what the student was saying, because the student's shoulder-length hair and general appearance had distracted the interviewer into being critical. This was even more apparent in our private discussion following the interview when he confessed that he heard almost nothing the student had said because the student's appearance was so distracting. This listener used a "different" appearance to rationalize poor listening. Many of us have fallen into this habit. If the speaker has an annoying mannerism, we focus on that and decide that we cannot listen. We spend the time mentally criticizing either the physical appearance or speech delivery at the cost of not receiving accurately or beneficially the information sent to us.

Faking attention. Almost any Sunday in church you can observe someone faking attention; and sometimes you can observe others who are not even bothering to fake attention. Faking attention can also be observed in classrooms, and it occurs frequently even in dyadic communication situations. The faker probably assumes that if he looks like he is listening, the speaker will be pleased. The speaker may indeed sometimes be deceived, but in most instances the only person deceived is the one faking the listening. Listening requires energy, effort, and the use of specific skills. When one's energy is used to fake attention, he cannot listen. On occasion, faking attention can be exposed by a carefully inserted question. Besides the embarrassment of being caught looking like a smiling statue, of being suddenly awakened to reality, or of failing to respond in the right way at the right time—in short, of being caught in the act of faking—one cheats himself of an opportunity to learn from what is being said.

Listening only for facts. Another problem in listening is that of listening only for facts. Focusing on "getting the facts" can develop into a bad habit in listening. One can become so busily engaged in listening for and trying to remember facts that the ideas are missed entirely. Memorizing facts is not a way to listen. Facts are useful in constructing and understanding ideas; as such they should be considered secondary to the idea. When people talk they want you to understand their *ideas*, and grasping ideas is the skill that is basic to effective listening.

Letting emotion-laden words arouse personal antagonism. Another habit detrimental to listening is that of allowing the emotions to take control of behavior. When that which we are hearing is something we do not want to hear—something that angers or frightens us— we may develop the habit of blocking it out. On the other hand, if the words are "purr" words for us, we are apt to react with positive emotions accepting everything that is said—truths, half-truths, or pure sham. Our emotions act as filters to what we hear, as we learned in Chapter 3. When we hear something that is opposite to our beliefs, values, attitudes, prejudices, or convictions, we react quickly and emotionally. We become fearful, and may begin to argue mentally with the speaker. We plan rebuttals to what he has said, and in the meantime have not heard anything else he has said; we think of questions we can ask him to "put him down"; or we may just turn to thoughts that support our own feelings on the topic. Any of these behaviors may become so habitual that as soon as we hear words, ideas, or arguments that strike our emotions, we react by not listening. Our antagonistic and negative behavior becomes as automatic as if an "antilistening" button were pushed. This may be our response *unless* we have learned to master our behavior, to break old habits, and to become good listeners.

Wasting the advantage of thought-speed over speech-speed. A final poor habit of listening has to do with how one uses the extra time available as a listener. We speak and think at different speeds. The average rate of speaking is about 125 words per minute, but the brain can handle words at a much faster rate. It is not uncommon, for example, to find people who can read at rates of 1,200 words per minute and easily understand what they have read. Some individuals have read as rapidly as 10,000 words per minute and then scored over 80 percent on factual tests of the material. Numerous experiments in compressed speech (speech that is speeded up mechanically) have shown that people can listen effectively at speeds four or five times faster than normal speech. The brain *handles* words at a lightning pace, but when we listen the brain *receives* words at a snail's pace. Hence, there is a gap between processing what we hear and receiving what we hear. We cannot think more slowly; we continue to think at high speed while the spoken words arrive at slow speed. What this means is that there is a lot of time available for our brain to sidetrack us. Our brain can and does work with hundreds of thoughts other than those spoken to us. We use the extra thinking time when we listen, but how do we use it? We often fall into the habit of wasting it, and sometimes this takes us into daydreams, fantasies, or other places unrelated to the message we came to hear. Even if you catch yourself and come back to what the speaker is saying, it will be more difficult to understand him. You have missed something in his line of thought, and it is now more difficult to grasp his ideas. What he is saying seems less interesting, and your old daydreams beckon you to return. Most of us have had such experiences as students in a classroom, but we must break the habit of wasting thinking time if we are to realize our full potential as listeners. The proper use of this spare time will be discussed in the following section.

IV How to Improve Listening Behavior

The objectives one should pursue to improve listening behavior include the elimination of poor listening habits already acquired and the development of basic skills and attitudes essential to good listening. If you desire to improve your listening, you may find the following eight suggestions worthwhile and helpful towards achieving your objectives.

Listen to difficult material. The poorest listeners are inexperienced listeners, listeners who are unacquainted with lectures, documentaries on radio or television, panel discussions or interviews on television, or public speeches given in lecture halls. Good listeners develop an appetite for a variety of spoken messages. They have even learned to enjoy the challange of difficult subjects. They like intellectual stimulation and growth. If you want to become a better listener but feel handicapped by the bad habit of avoiding difficult presentations, then you should resolve to eliminate this handicap by participating as a listener in a wide variety of communication situations.

Determine the purpose of the speech and your subsequent role in listening. If the speech is a persuasive speech, then you know that you will be engaged in critical listening. The next chapter section will identify specific skills involved in critical listening in addition to the objectives being presented in this section. If the speech is to inform or instruct, you will be concerned with receiving the ideas and concepts as clearly, accurately, and fully as possible. One objective for improving listening behavior is to acquire the habit of determining why you are listening.

Create an interest in the subject. The key to being interested in a subject is its relevancy or usefulness to you. Speakers do not always point out clearly how the speech is useful to you. Sometimes it becomes necessary for you to purposefully seek out ways in which this information can be beneficial. Sometimes, as a listener, you need to ask yourself: "What's he saying that I can use? What worthwhile ideas has he?" Research studies are unanimous in their discovery of the tremendous significance of the interest factor in listening proficiency. Good listeners seem to be interested in whatever they are listening to. Good listeners seldom find topics "dry."

We know that as interest goes up, concentration and learning efficiency increase also. The real problem is to determine what one can do when he is not interested that will provide a stimulus for his interest. For one thing, subjects tend to be interesting when they have immediate application. Hence, look for immediate reward. If necessary, however, discover for yourself how the information will be useful at a later time and place. Introspection to answer questions such as: "Why am I here? What initial motive brought me to hear this speaker? and What selfish uses can I find for this material?" usually helps one to discover genuine interest in the topic.

Effective listening is closely related to personal growth, and for selfish and personal reasons it is necessary for us to try to become genuinely interested in receiving ideas.

Adjust to the speaker. Another worthwhile objective is that of developing the ability to adjust to the speaker so that an optimal relationship for exchanging information is established. This objective relates to one of the common problems in listening discussed in the previous section—the problem of allowing distracting appearance or delivery to dominate one's attention and thinking. Our goal must be to listen to the message, not to the delivery or the appearance of the person. Our aim is to find out what the speaker is saying, to find out what knowledge he has that we need.

Every speaker has his peculiarities, and if a person allows himself to be bothered by a droning voice, a shrill pitch, a persistent cough, socially inappropriate dress, etc., he will hear few speeches during which he can concentrate fully on the message. Unfortunately, speakers often have some eccentricity. It may be poor eye-contact, an accent, or some distracting bodily activity. It is possible, however, for a listener to make the decision to adjust to those situations—to tell himself that it is the message he wants, and that the idiosyncrasy of the speaker is unimportant. In other words, man can be rational. He can learn to control his behavior. A listener can learn to adjust to the speaker, and when he makes that adjustment a natural part of his behavior, he will become a more effective listener.

Adjust to the physical situation. A good listener fights distraction. Sometimes problems in the physical environment are easily solved by closing a door, turning off the television, moving closer to the speaker, moving from behind the pole so you can see the speaker, or asking him to speak louder. If the distraction cannot be eliminated that easily, it becomes a matter of concentration. One should, of course, do all those things he can do to control the physical situation. One should make it a matter of routine to sit where he can easily hear and see the speaker.

Keep the emotions in check. An important objective for improved listening is to learn to hold your fire, to learn not to get too excited about a speaker's point until you are certain you thoroughly understand it. The aim is always to withhold evaluation until comprehension is complete. Effective listeners keep an open mind. They try to identify the words or phrases that are most upsetting emotionally and to purposely "cool" their reactions to them; otherwise, emotions are aroused and deaf spots are created which impair one's ability to perceive accurately and to understand. Deaf spots are always areas of great sensitivity— areas of our strongest values, convictions, and prejudices. A single emotion-laden word or an argument may trigger our emotional blockage and, when it occurs, our listening efficiency drops toward the zero point.

There are some steps you can take to strengthen your behavior control. When you hear something that really upsets you, you can extract those words or phrases that are most upsetting to you emotionally and make a list of them. Second, you can analyze why each word influences you as it does. Ask yourself what the original basis for your reaction to that word is. Third, it may be helpful to discuss each of these words with a friend or classmate. You may discover that these words carry unique and purely personal connotations for you that are without foundation. In any event, getting these words out into the open and identifying them will be of great help in enabling you to "cool" your reactions to them.

Listen primarily for ideas and patterns of reasoning. The seventh objective for effective listening is to attain the ability to recognize main points and central ideas. Good listeners focus on ideas. They have acquired the ability to discriminate between fact and principle, idea and example, and evidence and argument. Poor listeners tend to be unable to make these distinctions. They fall into the poor listening habit identified earlier in this chapter—the habit of listening for facts. Lee has found that only about 25 percent of the persons listening to a speech could identify the central idea of the speaker.[4] These good listeners are able to recognize conventional compositional techniques. They are familiar with patterns of organizing material, partitioning through the use of transitional language, and summarizing. Good listeners know that it is important to get the main idea as quickly as possible and to comprehend the underlying structure of the speech or the particular argument being given. This skill of detecting patterns of organization will be discussed further in this chapter when we consider note-taking in the classroom lecture situation.

4. Irving J. Lee, *How to Talk With People* (New York: Harper & Brothers, 1952), p. x.

Use spare time wisely. The final objective suggested for a self-improvement program in listening is to make the wisest possible use of the spare time created by the difference between speaking rate and thinking rate. The good listener acquires the ability to capitalize on thought-speed. Most of us can think easily at about four times the average rate of speaking, i.e., we have about 400 words worth of thinking time to spare during every minute a person talks to us. This major handicap to effective listening can be converted into our greatest single asset.

One should not attempt to synchronize thought and speech rates. The answer lies in using the spare time purposefully to enhance our understanding of the message we are receiving. Listening authorities suggest that the following mental activities be used to fill this spare time: (1) anticipate what the speaker will say before he says it; (2) note the adequacy with which each point is supported; (3) mentally review, after each point, the portion of the talk covered so far; and (4) listen "between the lines" for additional meaning. These are the ingredients of concentration in listening. The listener has time to engage in these "extra thoughts" while at the same time listening closely to the speaker.

Listening "between the lines" is listening for hidden or unstated meanings, new meanings—i.e., meanings other than those assigned by us initially—listening for what is not said as well as what is said. We can gain much knowledge about the speaker's competency, his integrity, and his creative ability from the careful study of his product—the speech he is giving. All of us can improve our ability to concentrate. Great gains in understanding or comprehending lectures can be made if one continually practices the four skills of concentrating so as to use spare listening time efficiently.

All of these objectives—listening to materials of varying degrees of difficulty, determining the purpose of the speech, creating a personal interest in the speech, adjusting to the speaker and the environment, holding the emotions in check, focusing on ideas and patterns, and using spare listening time efficiently—are quite worthwhile, especially for college students who spend an extraordinary amount of their time talking and listening.

Your successful effort to reach these objectives in your own listening behavior will be richly rewarded. You will not only improve your own listening ability, learning ability, and decision-making ability, but you will gain an appreciation of speech communication. You will gain new insights into the speaking process as well, and as you become a more competent speech communication critic, you may also become a better speaker. Further, you will be better prepared to handle the steadily increasing avalanche of communication in the world that threatens to inundate modern man. In this day of communication explosion and saturation, it is more necessary than ever that we acquire the ability to listen effectively and discriminatingly. In a world of conflicting views, half-truths, indoctrination, and propaganda, the competent person must be able to listen critically—to listen for valid information—to listen for enjoyment and renewal of spirit. The poor listener is severely handicapped today. Without the skills that permit him to be an effective receiver, he can easily be overcome by the streams of messages about him. It is understandable, though tragic, that some people give up and become apathetic, uninvolved beings, cut off from a powerful source of growth and knowledge—listening to others. The great personal satisfaction and reward which can be derived from listening is illustrated as follows:

Listening is a magnetic and strange thing, a creative force. The friends who listen to us are the ones we move toward, and we want to sit in their radius. When we are listened to, it creates us, makes us unfold and expand.

I discovered this a few years ago. Before that, when I went to a party I would think anxiously: "Now try hard. Be lively." But now I tell myself to listen with affection to anyone who talks to me. This person is showing me his soul. It is a little dry and meager and full of grinding talk just now, but soon he will begin to think. He will show his true self; will be wonderfully alive.[5]

The good listener opens doors to new, wholesome, and beneficial experiences. The objectives discussed in this chapter will aid you in becoming the good listener you can be.

5. Karl Menninger, *Love Against Hate* (New York: Harcourt, Brace & World, Inc., 1942), p. 275–76.

For Further Reading

1. Barbara, Dominick A. *The Act of Listening*. Springfield, Illinois: Charles C. Thomas, Inc., 1958.
2. Johnson, Wendell. *Your Most Enchanted Listener*. New York: Harper and Row, 1956.
3. Nichols, Ralph G., and Stevens, Leonard A. *Are You Listening?* New York: McGraw-Hill Book Co., 1957.

Chapter 13

Mass Communication.
The Responsibilities of
Senders and Receivers

Before beginning a discussion of the responsibilities of senders and receivers of mass communication, it is important to understand the distinction between mass communication and other types of communication.

If we were to consider the strict definition of "mass" to mean more than one person, then any speaker addressing an audience of two or more persons would be participating in the process of "mass communication." However, such a definition does not apply to our discussion of mass communication. Thus, we must look for other factors which differentiate mass communication from interpersonal communication.

One key factor which distinguishes the two is the presence of what we shall call a *gatekeeper*. The term was first used by the Austrian psychologist Kurt Lewin who defined gatekeeper as a person or groups of persons "governing the travels of a news item in the communication channel."[1] The gatekeeper acts as an agent in the communication channel between the source of information and the receiver, and it is the gatekeeper through which the communicated message must pass before it reaches the receiver. Figure 17 represents such a process. In the diagram, G_1 refers to the gatekeeper, R represents the receiver, and X, Y, Z become the actual sources of information from which the gatekeeper makes his selection. (Such sources may or may not represent an actual person.)

For example, if we are watching a television news program, we can assume that the information (X, Y, Z) we are receiving has passed

---

1. Kurt Lewin, "Channels of Group Life; Social Planning and Action Research," *Human Relations* 1 (1947): 143–53.

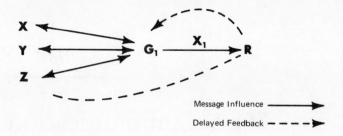

Figure 17. Basic Model of Mass Communication

through certain gatekeepers (G_1). A capsule report (X_1) of the day's news events (X, Y, Z) is selected by a "news editor" (G_1) and presented to the public (R) on a television news program.

In another example, the most important event of the day is selected from all possible events (X, Y, Z) and is presented to readers (R) in the evening newspaper in the form of headlines (X_1). The headline writer (G_1) of the newspaper determines what story (X_1), of all the possible stories (X, Y, Z), is to be communicated to the public (R).

It should also be remembered, that although the gatekeeper selects the information we receive, perhaps restricting our exposure to the gatekeeper's "informational environment," he also acts to *expand* our environment in the sense that he has access to information which we would not normally have access to. For instance, we may learn of a major political development at the United Nations through a news reporter (G_1) who describes the event to us. True, we may not receive *all* the aspects of the political development (X, Y, Z) since he has selected certain important events (X_1) to include in his report. However, since we were not at the United Nations to view the political development in a face-to-face communication process, had the reporter not told us of the development, we would not have received any information about the event. Thus, the same reporter who may have selected or restricted the communication we received, in the same sense expanded our "informational environment." Therefore, the role of the gatekeeper becomes two-fold; to select the information we receive while at the same time expanding our environment by supplying us with additional information.

Another quality of mass communication which distinguishes it from interpersonal communication is the presence of *delayed* feedback to the sender or information source. As opposed to interpersonal communication where the sender is usually in the physical presence of the receiver (as in an interview situation), in mass communication the sender of the communication is not within the physical presence of the receiver. Since the sender of communication or the information source is not physically present, alternative means of feedback must be employed. For instance, we can write a letter to the editor of the newspaper if we dislike the wording of the headline, or telephone the local news announcer if we dislike his interpretation of news events, but the transmission of the feedback is not instant, as in face-to-face communication. In some way it is delayed, and consequently the sender cannot instantaneously adjust the communication to meet his needs or the needs of the receiver.

Mass Communication and Contemporary Society

To this point we have discussed some of the specific qualities of mass communication. Now it becomes important to place in perspective the relationship of mass communication to our contemporary society.

In the twentieth century, such technological advancements as radio, television, film, and communication satellites have in fact enabled mass communication to fit the strict definition "communication to the masses" more aptly.

Eugene H. Methvin, Associate Editor of *Reader's Digest,* referred to mass communication and journalism in a speech to the Georgia Press Institute at the University of Georgia:

In 1776 news of the signing of the Declaration of Independence required a month to travel from Philadelphia to Savannah, a distance of 750 miles. Last March a woman in College Park, Georgia, watching a television newscast saw a young soldier in Vietnam cut down by a Viet Cong bullet. In horror she realized the soldier was her own son. The next day indeed an Army official came to confirm what she had seen; her son had been killed in action 10,000 miles away.
Thus technology has magnified explosively the speed and power American journalists can command. And this power is a little frightening.[2]

Perhaps Mr. Methvin's use of the phrase "a little frightening" is open to debate, but few people can deny that in today's world the "mass communications explosion" of radio, television, film, and the print media has had a commanding effect on our lives. No longer are walks on the moon a product of science fiction dreamers, they are a reality in the living room of every American possessing a radio or television. They become the front page stories of newspapers hours after the event occurs, not days or months later as in yesteryear when messengers relayed news by horseback, or even by ships to the continent of Europe.

2. Eugene H. Methvin, "Changing News Values in the Megamind Era," *Vital Speeches* 35 (May 15, 1969): 462.

If it seems astonishing, remember that the news of the signing of the Declaration of Independence took a month to reach Savannah. Today, it would be unthinkable to receive news of a disarmament treaty weeks after the signing. Yet over one hundred years ago the news of the end of the Civil War could not reach all of the fighting forces simultaneously, and consequently an undetermined number of lives were lost because the forces of the North and South were unaware that their respective generals had met at Appomatox, Virginia on April 9, 1865 and signed an end to the bloodshed.

Today, through the use of communications satellites, events can touch upon our lives as history is being made. As the last quarter of the twentieth century surrounds us, such phrases as "reporting from Moscow," "direct from Paris" are no longer atypical comments used by radio and television commentators. One's imagination need not travel too far into the future to hear a newscaster switch to news not only on the "international front" but on the "interplanetary front" as well.

However, accompanying the increased use of mass communication are increased responsibilities. When one considers that the attention of literally hundreds of millions of the world's population can in the same instant, through mass communication, focus on a single event, then this power does become "a little frightening."

The following paragraphs focus on mass communication, not so much in terms of its communicating facility, but rather on the responsibilities of those who send it, and perhaps even more important, on the responsibilities of those who receive it.

RESPONSIBILITIES OF THE SENDER—The responsibilities of the senders of mass communication have their foundation in a long tradition of legislation and "codes" which assure that senders will meet these responsibilities to their respective mass audiences. Some are self-imposed guidelines structured by the senders themselves. Others are in the form of laws and regulations which provide protection against abuse of the freedoms enjoyed by the senders of mass communication.

EARLY LEGISLATION—A review of some of the major laws and codes provides some insights into the understanding of these responsibilities.

One of the first laws, the United States Constitution, was not so much concerned with regulating and restricting freedom but instead, guaranteeing it. The First Amendment spells out the basic foundations of the frequently heard phrases, "freedom of the press" and "freedom of speech":

Congress shall make no law respecting an establishment of religion, or prohibiting the free exercise thereof; or abridging the freedom of speech, or of the press; or the right of the people peaceably to assemble and to petition the government for a redress of grievances.

But even when the Constitution was being formulated, responsible men in government saw the possibilities of abuse resulting from irresponsible or devious use of the freedoms. One critic of the early Constitution was Alexander Hamilton who referred to the First Amendment as actually being "dangerous" and asked, "Who can give it any definition which would not leave the utmost latitude for evasion?" Although Hamilton lost his plea for exclusion of the First Amendment from the Constitution he would have seen, were he alive today, another part of the Constitution (Article I) used as a safeguard against abuse of the First Amendment. Article I, Section 8, states:

The Congress shall have power ... to regulate commerce with foreign nations, and among the several States, and with the Indian Tribes.

This power to regulate commerce was exercised in 1910 when the 61st Congress enacted The Wireless Ship Act, insuring the safety of passengers of ocean-going ships by requiring ships carrying fifty or more persons to be equipped with radio communication.

The Act fell under the jurisdiction of the Secretary of Commerce and Labor and was enforced "by collectors of customs and other officers of Government."

Two years later further power over mass communication was granted to the Secretary of Commerce and Labor in the Radio Act of 1912. This Act prohibited the operation of any radio transmitter without a federally issued license. Again with a strong reference to "commerce with foreign nations," the Act read:

That a person, company, or corporation under the jurisdiction of the United States shall not use or operate any apparatus for radio communication as a means of commercial intercourse among the several States or with foreign nations, or upon any vessel of the United States with a license, revocable for cause ... so unlawfully used and operated may be adjudged forfeited to the United States.

The need for such licenses and regulations became apparent, when in 1920, radio station KDKA in Pittsburgh, Pennsylvania went on the air with a broadcast of the Harding-Cox election. Shortly thereafter other stations also began to broadcast. Station KYMN Chicago in 1921, just one year after KDKA, programmed to an audience of over 20,000. WDAP (later WGN), pioneered with live broadcasting in the mid 1920s with such broadcasts as the Prohibition debate featuring the famous lawyer Clarence Darrow. The roar of the Indianapolis 500-mile auto race from the Indianapolis Speedway, the crack of bats from the Cubs and White Sox parks rocketed radio and the new "mass communication" into exploding popularity.

As the mid-1920s approached, it became evident that renewed responsibilities had to be accepted by broadcasters if the airways were not to become chaos with stations competing for frequencies and listening audience. Station operators knew that by changing frequency and wattage they could reach far beyond the confines of metropolitan centers to the continents of Europe and Asia. To prevent "jamming," control of power output and frequency had to be considered.

President Calvin Coolidge, in a message to Congress on July 8, 1926, recommended legislation to insure broadcasters met these responsibilities:

Many more stations have been operating than can be accommodated within the limited numbers of wave lengths available; further stations are in course of construction; many stations have departed from the scheme of allocation set down by the Department ... I most urgently recommend that this legislation should be speedily enacted.

Eight months later Congress took the President's advice and passed the Radio Act of 1927 which established the Federal Communications Commission (FCC) as an agency to regulate broadcasting. The Act encompassed all phases of broadcasting and divided the United States into five zones to assure proper regulation. Provisions for acquiring and revoking licenses were also included in the new legislation.

Despite the fact that the Act clearly established certain guidelines in the operation of radio, the one area which remained questionable was the permanent status of the FCC. The Act of 1927 had established the Commission as a temporary unit of government only, so those in mass communication wondered exactly what the future held for them since only this body insured a broadcaster's responsibility to the public.

Then in 1934, President Roosevelt, realizing the problem faced by the medium, addressed Congress saying that he felt certain "utilities" in America should be divided into three parts and each placed under the direction of a separate area of government. Specifically the President noted that transportation was under the auspices of the Interstate Commerce Commission; the problems of power, its development, transmission, and distribution "were under the auspices of the Federal Power Commission"; but communication still did not rest under a permanent government agency. President Roosevelt proposed to Congress that such an agency be formed, responsible not only for radio broadcasting but for all communication using wires or cables as well.

Four months later the Congress acted and passed the Communication Act of 1934. Largely based on the Radio Act of 1927, the new legislation officially created the Federal Communications Commission as a permanent and separate governmental agency. Expanded from the

Radio Act of 1927, the 1934 Act defined the role of mass communication "to serve the public's convenience, interest and necessity." Since 1927, air travel had come into its own and the Communication Act of 1934 included guidelines for those persons using both ground-based and airborne aeronautical stations. In the area of programming responsibility there was included the well known Section 315 which stated that broadcasters would provide equal time to opposing political candidates. Carefully avoiding infringement on the freedom of speech and press as defined in the Constitution, Section 315 did not include governance over a:

legally qualified candiate on any (1) bonafide newscast, (2) bonafide news interview, (3) bonafide news documentary (if the appearance of the candidate is incidental to the presentation of the subject or subjects covered by the news documentary, or (4) on-the-spot coverage of bonafide news events (including but not limited to political conventions and activities incidental thereto) . . .

The interpretation of Section 315 has been called to the recent attention of the FCC by political parties different from those of the President of the United States. The parties contend Section 315 permits reply and rebuttal to a President addressing the nation on a given issue.

RADIO COMES OF AGE—By the time the Communication Act of 1934 had passed Congress, broadcasting had ventured into what has commonly been called the "golden era of the 1930s" and there were new responsibilities to be met by persons in radio.

No longer was the only asset of broadcasting its listening audience. By the 1930s the dollar assets of paid advertising sponsors had taken broadcasting beyond the experimental stages into a commercial enterprise. The National Association of Broadcasters (NAB) had been founded in 1923 and by the late 1940s had over 1400 members and reported an annual income of over $600,000.

Perhaps most important was the fact that now broadcasters were getting together on their own to assume responsibilities without waiting for government prodding. In 1939 the NAB adopted a manual as a guide to members. The manual, commonly called the "Radio Code," covers such areas as unacceptable advertising accounts, length of commercial copy, and other practices and problems encountered by broadcasters. In a subsequent revision of the Radio Code, the NAB established further guidelines captioned "Business Not Acceptable." Some of the suggested restraints include refusal of advertising for hard liquor, for those products which by use or by physical makeup represent a violation of the law, for gambling, and for speculative finance.

Currently the Radio Code has been extended to include such modern day concerns as "bait switch" whereby a broadcaster must accept the responsibility of guarding his community against an advertiser who advertises goods or services which he has no intention of selling but offers merely to lure customers into buying higher priced goods or services. The broadcaster has the responsibility of seeing to it, among other specifics, that testimonials are an accurate reflection of the product being described; that claims of those offering special instruction classes do not boast untruthfully of opportunities awaiting those who enroll; that advertising of firearms and ammunition be limited to portraying such goods for sports use and adhering to good safety standards. Also related to firearms and ammunition, and as a direct result of the 1963 assassination of President John F. Kennedy, the Code discourages mail order advertising firearms. Other suggested guidelines established by the NAB include maximum time "allowable to a single sponsor."

Responsibility in the area of handling contests is also clearly outlined. It includes making sure "rules, eligibility requirements, opening and termination dates" are announced and made readily available to the listening public, including the fact that the names of winners "be released as soon as possible after the close of the contest."

With the increase in free offers, the gas station "giveaway" explosion, and other syndicated programs such as "Dialing for Dollars," the NAB established guidelines for radio broadcasters to make sure that there are "no misleading descriptions or comparisons of any premiums or gifts which will distort or enlarge their value in the minds of the listeners."

A further analysis of the Radio Code points out some of the factors peculiar to this medium. For instance, radio as a form of mass communication is unique in its ability to reach the largest number of people on a first time basis with major events, usually news coverage. As can be seen in our discussion of the Constitution, any form of regulation over news coverage runs a dangerously thin line of infringement on the concept of freedom of the press. Thus, the Radio Code instead of legislation outlines the responsibilities for news coverage. Its guidelines are based on the unique role radio plays in mass communication. One area is the responsibility in the selection of news sources "to uphold the reputation of radio 'as a dominant news medium' which depends largely upon the reliability of such sources." Such a responsibility may seem like common sense to the average reader who naturally expects and assumes such "reliability" and "credibility" from radio, or for that matter from any of the news media. But a further understanding of the role radio plays in mass media news points out the need for increased responsibility. It may seem strange to learn that much of the news seen on television or read in the evening newspaper, was probably received directly or indirectly by radio. Why? Because radio—unlike most television stations which usually meet two deadlines per day, or newspapers which meet one—meets anywhere from five deadlines (on small stations) to forty-eight for larger metropolitan stations (which present "local" news on the hour and half-hour twenty-four hours a day).

In many cases when a news event occurs, it is the radio reporter who is at the scene doing a live broadcast. And it is usually this reporter who is responsible for feeding news to the wire services such as United Press International and Associated Press. The radio reporter identifies the "sources" of news from which television stations may later film additional interviews and newspapers may obtain additional information for in depth stories. Hence, the radio reporter's knack for obtaining reliable sources becomes of paramount importance.

Other responsibilities covering news reporting and stated in the Radio Code include broadcasting in good taste and the responsibility to avoid the use of words and phrases which tend to sensationalize the news and which are "not essential to factual reporting." A typical reporting situation provides an example of why sensationalism must be avoided. One's imagination need not stretch too far to foresee the different reactions in a college dormitory if students were to look outside and see fire trucks racing to their residence hall. Turning to their radios they hear two separate reports of what is taking place. One radio station reports it's merely a fire in a wastebasket and the numerous fire trucks are there as a precautionary measure. Another station reports the building is "exploding in flames." Without a doubt the second broadcast could instill mass panic and far more injuries could result from students running to get out of the building than could possibly result from the fire itself. The elimination of sensationalism becomes especially important when broadcasting such things as disasters or civil unrest where there is an inherent need to prevent undue panic and alarm.

The responsibility of broadcasters for policing radio advertising, as discussed earlier in this chapter, also applies to news broadcasting and the use of advertising in news programming. The broadcaster has the responsibility of seeing to it that advertising is clearly distinguishable from news. Most radio stations frown on the practice of using an announcer's voice, normally heard on newscasts, to be used in the selling of a sponsor's product.

In the second half of the twentieth century, there are some further responsibilities associated with radio broadcasting which have been a result of technological advancements. The invention and universal distribution of the tiny, relatively inexpensive transistor, and the increased allocation of FM frequencies have resulted in radio being within instant reach of almost everyone—teenagers and young adults particularly. For this age group the transistor radio has become as common a possession as a wristwatch—perhaps more so. It is the transistor radio that accompanies the cycle riders, and the gang headed for the beach party—not a newspaper and rarely television. Thus, new responsibilities sit astride the shoulders of the broadcaster who realizes he is constantly reaching this age bracket with more "attentive hours" per day than any other medium. It is for this very reason that the recent revisions of the Radio Code detail those areas which are intended to make sure that radio broadcasters will meet programming responsibilities with "accepted moral, social and ethical ideas characteristic of American life."

As radio continues its growth there will undoubtedly be additional responsibilities assumed by broadcasters. Much like the tremendous growth of AM frequencies in the 1930s and 1940s, the 1970s and 1980s show the same potential for growth in the FM frequencies. The "specialized" radio station is coming into its own as "all news," "country-western," "top 40," and others transmit messages to their "specialized" listening audiences.

TELEVISION—While radio developed as the dominant mass communication medium in the '30s and '40s, the technical advance of television was just getting underway. It started in the late '20s when a closed circuit television picture was transmitted inside a New York industrial plant. By the late 1940s television was becoming as popular as radio had been twenty years before.

Many of the responsibilities first shouldered by television had foundations in that legislation which had placed responsibilities upon radio broadcasters. Although there was no specific mention of television, it seems safe to assume that when the Communication Act of 1934 was created there was some cognizance on the part of the lawmakers that television would follow. As with radio, television stations were required to obtain a license to broadcast. Frequency allocations were awarded only after the licensee agreed to meet certain responsibilities in programming. In the early 1960s, as station applications increased, the FCC awarded channels in the VHF (very high frequency) bands. Certain channels became "specialized" such as educational television (ETV) stations.

Recent developments in cable television (CATV) have caused considerable interest in broadcasting. What started as a business to permit long range reception and multi-channel choice of stations from distances greater than an audience's local area, have now become in themselves, individual stations. The FCC in the late 1960s ruled that cable television came under FCC jurisdiction and that CATV was responsible for meeting the programming needs of local communities. Individual cable companies are now initiating their own local programming. In many cases, where CATV companies have never had experience in local programming they have delegated the responsibilities to local educational institutions which possess the facilities to produce programs and in turn provide an excellent training ground for students. In other cases many syndicated programs are helping to meet the responsibilities of cable broadcasters.

As television mushroomed and additional stations appeared, "code" authorities within the profession itself created a form of "professional criticism," the veiled threat of which is used to assure high standards of programming. The most adhered to is the National Associations of Broadcasters Television Code. First established in 1952 and in the process of continuous revision to meet the changing needs of broadcasters, the Television Code establishes guidelines of responsibility for television broadcasters, dealing not only with "audio" (as for radio), but more particularly with the added dimension of "video." Also taken into consideration for television broadcasters is the tremendous social force of the medium which, as opposed to radio, is an attentive medium demanding and getting two dimension of the senses, sight and sound. It is usually viewed in the confines of the home and thus as stated in the NAB Television Code:

It is the responsibility to bear constantly in mind that the audience is primarily a home audience, and consequently that television's relationship to the viewers is that between guest and host.

Given that this guest-host relationship exists, we can begin to see some differences in the make-up of the television audience and how television meets certain responsibilities to these audiences.

One such audience is small children. Such programs as Captain Kangaroo and Sesame Street have become to children nothing less than a ritual of American Tradition. In such programming, television finds an opportunity to present features which in fact act as instructional tools for the younger generation. Other responsibilities within the confines of programming for children, and clearly worded in the NAB code, specifies such things as not presenting crime "as attractive or as a solution to human problems, and the inevitable retribution should be made clear". The programming of excessive violence creating "undesirable" reactions in children is also shunned by the medium. Such guidelines take on major importance in light of the increasing backlog and reruns of western films in prime time (preschool and elementary school) viewing periods. Cartoons too give cause for concern since, to young children, their animated characters are real people, whose pranks, in a society which children perceive as very much like real life, take on considerable significance.

The responsibility to "afford opportunities for cultural growth" presents an opportunity for other types of children's programming such as the New York Philharmonic Orchestra and its "Young People's Concerts," as well as special programs on art and the theatre, pioneered by television on a national scale. When we look in retrospect at the fact that literally an entire national population is exposed to television during the critical formative years of learning, we think back to Eugene Methvin's phrase—"a little frightening."

Television also has responsibilities to adults and young adults which point to the need for cognizance by industry management of the potential social force television commands. Two social issues which are geared more to the adult and young adult deal with automobiles, specifically drunken driving—and drugs, specifically narcotic addiction.

Prime viewing time has been used by management in cooperation with various national organizations and agencies, such as the National Safety Council and the Department of Health, Education and Welfare, to direct messages to the viewing audience presenting narcotic addiction as a vicious habit and, oriented to the young adult, the use of hallucinogenic drugs as unacceptable.

Catering to the adult audience, television management has found sports programming to be one of the most productive, financially, of any type of programming. Sports telecasts have the advantage of drawing an upper middle-class high income audience with tremendous buying power. Besides the numbers of sponsors wanting to reach this type of audience there is the added advantage of low production costs. To buy television rights to a New York Jets football game is relatively inexpensive compared to what the cost would be for paying the salaries of each individual team member, plus those of the opposition team, for a three-hour television spectacular.

With the increased use of sports programming the issue of gambling has become of concern to television. Television is inclined to avoid showing gambling with any degree of frequency or as a dominant, acceptable theme. However, it should be remembered that complete elimination of the subject would be to take away from some of the excitement of certain sports events—especially horse racing. It is difficult, if not impossible, to report the activities leading up to the running of the Kentucky Derby without some mention of the betting and odds on certain entries. It would be equally impossible to report an election campaign when a state lottery or pari-mutual betting is included as a major plank in a candidate's platform. In cases like these the presentation of situations involving "chance" is permissible.

Since the launching of the first Sputnick in the 1950s, and space travel in the 1970s, increased responsibility in the area of news programming has been laid on television's shoulders, even more so than on radio's. A screech of tires and a crash of metal may achieve interest on radio, but the sight of twisted metal and blood-stained pavement on television achieves an even greater interest. The voice of Neil Armstrong as he first set foot on the moon was exciting, but the response of most of the world's population to actually seeing live television pictures of a man in the moon could only be characterized as fantastic!

It should be remembered, however, that in order to avoid any infringement on freedom of speech and press as stated in the Constitution, the responsibilities for avoiding irresponsible or devious use of those freedoms are founded in guidelines and codes emanating from the industry itself, not from legislation.

With the increased news coverage of social issues in society and the Vietnam war, there has been considerable concern over the amount of conflict and violence which television news coverage should entail. Critics have charged too much violence on television and national commissions have attempted to analyze the effects of television violence and conflict on the viewing audience. Those in the medium have rebutted saying it is impossible to report war without showing the bloodshed which is taking place, and television is meeting its responsibility to the public and truthfully telling what is taking place.

Of late, television is taking a renewed critical look at itself. Even in local communities station managers are looking at their news departments in a different perspective. No longer do they hire men to simply "rip and read" wire copy. The local news reporter has become the center of attention as a man who must have the ability to interpret the trends, needs, and specific problems of his local community. Television is making new efforts to review the needs of communities and to institute changes in the form of increased documentary production and extended local news coverage. In such fields as reporting civil unrest, individual decisions were made by some stations which instituted what is commonly referred to as "code 30s" or "code 60s". These localized codes meant that in high tension areas beset with civil unrest, where the presence of television cameras could possibly spur violence, television crews would wait 30 to 60 minutes before approaching an area to give the police an opportunity to bring things under control. Some stations choose to "hold down" the film coverage of such events in the belief that they have aided by not precipitating further unrest. On the other hand, there are those who consider television as not meant to be an instrument of social control and feel that responsibility to the public is best met if the total picture is told and news filmed when it is in the process of being made, regardless of the consequences.

No matter what measures are being undertaken the medium is continually making an evaluation of itself to determine the needs of the community and how it can best serve these needs. Even FCC license renewal applications require proof of community involvement; thus television has made a concerted effort to meet these requirements.

There are also supplementary organizations to insure that broadcasters meet their responsibilities. The Radio Television News Directors Association (RTNDA) has established a code of ethics for broadcast news reporters which sets up certain responsibilities for news broadcasters. Some of the areas affecting television which are covered under the RTNDA "Code of Ethics" includes frowning on the "undue use of sound and visual effects."

As television continues its growth in the last quarter of the century, it will be making practical application of the lessons learned in the "experimental" decades—the '50s and '60s.

THE PRINT MEDIA—Although the print media (i.e. newspapers, books and magazines) are an important part of our society, they have not been scrutinized as closely as radio and television. Print media do, however, possess some unique qualities worth studying. Where the broadcast media are controlled by federal legislation in such areas as frequency allocation and programming standards, the print media has traditionally been the more closely tied and protected by the basic legal foundation of government, the Constitution. The Communication legislation discussed earlier in this chapter in no way covered newspapers and the print media. The only real control by the federal government is in methods of transmission or distribution, i.e. the U.S. Mails. Where radio and television are assigned certain frequencies, and a limited number of those to a specific area, there is no control over the number of newspapers which covers an area, no license required to print, and only vague legislation controlling content. Instead, the responsibilities are vested in "codes" but without the threat of legal recourse if they are broken. Thus, the print media must, figuratively speaking, live with their own conscience.

Fortunately, however, the journalism profession, with standards set forth in various organizations, have assured meeting certain responsibilities on news reporting. One such code is the American Society of Newspaper Editors' Code of Ethics, commonly referred to as the "Canons of Journalism". It deals with maintaining freedom of the press, truthfulness, divisions between news and editorial opinion, and an opportunity for the presentation of opposing sides of controversial issues.

In newspapers, guidelines are found only in the "Canons" whereas in radio and television, responsibility is assured by law. Newspapers also have some unique qualities due to their peculiar content style. Modern newspapers no longer send a news development onto the street in the form of an "extra;" the "flash and the bulletin" have been left to the broadcast media.

But, along with this change, newspapers are developing increased responsibility for in depth reporting. A broadcast journalist's short comment about a news event is reported in depth in the newspaper. The surface details become the foundation of an analysis of the issues and background surrounding the event. Thus, knowing that the reader will turn to the newspaper to better "understand" the news instead of just "hearing" or "seeing" it, the print journalist has to spend much of his time checking out additional facts—facts that must be not only accurate but objective as well. He must also accept full responsibility for relating these facts to the event they describe. The American newspaper is still struggling to shake the image of the one-sided political press of yesteryear. Although not necessarily true, the charge of Republican, Democratic, conservative, liberal, and radical press are all too frequently applied as labels.

The paperback book is another print medium which has created an impact on American society. The classics of the Greeks or the motion picture of the 1970s can be purchased at the newsstand, in transportation terminals, in book stores, and on sidewalks. Paperback books enjoy some advantages that other print media do not. For instance, they are small and light, a far greater number can be shipped in the same amount of space than can corresponding hardback volumes; they are less expensive than hardback volumes and unlike most magazines, make their profit exclusive of advertising. That is to say they are not hampered by restrictions which advertisers may place on other media. For example, an advertiser may appeal to certain responsibilities of newspaper, radio or television management, by suggesting the removal of an ad or media content which he does not consider "fit for public consumption." The implication is that he will withdraw his advertising if his suggestion is not acted on. Paperback books are not hampered by such possible restrictions.

It should not be inferred by the reader that everything found in a paperback book does not meet public standards and falls into the broadly interpreted "censored" category. Quite the contrary, many of the textbooks you use in college are paperback books. The above conditions are mentioned only to make the reader cognizant of the fact that there are few existing safeguards capable of restricting the content of paperback books.

MOTION PICTURES—The responsibilities of the motion picture industry are in some ways similar to those of the newspaper and paperback book publishing fields. Motion pictures have enjoyed steady growth throughout the past fifty years and will undoubtedly continue into the 1970s and 1980s. The responsibility of the industry is defined in the "Motion Picture Code." A general interpretation is found under the General Principles section of the Code which states:

1. No picture shall be produced which will lower the moral standards of those who see it. Hence, the sympathy of the audience shall never be thrown to the side of crime, wrong-doing, evil or sin.

2. Correct standards of life, subject only to the requirements of drama and entertainment, shall be presented.

3. Law—divine, natural or human—shall not be ridiculed, nor shall sympathy be created for its violation.

Like print media, most of the responsibility falls on the receiver of the communication. As an aid in meeting these responsibilities, the industry and participating theatres have subscribed to a rating system which varies somewhat depending on locale but, in general, rates films as: G—General audience, all ages admitted; GP—Parental guidance recommended; R—restricted to those accompanied by a parent or guardian; and X—No one under 18 admitted.

Although not a foolproof method of selection, it does provide some public guidelines, especially where there is a concern about children viewing certain pictures.

Responsibilities of the Receiver

To be receivers of mass communication, and to insure proper feedback into the system, we must understand more about the process itself. To obtain this understanding, we refer back to the beginning of this chapter, which dealt with the distinctions between mass communication and interpersonal communication.

THE GATEKEEPER "CHAIN"—The gatekeeper was defined as a person or groups of persons "governing the travels of a news item in the communication channel." As receivers of mass communication, we must be aware of the problems arising when more than one gatekeeper is employed in the communication process. Considering the concept of a single gatekeeper, we may conclude that under such circumstances, a minimal amount of distortion will exist. For instance, a radio reporter describing a news event in a live broadcast, or a newspaper reporter describing in his daily the routine details of the police beat, can provide us with rather accurate details of what he is observing. However, when more than one gatekeeper is employed, as is many times the case, such factors as "informational distortion" may result.

In other words, owing to such things as misunderstandings, word misinterpretation, even technical breakdowns, the message that leaves the informational source may not be the same message that reaches the receiver. The communication channel becomes filled with "noise" much the same as the "noise" factor present in the model of interpersonal communication. In mass communication, when more than one gatekeeper is involved, channel noise has an even greater opportunity to flourish. With every added gatekeeper we add the probability of additional noise input into the channel.

Theoretically, instead of a single link between the gatekeeper and the informational source, there are numerous interpersonal links between gatekeepers. Such a condition, as is represented in Figure 18, can be labelled the "chain" relationship of gatekeepers.

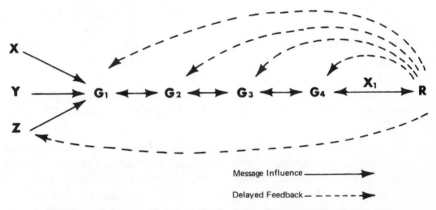

Figure 18. Model of Gatekeeper "Chain" in Mass Communication.

To illustrate the "chain" relationship, let us describe the problem of a communicated message traveling through a series of "gatekeepers" and the resultant effect of the message. Most of us are familiar with the game of "rumor" played among elementary school students. One student (G_1) will whisper a message to another (G_2), who will then tell still another (G_3), and so on around the room until the last student (G_4) to receive the message announces it (X) in front of the class (R), only to find it considerably different than the message transmitted by the first participant.

A similar phenomena can take place in the transmission of a message in the mass media. For example, suppose a local reporter (G) in a small community awakens one morning to learn that a tornado has touched the outskirts of town. He must report the story to the local newspaper. Upon arriving at the scene, he finds that two homes have been destroyed and three persons have been injured. He then calls his local newspaper and gives his observations to the city desk reporter (G_2), who may write the story to read:

A tornado struck the outskirts of Elmville this morning near the intersection of Route 30 and U.S. 421. First reports indicate two homes have been destroyed and three persons injured.

From here the story is routed to the city editor (G_3) who checks for additional facts with the Weather Bureau, learns the direction the tornado traveled, and rewrites the story:

A tornado swept eastward over Elmville today destroying a number of homes and injuring residents in a housing development near U.S. 421.

Although still factual, it is different from the version filed by the original reporter.

At this point, the city editor receives a call from the state wire service. The wire service editor (G_4) is preparing a "wrap-up" summary of tornado damage over the state and wants to include information on what happened at Elmville. He combines the Elmville story with information from other reports and writes:

A series of tornadoes swept the state today injuring scores of persons and causing millions of dollars in damages. Elmville and other cities were hit by this spring's first major disaster.

The wire story is sent to an out-of-town television station where an announcer reads the story in the evening newscast. A person hearing this story receives a much more terrifying version of what happened at Elmville than the Elmville reporter who witnessed the event. The "chain" of gatekeepers has permitted semantic "noise" to enter the communication channel and distort the message.

Perhaps the person hearing the television newscast is from Elmville and calls the local paper (- - - - -➤ G_2) to check the exact amount of damage. Wishing further information, he may drive to Elmville to see for himself what happened (- - - - - ➤X,Y,Z). Calling the local paper or driving to Elmville to view the damage firsthand are both examples of delayed feedback.

THE GATEKEEPER "GROUP"—Another arrangement of gatekeepers which we can term the "group" effect, is also important to consider. In the "group" there is still more than one gatekeeper but such a relationship permits a certain amount of direct influence and feedback among gatekeepers. In such cases, information is fed to a gatekeeper who has direct contact with other gatekeepers, who in turn discuss the informational qualities of the message before it is sent to the receiver. Such a process is described in Figure 19.

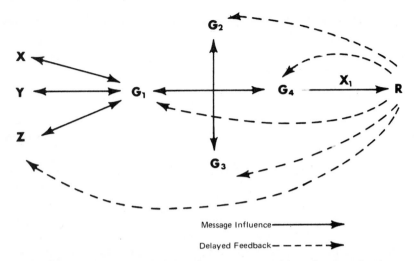

Figure 19. Model of Gatekeeper "Group" in Mass Communication

The important thing to remember is that in the gatekeeper group, all gatekeepers can directly influence and give feedback to all other gate-keepers. In the "chain," a gatekeeper can only directly influence and give feedback to gatekeepers on either side of him on the chain.

To better understand such a group relationship, we can refer back to the Elmville tornado. Imagine that the reporter (G_1) who witnessed the event returned to the newspaper office and sat down in conference with the city desk reporter (G_2), the headline writer (G_3), and the managing editor (G_4). The following could be a typical dialogue:

G_4 "How bad was it?"

G_1 "Well, the homes that were hit were totally demolished."

G_3 "Could we call it a disaster?"

G_1 "No, it wasn't that bad. Let's go with tragedy."

G_2 "Tragedy is too strong a word, there were only three people hurt."

G_1 "But all the same family, a mother, father and baby."

G_2 "Are they hurt bad?"

G_1 "Didn't have time to check."

G_4 "I'll check the hospital, then we'll get a better perspective."

G_2 "Good idea. I'll check State Police to see if any other area was hit. There's a mobile home park just north of the 30-421 intersection."

G_1 "It missed the mobile home park, I talked to the manager. They were lucky."

G_3 "I'll make note of that."

G_4 "OK, check facts, watch the use of those hard words like 'tragedy' and 'disaster' until we know what we've got. Write up a draft and check back with me."

What is occurring is interpersonal communication, direct influence and feedback among gatekeepers. They are all discussing "informational qualities" of the event (X, Y, Z) to be transmitted to the Elmville readers (R). It is easy to see how such a process will insure a fairly accurate description of what took place and the events will be put into their proper perspective. Such direct influence and feedback was not possible when information passed through the gatekeeper chain.

As receivers of mass communication, it is important to realize that such gatekeeper "chains" and "groups" do exist and are a daily influence on the information we receive. Such an understanding of this process permits proper feedback into the communication channel—feedback which will help to assure that we receive from the gatekeepers an accurate presentation of the message leaving the information source.

INTENTIONAL AND UNINTENTIONAL MASS COMMUNICATION—Most of our discussion up to this point has dealt with the factors which operate on and affect the message within the communication channel. But there are also other types of messages as well which are important to understand.

In terms of the message stimuli or communication fed to the receiver, they may for our purposes be classified as "intentional" and "unintentional" communication. For a proper understanding of intentional and unintentional communication, it is important as receivers to be able to differentiate between two additional qualities, message "content" and message "purpose." Content refers to the actual information contained in the message, whereas purpose refers to the motive behind the message. For instance, if we are viewing a television commercial for a particular product, the content of the message would be the actual qualities or facts about the product which are being communicated to us. The product may be soap, which comes in a certain "size," a specific "color," and "smells" clean. Those qualities—size, color, smell—make up the "content" of the communicated message. On the other hand, the advertiser presenting the commercial message chose to emphasize the qualities of size, color, and smell to convince us of the excellent quality of his soap. He may have wanted to compare his soap with a larger size which was too big to hold in one's hand, or to convince us the color of his soap would blend with the bathroom. If we were already purchasing his product, he would want to reinforce our approval of it so we would continue to use it. If we were using another brand of soap, he would want to change our attitude so we would use his brand. In the above example, the desire of the advertiser to convince, to reinforce, to change attitude, becomes the "purpose" behind the communicated message.

To understand the difference between intentional and unintentional mass communication, one must analyze the content and the purpose of the communicated message.

Unintentional mass communication will possess only content without the presence of a motive or purpose. Thus, unintentional communication is that communication which is directed to us and is free from symbols or stimuli which were placed there by a gatekeeper for the purpose of influencing us. For example, light blue shaded scenery may appear behind a television announcer. We can see it and identify it as light blue. Yet the director who placed it there did not intentionally place it there for the purpose of influencing us or creating attitude change. On the other hand, if a political candidate wants to impress upon the voters that he has some association with Washington D.C., he may place behind him a backdrop of the Capitol. In this case the picture of the Capitol is considered intentional communication since the selection of the scene contains a motive or "intentional" desire to change or reinforce attitude. As receivers we have the responsibility to recognize these subtle "intentional" means of communication. Other intentional means of communication are more easily recognized such as a television or radio commercial, the advertisement in the newspaper, the pictures of the refreshment stand during an "intermission" at the outdoor movie theatre, or the cover on a book or magazine. Other types of intentional programming are contained in longer time segments which may be directed to us in the form of actual programs or feature stories. For instance, the use of the political documentary during campaign time is appearing with increasing frequency. Such programs usually take the form of a one-half to one-hour program which describes the life of the candidate. These are ended with an announcement that the message has been a paid political broadcast. The receiving public hearing such an announcement are made aware of the fact that the message was intentional communication, i.e., the receiver knows it was intended to influence his vote.

One area which demands responsible and critical use of our skills as receivers of mass communication is in the area of news programming, since at this point much of the content of the news may be intentional in nature. This is not to say that the gatekeeper, as a journalist delivering an unbiased news report, is lax in his responsibilities. It simply means that some events or persons may have been made to become news for the purpose of directing "intentional" communication at us. For instance, a politician may call a news conference in which he lauds the accomplishments of a special fact-finding commission. He may not specifically state that the commission is made up of members from the same political party. Watching a telecast of the news conference we may react by expressing approval of such a commission and all those associated with the political party it represents. Or, we may disregard the comments as partisan. One may argue that the gatekeeper who is responsible for selecting the communication he transmits, has an equal responsibility to select those events which are nonpartisan in nature. This is partially true, and an alert, objective gatekeeper will point out that the commission was perhaps politically partisan. Yet in many cases the mere "news" or "informational value" of a message may warrant its transmission. It would seem ridiculous for a gatekeeper to refuse to use any news concerning the President of the United States since he in turn belonged to a political party, and in using news of the President the gatekeeper "plugged" the political party. Yet as receivers, we must realize that at any time such messages are sent to us there may be intentional as well as unintentional communication taking place and in such cases, although difficult, we must accept the responsibility to separate content and purpose to properly evaluate such messages.

There is another area in which we must examine unintentional and intentional communication, and that is the area of message transmission. For example, we are all familiar with the common "paperback." As discussed earlier, such books have become increasingly popular and appear quite frequently in newsstands and other places. In such cases, the usual intentional purpose of the publisher of such a book is to sell this product and make a profit. Thus, such things as attractive covers or catchy titles are employed as means of attracting our attention. As receivers of mass communication we are aware of this and even look for such attention factors. We assume, and usually rightly so, that the publisher has no motive which would include "intentional" communication within the covers of the book. Yet there are occasions when such books, simply through increased transmission (i.e., distribution), can result in desired "intentional" communication. As an example of this, take the biography of a candidate for political office. Such books appear with increasing frequency during campaigns when they are distributed for the purpose of publicizing the candidate. Although the actual content of the book may be unintentional communication (free of political motive), the increased distribution of such a book makes it intentional communication. Theoretically speaking such distribution is an "intentional" increase in frequency of transmission of message stimuli fed into the channel.

Another example of such intentional transmission may occur by increasing exposure to the message: in radio or television by increasing the number of times the commercials are used; in newspapers by increasing the number of times the advertisement is run. These are examples of intentional transmissions of a communicated message. Thus, we can see a total of four different combinations for receiving such communication. Figure 20 represents these possibilities.

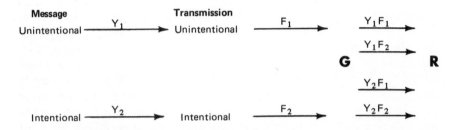

Figure 20 Unintentional-Intentional Mass Communication

Hypothetically we could view such possibilities as being combinations of Y_1, Y_2, F_1 and F_2. For instance, the message influence of Y_1F_2 would indicate a combination of an unintentional message and intentional transmission or distribution. If a combination of Y_2F_2 were used, it would indicate an intentional message containing both content and motive, and an intentional transmission or distribution with a frequency (F) of presentation greater than one. As receivers of mass communication, we may not be exposed to the entire content or transmission of messages, but we must remain aware that combination of message content and transmission exist and are continually bombarding our population.

Summary

The process of mass communication is becoming increasingly complex. It encompasses at some point all the qualities which are part of the intrapersonal and interpersonal communication process. As technological advancements continue the process is destined to become even more complex. Yet at the same time the world's population is made a "witness" to many important events of the twentieth century. The Olympics in Europe, for example, instead of being reported in America by rewriting accounts of European newspapers, is now presented "live" via satellite to an entire nation. Although there is an increasing freedom in mass communication—plus increasing freedom of interpretation as well as increased capacity for transmission—there are increased respon-sibilities also accompanying use of mass communication. This chapter has presented some of the responsibilities of receivers and senders. It now becomes important to apply these responsibilities in order to become "responsible" participants in a communicative society.

For Further Reading

1.   Green, Maury. *Television News: Anatomy and Process.* Belmont, Calif.: Wadsworth Publishing Co., 1969.

2.   Hoffer, Jay. *Managing Today's Radio Station.* Blue Ridge Summit, Pa.: Tab Books, 1968.

3.   Katz, Elihu, and Lazarsfeld, Paul F. *Personal Influence: The Part Played by People in the Flow of Mass Communications.* New York: Free Press, 1955.

4.   Kahn, Frank J., ed. *Documents of American Broadcasting.* New York: Appleton-Century-Crofts, 1968.

5.   Kuhns, William and Stanley, Robert. *Exploring the Film.* Dayton, Ohio: George A. Pflaum Pub., Inc., 1969.

6.   Johnson, Nicholas. *How to Talk Back to Your Television Set.* New York: Bantam Books, Inc., 1970.

7.   McLuhan, Marshall. *Understanding Media: the Extensions of Man.* Signet Books, 1964.

Chapter 14

Protest Communication

The decade of the 1950s has been described as quiet and apathetic.[1] It was a decade of peace and prosperity when the growth of industry and business, as well as the high wages, distracted attention from the pockets of poverty and the plight of millions of Americans who did not enjoy equally the rights and opportunities of millions of other Americans. But Americans soon forgot the calm and serenity of the fifties in the alarming, social upheavals of the sixties—a decade marked by violence. It struck in Dallas, Watts, Chicago, Detroit, Vietnam, Cambodia; at San Diego State College, Columbia University, Kent State University, and other places as well. Many students became activists and participated vigorously in demonstrations; and some students joined radical groups in destructive criminal acts and riots. Organized groups emerged preaching anarchy, and militants appeared demanding sweeping social and political changes. Dr. Spock was jailed for his publicly stated prescriptions of dissent; Columbia University and San Francisco State College nearly collapsed in chaos; and the August 1968 battles in Chicago constituted a momentous apex of the violent protest that characterized the sixties. The high scene of conflict was described in the *Walker Report*:

Many policemen charged with preserving law and order in the nation's second largest city at a crucial moment in history responded to the misbehavior, obstruction, obscenity, and occasional violence of bands of provocateurs midst crowds of peaceful dissenters with frequently unrestrained and indiscriminate violence of their own in thought, word, and deed. ... Running through this report are cogent accounts of the accumulated grievances of the clever or

1. Charles W. Lomas, *The Agitator in American Society* (Englewood Cliffs, N. J.: Prentice-Hall, Inc., 1968), p. 1.

277

merely desperate young men and women who seek to organize dissent somewhere between the established world of political conformity and the underworld of violent revolution, through the now=challenged devices of free
speech and assembly to the deliberately provocative tactics of disobedience and
violent confrontation.[2]

There is no disagreement as to the importance of urban violence
to the future of America, but there is disagreement as to how this
society and other societies should cope with such violence. This chapter
is included in this basic text, not because we have an easy answer to this
difficult problem, but because demonstrations and violence are,
primarily, communicative acts. They are types of public communication, and they comprise a phenomenon extremely relevant to the concerns of teachers and students of communication. It is imperative that
the role of communication in the political and social issues of our day
be investigated, and that the understandings and skills of communication be applied to the real issues of today. There are few current,
domestic problems more crucial in urban areas than violence. Rioting
and violence are the lowest forms of communication for achieving
goals. The objectives of *speech* communication have not been realized
when significant numbers of the populace go into the streets in violent
protest and use destructive coercion to make known their grievances
and obtain solutions to their problems. This final chapter, then, focuses
on dissent and protest.

Violence is *Not* a New Phenomenon

Although the fifties in America were peaceful and apathetic, and the
sixties violent by contrast, violence is not a new phenomenon. Rather,
violence and riots have occurred at various places, at different times,
involving many races, religions, and social issues. Consider the following example:

It was a warm June morning, the beginning of a long hot summer
in one of the largest cities in the world, and on a street in that city there
began a quiet demonstration on behalf of civil liberties. But, as the
demonstration gathered momentum, it turned into a riot, and for six
days and nights thousands of persons engaged in senseless destruction,
plundering, and looting. More than eight hundred persons were killed
or injured; jails were opened and prisoners let out by the hundreds;
government offices were raided; a large bank was broken into and
destroyed; and thousands of people wandered the streets in gangs that
not even the military could restrain.

2. David Walker, *Rights in Conflict* (New York: Bantam Books, 1968), pp. vi–vii.

It sounds like an American riot in the 1960s, but the city was London, the year was 1780, and the demonstration was by Protestants against Catholics.

At another time in history another demonstration began as a group of men gathered to march and carry signs protesting the draft. Again the demonstration grew in number and emotional power, and violence erupted. The mob broke into a draft office, destroyed the lists of potential drafties, and battled with federal troops who rushed to the scene. Fires were started. Pillaging, looting, and killing raged for three days. The estimates of the number of persons killed ranged from four hundred to two thousand. The city was New York, the date was Monday, July 13, 1863, and the demonstrators had gathered to protest the first federal draft law and the initial drawing of names that had occurred two days earlier.

Riots and protest are not new. Scholars have identified thirty-three major interracial disturbances in the United States between 1900 and 1949. Eighteen race riots occurred in America at the time of World War I, between 1915 and 1919. Labor riots, as an outgrowth of strikes, have been common. During one such outbreak in East St. Louis in July 1917, thirty-nine strikebreakers were killed. Two years later a race riot lasting for two weeks in Chicago left thirty-eight dead, hundreds injured, and thousands homeless. During World War II there were several major riots, among which were the Harlem riot, the anti-Mexican and Negro violence in Los Angeles, and the intense Detroit riot of 1943. For those who believe that all the recent riots are un-American and new phenomena, it may help to recall two events linked with American patriotism—the Boston Massacre and the Boston Tea Party. Both were riots in terms of dictionary or political science definitions; i.e., "a wild and loose festivity; disorderly behavior, the tumultuous disturbance of the public peace." Both incidents were based on grievances and were attempts to force change by using methods of physical coercion. These incidents are cited not to justify violence, burning, and killing, but to illustrate that violent protest is *not* new, and to contradict those prophets of doom who predict that the violence of the sixties means the end of everything American.

Causes of Protest

Every protest is created by pre-existing factors—usually many factors that have accumulated without any attempts by those in power to redress the wrongs. No specific, single cause can be assigned to all riots. Any unjust denial of man's basic rights, needs, or aspirations can create feelings of frustration, despair, and rage. When no socially acceptable method for redress can be found, then violent methods may emerge.

The most convenient explanation of the current riots and violence by many Americans is that a conspiracy is responsible; that groups, either foreign or domestic, plan strategies to incite violence. The use of violence and riots may of course be used to achieve revolutionary goals, but the 1967 commission on civil disorders, the Kerner Commission, found little evidence of foreign or domestic conspiracy, and other scholarly research studies also have found little evidence of national plotting.[3]

Another theory for explaining riots is that man is instinctively aggressive, that aggression is a basic drive, as is sex or hunger. According to this theory, when man is frustrated through a denial of some goal, his aggressive tendencies emerge. This "human nature" theory is held by some psychiatrists and many popular authors.[4]

Closely allied to the human nature theory is another to the effect that prosperity alongside poverty, freedom alongside oppression, and unlimited opportunity alongside prejudice and discrimination heighten the awareness of injustice and increase the desire for redress of wrongs and grievances.

If all men's needs and desires were fulfilled there would be no protest or riots, but when individuals have goals which they want to attain—a good environment in which to live and rear their children, good educational opportunities, and fair treatment under the law—and when some individuals succeed in attaining such goals, others who cannot attain them become dissatisfied with their lot. Some persons achieve their economic goals,—others do not. Some own new cars and suburban homes, while others walk, and live in rat-infested hovels. Some eat rich foods, while others eat government-surplus foodstuffs or even go hungry. As long as persons find a disparity between what they have and the privileges and rewards others enjoy, society must maintain ways of meeting and handling the resulting grievances. All genuine protest and dissent rests on *real grievances*. Without grievances, distress, and political and social discomfort, there would be no motivation for protest, nor fuel for agitation (active protest). Protest is aimed against the status quo, and is, therefore, aggressive rather than defensive.

The 1919 Chicago race riot resulted from a combination of many varied problems and inequities. The gathering of arms by members of both races was well known to authorities and the public. Several minor

3. Rodney F. Allen and Charles H. Adair, eds., *Violence and Riots in Urban America* (Worthington, Ohio: Charles A. Jones Publishing Co., 1969), p. 51.
4. See, for example, Konrad Lorenz, *On Aggression* (New York: Harcourt, Brace & World, Inc., 1966).

clashes and incidents preceded the main riot. A white saloon keeper who died of heart trouble was incorrectly reported by the press to have been killed by a Negro. There were cases of individuals beaten by gangs; persons fired on by snipers at night; and inflammatory notices posted in conspicuous places. Prior to these kinds of incidents unrest had been created by increasing competition between black and white laborers in industry following the sudden and steadily growing increase in the number of Negroes migrating from the South. A housing crisis had developed, and the Negroes had begun to take houses outside the recognized area of Negro residence. Homes of Negroes were bombed and burned. The specific incident that touched off the riot on July 27, 1919, occurred at the lake front beach from Twenty-sixth to Twenty-ninth Street. A line supported by a float indicated the area for white swimmers and the area for black swimmers. When Eugene Williams, a Negro boy of seventeen, entered the water from the side used by Negroes and drifted across the line, he promptly became a target for stones. He was struck by a stone and went down. A white man, Stauber, was accused of throwing the fatal stone, and although Negroes demanded that Stauber be arrested, the policeman present refused to arrest Stauber. Instead, he arrested a Negro on a white man's complaint. Negroes then attacked the officer and the full scale riot was set off. Raids, sniping, and battles ensued. The causes of the riot were many, but they involved the negation of rights, opportunities, and aspirations; and were characterized by the blocking of peaceful avenues for redress of grievances.

Insecurity, frustration, overcrowding, inadequate housing, inadequate incomes, denial of rights, and many other injustices cause dissent and protest. As summarized by Kenneth Boulding:

Protest arises when there is strongly felt dissatisfaction with existing programs and policies of government or other organizations, on the part of those who feel themselves affected by these policies but who are unable to express their discontent through regular and legitimate channels, and who feel unable to exercise the weight to which they think they are entitled in the decision-making process. When nobody is listening to us and we feel we have something to say, then comes the urge to shout.[5]

Forms of Protest and Dissent

The right to dissent is *fundamental* to democracy, but the expression of that right has become one of the most serious problems in contemporary democratic societies. That problem was dramatized on television

5. Kenneth E. Boulding, "Towards a Theory of Protest," in *The Age of Protest*, ed. Walt Anderson (Pacific Palisades, Calif. : Goodyear Publishing Co., Inc., 1969), p. vi.

and in the newspaper coverage of the crowd-police battles at the Democratic National Convention in Chicago in 1968. Anarchists, revolutionists, peaceful protesters, and bystanders were merged together and caught up in the events of the week of August 25–30. The response of people in the United States and throughout the world ranged from horrified condemnation of the police (news commentators sympathetically relayed the position taken by the demonstrators who compared the Chicago police to the Soviet troops then occupying Prague) to the feeling that the demonstrators got what they deserved and the city had no alternative.

Most Americans acknowledge the right to dissent, and most dissenters acknowledge the right of a city or state to protect its citizens and its property; but when these rights are brought into conflict, conditions are created which encourage violence. The crucial concern of this society, and other societies facing the same problem, is to discover alternatives to violence—to facilitate the use of other forms of protest. The forms that protest may take are shown in Figure 21.

P	L	1. Direct persuasive influence on government or other
	E	organizational representatives
R	G	2. Voting power
	A	3. Demonstrations
O	L	4. Boycotts, strikes and other legal persuasive acts
T		Nonviolent—Civil disobedience
	I	
E	L	Violent—Criminal disobedience:
	L	1. Individual violence: attacks by individuals on
S	E	persons or property
	G	2. Riot: mob attacks upon persons or property
T	A	3. Insurrection: organized uprising against a law
		or policy
		4. Revolution: organized uprisings against a government
		with the goal of establishing a new government

Figure 21 Forms of Protest

As Figure 21 shows, forms of protest can be classified as legal or illegal with legal protests falling into four general types: (1) direct verbal persuasive influence upon lawmakers, governmental agencies, or other groups legally constituted to establish policies or to enforce and administer established policies; (2) the right to express protest through voting power; (3) demonstrations by pickets, rallies, marches, or other legal means; and (4) legal persuasive acts (collective or individual) such as economic boycotts, strikes, etc.

Illegal forms of protest can be classified as nonviolent (civil disobedience) or violent (criminal disobedience). Criminal disobedience, or violence, may be further classified as: (1) individual violence, (2) riots, (3) insurrections, and (4) revolutions.

As previously noted in this chapter, examples of most of these forms of protest can be found throughout the history of man. Among the many persons who have used civil disobedience as a means of protest when legal forms of protest seemed inadequate are Mahatma Gandhi and Dr. Martin Luther King, Jr.

One of Gandhi's first large, successful civil disobedience campaigns took place in Africa to secure rights for the indentured Indians working in South Africa. A group of Natal "sisters" were to court arrest by entering the Transvaal without permission, and simultaneously a group of Transvaal "sisters" would enter Natal. The Natal "sisters" were imprisoned; indignation flared and brought new recruits. The Transvaal "sisters," were not arrested, so, obeying previous instructions, they proceeded to the Newcastle coal mines and urged the indentured Indian miners to go on strike. Thereupon the Transvaal "sisters" were arrested and each given a three months' jail sentence. The strike began. Gandhi went to Newcastle. The mine owners turned off lights and water in the company houses in which the Indian strikers lived. Gandhi then advised them to leave their homes and pitch camp in the open. In a few days over five thousand Indians were living under the sky. Not knowing how to feed so many, Gandhi decided to organize a march into Transvaal where they would be arrested for illegal entry and safely deposited in jail where they would be fed. Gandhi's orders were: "Do not resist arrest; submit to police flogging; conduct yourself morally and hygienically."[6] When the marchers reached Balfour, they were herded into waiting trains and shipped back to the mines in Natal where they were imprisoned in wire-enclosed stockades and guarded by company employees sworn in as constables. Other indentured servants, whom the state considered slaves having no right to strike, went on sympathy strikes. Soldiers were sent to suppress the strikes and fired on strikers, killing and wounding several Indians. Soon over fifty thousand indentured laborers were on strike. By June, 1914, the Indian Relief Bill was a reality. The grievances (cessation of importation of indentured Indians, annulment of the tax on indentured laborers, and others) were settled along the lines sought by Gandhi.

During World War I civil liberties were taken away in India. Censorship was rampant; and secret tribunals sentenced people in all parts

6. Louis Fischer, *Gandhi: His Life and Message for the World* (New York: Mentor Books, 1954), p. 45.

of India to prison for innumerable trumped-up charges. Following the end of the war, the Rowlatt Acts were passed to increase the wartime control even more. Gandhi and others attempted to gain redress of wrongs through the courts and through the legislative bodies of India, but their efforts were to no avail. Once again, Gandhi put into effect the strategy of strikes and civil disobedience to communicate the Indians' protest. It included first, a "general hartal"—the complete suspension of economic activity. Shops closed, factories were idled, ships floated at the docks unloaded, and banks closed as vast masses of persons observed the hartal. It was enormously successful. Accompanying the hartal were acts of civil disobedience. They sold prohibited literature, a civil crime. Proclamations were issued by the government forbidding processions and meetings, but the meetings and marches continued as acts of civil disobedience. Gandhi cautioned: "We may no longer believe in the doctrine of tit for tat; we may not meet hatred with hatred, violence with violence, evil with evil. . . . Return good for evil."[7] Gandhi's non-cooperation policy followed in which British goods, British homes, British courts, British schools, and British jobs were boycotted. By December, 1919, the demands of Gandhi began to be won and culminated in the Montagn-Chelmsford reforms.

Again in 1930 Gandhi protested unjust taxes and practices, particularly the tax on salt, a tax that fell heavily on the poor. Gandhi wrote: "Nothing but organized non-violence can check the organized violence of the British government. . . . This non-violence will be expressed through civil disobedience. . . . My ambition is to make the British see the wrong they have done to India." And then he pleaded for nogotiation. "I respectfully invite you to pave the way for the immediate removal of these evils, and thus open a way for a real conference between equals."[8]

When no results followed, Gandhi led his followers in breaking the salt laws. At 61 years of age he led the marchers fifteen to sixteen miles per day on the famous salt march. From village to village they marched, and at various villages Gandhi gave speeches urging the population to make and wear homespun clothing, to abandon child marriage, and to live pure lives. By the time Gandhi reached the sea his small band had grown to a non-violent army of several thousand. At the sea they dipped into the water and began to refine salt. Gandhi, in a single gesture of civil disobedience, picked up a palmful of salt and broke the British law which made it a punishable crime to possess salt not purchased from the government salt monopoly.

7. Ibid., p. 64.
8. Ibid., p. 97.

These are but a few of the acts of civil disobedience which Gandhi used to express the protest of India to British injustice.

In the United States, a major advocate of demonstrations and civil disobedience was Dr. Martin Luther King, Jr. In 1958, Dr. King outlined some aspects of the non-violent philosophy:

First, it must be emphasized that nonviolent resistance is not a method for cowards; it does resist. If one uses this method because he is afraid or merely because he lacks the instruments of violence, he is not truly nonviolent. . . . This is ultimately the way of the strong man. . . . The phrase "passive resistance" often gives the false impression that this is a sort of "do-nothing method" in which the resister quietly and passively accepts evil. But nothing is further from the truth. For while the nonviolent resister is passive in the sense that he is not physically aggressive toward his opponent, his mind and emotions are always active, constantly seeking to persuade his opponent that he is wrong. The method is passive physically, but strongly active spiritually. It is not passive nonresistance to evil, it is active nonviolent resistance to evil.[9]

The second principle of King's policy of nonviolence is that it does not seek to defeat the opponent, but to win his friendship.

The nonviolent resister must often express his protest through noncooperation or boycotts, but he realizes that these are not ends themselves; they are merely means to awaken a sense of moral shame in the opponent. . . . The aftermath of nonviolence is the creation of the beloved community, while the aftermath of violence is tragic bitterness.[10]

The third principle emphasizes that the goal is justice, not the defeat of persons.

It is evil that the nonviolent resister seeks to defeat, not the persons victimized by evil. . . . I like to say to the people in Montgomery: "The tension in this city is not between white people and Negro people. The tension is, at bottom, between justice and injustice, between the forces of light and the forces of darkness. And if there is a victory, it will be a victory not merely for fifty thousand Negroes, but a victory for justice and the forces of light. We are out to defeat injustice and not white persons who may be unjust."[11]

King's fourth principle is the key one for a policy of nonviolence and is taken from Gandhi's theory:

[Nonviolent resistance requires] a willingness to accept suffering without retaliation, to accept blows from the opponent without striking back. . . . The

9. Abridged from pp. 102–103, 106 in *Stride Toward Freedom* by Martin Luther King, Jr., Copyright © 1958 by Martin Luther King, Jr. Reprinted by permission of Harper & Row, Publishers, Inc.
10. Ibid.
11. Ibid.

nonviolent resister is willing to accept violence if necessary, but never to inflict it. He does not seek to dodge jail. . . . Suffering, the nonviolent resister realizes, has tremendous educational and transforming possibilities. "Things of fundamental importance to people are not secured by reason alone, but have to be purchased with their suffering," said Gandhi.[12]

The fifth principle of King's theory of nonviolence focuses on the mental health of the protester:

[Nonviolent resistance] avoids not only external physical violence but also internal violence of spirit. The nonviolent resister not only refuses to shoot his opponent but he also refuses to hate him. . . . Along the way of life, someone must have sense enough and morality enough to cut off the chain of hate. This can only be done by projecting the ethic of love to the center of our lives.[13]

The sixth principle is a philosophical view of the nature of the universe:

[Nonviolent resistance] is based on the conviction that the universe is on the side of justice. Consequently, the believer in nonviolence has deep faith in the future. This faith is another reason why the nonviolent resister can accept suffering without retaliation. For he knows that in his struggle for justice he has cosmic companionship.[14]

Nonviolent resistance as practiced by Gandhi and King has been shown to be a potent form of protest. The term civil disobedience is used in conjunction with nonviolence, and although nonviolence may not constitute civil disobedience, as is the case when a custom is violated rather than a law, it usually involves civil disobedience.

Legal demonstrations are another form of protest. They have been used frequently in the United States to call attention to wrongs and injustices, and to win support from the general public as well as to consolidate and reinforce the belief of the participators or segment of society associated with the demonstrators. Although numerous examples of demonstrations in the sixties by various economic and social groups in America (farmers, teachers, union members, hard-hats, blacks, anti-Vietnam war groups, etc.) could be discussed, let us consider as an example the demostration march in New York City in April 1967, a march led by Dr. Martin Luther King, Jr. The march was from Central Park to the United Nations Plaza, and it was carried out to protest the war in Vietnam. The city issued a parade permit, and demonstrators representing nearly 150 separate organizations filled ten

12. Ibid., p. 392.
13. Ibid.
14. Ibid., p. 395.

city blocks and marched peacefully to the United Nations Plaza. They listened to speeches by Dr. Martin Luther King, Jr. and others. The demonstration was nonviolent and, in the main, nondisruptive. The attitude of the demonstrators was serious but friendly—an example of a legal demostration. Several such anti-Vietnam war demonstrations occurred in 1966, 1967, and 1968. Some, however, resulted in violence.

One of the difficulties in the last few years has been that of keeping demonstrations from evolving into riots. In part, the problem may be that too many individuals and groups fail to distinguish between demonstrations and riots—between legal forms of protest and illegal violence. Another difficulty is that too many persons are too vulnerable—too incapable of keeping their own intrapersonal communication operating efficiently. As the Chicago riots at the time of the National Democratic Convention showed, too many police and demonstrators ceased to communicate effectively both intrapersonally and interpersonally. A riot was *not* what the majority of persons on either side wanted, but a riot was what developed. The *Walker Report* found and reported:

> The protesters wanted to expose the inhumanity, injustice, prejudice, and hypocracy. . . . It is clear that the great majority of protesters in Chicago had no preconceived intention to initiate violence. . . . Most of those who intended to join the major protest demonstrations scheduled during convention week did not plan to enter the Amphitheatre and disrupt the proceedings of the Democratic convention, did not plan aggressive acts of physical provocation against the authorities and did not plan to use rallies of demonstrators to stage an assault against any person, institution or place of business.[15]

Although the large majority came to demonstrate legally, too many found themselves participating violently. Several analysts of violence and riots in the United States are of the opinion that the highly charged emotionality that sometimes is created in mobs causes individuals to behave in a way uncharacteristic of their usual *individual behavior* in large audiences. One writer states:

> The failure of internal control [intrapersonal communication] is particularly likely to occur where the individual is caught up in the "maddening crowd" and where the agencies of external social control, such as the police, appear to be intimidated or even absent. Needless to say, this view is a particular favorite of those whose training is in psychiatry.

As admitted above, there is some evidence to support this view. There are numerous reported instances of looted merchandise being returned by individuals claiming they did not know how they got it. Presumably the superego norms have reasserted themselves strongly enough by the time this happens that they work to repress even the memory of having looted the goods in the

15. Daniel Walker, *Rights in Conflict*, p. 18.

first place. There are equally numerous reports by rioters of a sense of almost orgiastic release in the early stages of a riot. . . . Such reports are so widespread that Dr. John Spiegel of the Lemburg Center for the Study of Violence has characterized the crowd-gathering and looting stages of a riot as a "Roman Holiday" or "carnival."[16]

This description accords well with the distinction made in Chapter 11 between audiences and mobs. Riots are especially characterized by high emotionality and inefficient intrapersonal communication. A major variable in the situation is public communication. The role of public communication in protest situations such as the riot will be investigated in a later section; but at this point in the chapter we will look at another form of protest—revolution.

A Violent Protest: The Black Revolution

Until the 1960s, northern ghettoes were relatively quiet except for internal violence—fighting among family members, brawls incident to drinking and gambling, mayhem, and homicide. These are traits associated with the poverty culture everywhere, induced by insecurity, frustration, overcrowding, and inadequate incomes.[17] (It was characteristic of Irish, Italian, and Polish communities in the United States before World War I.) Violence in black ghettoes was limited to the above mentioned characteristics until the 1960s. In the early sixties, especially in 1964, rioting and violence emerged. Ghetto dwellers began to focus their anger and rage outward, venting their fury upon "Whitey's" property. The incidents were usually set off as unplanned, spontaneous protests against two specifically vicious repressions or practices that had rubbed the sores raw among ghetto dwellers—police brutality and economic exploitation by white businessmen. The stores who did business in the black community were the first to suffer the consequences of black wrath. This type of violent protest, riots and burnings, has escalated during the sixties, culminating in the arson and looting in more than 100 cities when Dr. Martin Luther King, Jr. was assassinated in 1968. Throughout the sixties there was an increasing movement within the black masses away from the nonviolent demonstrations and civil disobedience policies of King and toward policies of violent protest and, for some, revolution.

Smith states that the present rhetoric of black revolution first appeared after the Montgomery bus boycott and the Supreme Court School Decision of 1954 (*Brown vs. Board of Education*).[18] Before these

16. Louis H. Masotti and Don R. Bowen, *Riots and Rebellion* (Beverly Hills, Calif.: Sage Publications, Inc., 1968), p. 16.
17. Allen and Adair, *Violence and Riots*, p. 48.
18. Arthur L. Smith, *Rhetoric of Black Revolution* (Boston: Allyn & Bacon, Inc., 1969), p. 2.

events, the protest of blacks was directed by the policies of the NAACP under the leadership of Dr. Martin Luther King, Jr., but after these events black Muslims and black nationalists groups began to preach revolution. They preach pride, self-respect, and self-assertion to establish a black identity. They tell their audiences to use African names, to wear Afro hair styles, to wear dashikis. Bleaching creams, processed hair, and even the conventional western hair comb are despicable symbols to the black revolutionists. Black Power advocates and black nationalists are insisting on immediate change in the social, political, and economic structure of the United States. As Smith has written:

> Whereas Martin Luther King, Jr. had been content with gradual change brought about through protest and social legislation, the black revolutionists argued that the black man could never be free until he accepted and asserted his freedom even in the face of physical death. ... Tired of begging, they intended to earn or take, as circumstances dictated. Given the American situation with political juggling of social legislation, disdain for the black man's cry of police brutality, white backlash, and many other injustices, the black revolutionist decided that the white man had no intention to move until the black man did.[19]

By the late 1960s there emerged a new black rhetoric, the rhetoric of black revolution—a rhetoric that demands; warns that if demands are not met, only one alternative remains, violence. According to Smith, revolutionary rhetoric utilizes four strategies or objectives: (1) vilification, (2) objectification, (3) mythication, and (4) legitimation. [20] Vilification is using language to degrade a person associated with the status quo. The person vilified is usually a political leader, a person who has been publicized enough to be well known to the audience. Therefore, men who have been vilified in agitational rhetoric include former President Johnson, President Nixon, Robert MacNamara, Dean Rusk, Ramsey Clark, and others. Vilification normally utilizes language that is highly charged emotionally.

Objectification is the directing of the grievances of the protesting group toward another collective body such as Congress, the Supreme Court, the nation, or a political party. Sarcasm and low humor are often used in objectification as the speaker seeks to make fun of and to embarrass the body that is the object of the attack. This body is shown to be responsible for the evils felt by the protestors. Reference to the "white power structure" is a clue to the use of objectification. Derogatory names are often used in objectification. Whitey, racist, racist honkey government, and pig are examples.

19. Ibid, p. 12.
20. Ibid., p. 26.

A third characteristic of revolutionary rhetoric is mythication, the use of language that suggests the sanction of supra-rational forces. Mythication creates a spiritual dynamism for the revolutionary movement. Biblical references, historical sanctions, and ordained destiny are used to provide the sustaining spiritual power of the movement.

Finally, the black revolutionist speaker makes use of legitimation —the explanation, vindication, and justification of the actions of the revolutionists. As Smith states:

> Historically, it has made little difference to revolutionists whether their friends engaged in burning and looting Colonial Boston, emptying private tea into the harbor, or setting fire to liquor stores in the black ghettoes, so long as the activists did it for the cause. Indeed, after the conflagrations in Watts, Detroit, and Newark, the black revolutionists explained that the buildings were burned down because the people were tired of oppression and discrimination. Squirming to evade the charges of riot and hooliganism, the agitator defines the actions as a rebellion or a revolution.[21]

After several of the major riots of the late 1960s, black nationalists explained the nature of the conditions that provoked the violence. They legitimized the violence.

All these strategies—vilification, objectification, mythication, and legitimization—are found in revolutionary movements. The rhetoric of the current black revolution is no exception.

The Role of Communication in Riots

Of all the forms of protest short of revolution or war, riots are the most destructive. As we have noted, riots often grow out of peaceful demonstrations, usually marches or rallies. Things sometimes happen to turn peaceful demonstrations into violent riots. Some of the factors involved in this change are communication factors. Instead of communication being used to "cool it," it is used to "heat things up." Feelings are inflamed and a highly charged emotional mood is created through the use of irresponsible but purposeful communication tactics by a few revolutionists and the *inability* of the many peaceful demonstrators to recognize and cope with the manipulation of professional agitators or irresponsible persons filled with hate. Other communication factors play a role in riots. Let us consider four such factors: (1) the use of the mass media, (2) rumor, (3) inflammatory communication (obscene language and obscene nonverbal communication), and (4) identifying and solidifying communication.

21. Ibid., p. 41.

Use of Mass Media—In violent forms of protest, the protesters must win social support for their cause and public acceptance of their ideology, values, beliefs, and policies. Pickets, posters, leaflets, and protest meetings are likely to reach only a few people. Therefore, to communicate the message of dissent, the protesters need the wide coverage of the mass media, particularly television, exploitation of which enables them to reach millions with little effort. Although the protesters want their ideology and values carried on the mass media, those who control are not interested in carrying ideological messages. Such messages make for dull viewing or dull reading. Newspapers and television, therefore, seek *unusual events* and especially those *events involving conflict.* If no real conflict is available to report, newspaper and television personnel are likely to select words or scenes that seem to imply conflict. This problem was discussed in Chapter 13 and corrective solutions were proposed. Nevertheless, during and since the sixties there has been a great amount of selective reporting by the mass media because it provides exciting news; and there has been wide exploitation of the mass media by the protesters.

The practice by the media people of selecting, interpreting, and slanting what is reported is illustrated by one of the leading protesters, Malcolm X: I don't care what points I made in the interviews, it practically never got printed the way I said it. I was learning under fire how the press, when it wants to, can twist, and slant. If I had said "Mary had a little lamb," what probably would have appeared was, "Malcolm X Lampoons Mary."[22] When the press called him a "fomenter of violence," he said point blank, That is a lie. I'm not for wanton violence, I'm for justice. I feel that if white people were attacked by Negroes— if the forces of law prove unable, or inadequate, or reluctant to protect those whites from those Negroes—then those white people would protest and defend themselves from those Negroes, using arms if necessary. And I feel that when the law fails to protect Negroes from whites' attacks then those Negroes should use arms, if necessary, to defend themselves. The press reported, "Malcolm X Advocates Armed Negroes!"[23]

Besides the misuse of the mass media by media persons, there is the exploitation of the media by the protesters. One way the protesters get mass media coverage is to seek legitimizers, famous persons who are newsworthy and who will speak the message of the protesters. Dr. Benjamin Spock, Senator Eugene McCarthy, and Senator William Fulbright could gain media exposure during the agitation against the war

22. *The Autobiography of Malcolm X* (New York: Grover Press, Inc., 1964), p. 243.
23. Ibid., p. 366.

in Vietnam. A second way by which protesters exploit the mass media is through staging or creating events that are unusual or involve conflict. The *Walker Report* emphasized the role of exploitation and misuse of the media in the 1968 Chicago riots:

Perhaps the most influential contributing factor to the strength of dissent was the existence of communications media of all kinds. There is no question that the protesters in Chicago, as elsewhere, played to the cameras or that they often did it very effectively and, this, too, has been learned in earlier protests.[24]

Walker reported that protesters and television cameramen collaborated in staging scenes inferring police brutality, i.e., uninjured persons held fake bandages on their heads while they were filmed.

Certainly, one communication factor in protests is the use of the mass media.

RUMOR—A second factor is rumor. A rumor is the passing of information from one person to another without official verification or in the absence of any trustworthy official source. Rumors are most likely to occur in ambiguous situations in which trustworthy official interpretations are absent, and in which there is an element of drama or conflict. In the case of riots, all these conditions are met; consequently, rumors often run rampant and fan the flames of riots into even greater conflagrations.

Three processes have been identified in rumor—leveling, sharpening, and assimilating or contrasting. Leveling is a process in which details are lost as the rumor is told and retold. Sharpening is the exaggerations of one or two details as the rumor spreads. Assimilating or contrasting refers to the process by which an individual makes the rumor fit into his own system of beliefs and values. The individual *distorts the rumor* either towards what he wants to believe (assimilation) or in a negative direction; i.e., in the direction of what he would least like to believe (contrast).

In the 1968 Chicago riots rumors ran rampant. Both the police and the protesters appeared to use contrast in their promulgation of rumored happenings. The protesters sustained rumors about police brutality, and the police sustained rumors about the number of protesters coming to Chicago and at Chicago, as well as about their motives. In some instances the mass media helped to combat rumors in Chicago, but in other instances the media may have aided the spread of rumor. Such was the case, also, in the Chicago riot of 1919. Allen and Adair report that rumor was a primary cause of the *continuance* of the 1919

24. Walker, *Rights in Conflict*, p. 16.

riot for several days. Rumors, given wide dissemination by the press, kept the crowds in an excited, mob state.[25] The rumors circulated by word of mouth and in the press included stories of atrocities committed by one race against the other, and numerous references to the arming of Negroes. In the *Daily News* of July 30, 1919, for example, appeared the sub-headline: "Alderman Jos. McDonough tells how he was shot at on South Side visit. Says enough ammunition in section to last for years of guerrilla warfare." The story described bombs going off: "I saw white men and women running through the streets dragging children by the hands and carrying babies in their arms." There is no record in any of the riot testimony in the state's attorney's office of any bombs going off during the riot. In the 1919 riot, as well as in other riots, including those at Watts and Columbia University, the widespread effect of rumor has been well documented.

INFLAMMATORY AND OBSCENE COMMUNICATION—A third type of communication problem is the inflammatory communication that leads to violence. Although a majority of demonstrators may not want killing and other violence, they may create it by inflammatory communication; or, as is more likely the case, the minority that is committed to violence and revolution may take advantage of the demonstration, and through inflammatory communication (inflammatory verbal messages as well as inflammatory acts) instigate a riot. Any one of several riots might be used to illustrate this problem, but the detailed descriptions included in the *Walker Report* of the 1968 Chicago riot show explicitly how inflammatory communication (acts and verbal messages) triggered violence. The *Walker Report* describes one of the confrontation scenes:

> The police had not initiated the barrage of abuse, and they were not responding to it any way. As the crowd, attracted by the lights, kept growing, the abuse mounted. But the police stood impassively and said nothing. At first the demonstrators had kept a distance of about 20 feet, but as their numbers increased they moved in, and soon the police were clearly trapped. ... This went on for about half an hour, the crowd still jeering and taunting, the police silent. ... Suddenly the police charged. ... The charge was fierce, with police hitting everyone they could reach.[26]

Inflammatory language played a strong role in triggering the Logan statue incident. The U.S. Attorney stated: "The vilest conceivable language was used by both men and women" and there were

25. Allen and Adair, *Violence and Riots*, p. 43.
26. Walker, *Rights in Conflict*, p. 146. Pages 146–58 give a running account of the vicious and inflammatory language of police and demonstrators.

"many incidents of demonstrators spitting on police."[27] The language
of some of the police was no less inflammatory. The *Walker Report*
quotes a Chicago attorney who may have been mistaken for an official
by the police since they allowed him to roam among them. He heard
their conversation and remarks and reported that:

> There seemed to be almost without exception, an attitude or mentality of
> impatience about "getting started" and it was the normal thing for policemen
> to talk about how anxious they were to crack some heads. . . . [Some] were
> obsessed with getting a "Commie" or "Hippie" and what they would do to
> them. I am sure that there were many policemen who did not feel this way, but
> they were not talking or protesting what their fellow officers were saying.[28]

In reply, demonstrators shouted obscenities and filthy taunts at police,
several times directly in the faces of police officers; and human excre-
ment and cans of urine were hurled at police. They spit at police,
offered them sandwiches filled with feces, disrobed in front of police;
and a blond female, dressed in a short red minidress, pulled up her skirt
and made lewd, sexual motions in front of a police line.[29] A *Washington
Post* reporter said, " It was clear that the Chicago police had 'had it.'
They were showing visible signs of the strain they had been under. The
kids knew full well, and they knew they had made them 'lose their cool.'
"[30]

There is little doubt that obscenity was instrumental in producing
violent confrontation in Chicago. Typical police explanations of their
behavior included references to the obscenity of the protesters. The
tactic that prompted the violent police actions was the use of obscenity
—verbal and nonverbal.

By way of contrast, the *Walker Report* cites several instances when
the National Guard stood its ground, despite a level of abuse called
"unbelievable," with no significant response—physical or verbal—to
the demonstrators. In these situations, even after several days of violence, the crowds gradually quieted and slowly drifted away.[31] There
can be little doubt that the quality of communication in tense and
emotionally charged moments is an important factor in creating or
preventing violence.

IDENTIFYING AND SOLIDIFYING COMMUNICATION—A fourth use of communication in protest is to weld the protesters into a strong, cohesive
group. Identifying and polarizing communication can serve that func-

27. Ibid., p. 166.
28. Ibid., p. 195.
29. Ibid., p. 210.
30. Ibid., p. 211.
31. For a description of such an incident, see Walker, *Rights in Conflict*, p. 214.

tion for the protesting group. Protesters are at odds with the status quo —the institutions and groups in power—hence, if a protest movement is to survive, it must contain committed and strongly supportive members. Communication serving this function includes songs, slogans, symbols and in-group publications.

Songs of the protest groups serve to identify those groups—the songs are theirs. The lyrics of such songs often talk of unity, of courage, of overcoming, and they often describe the conflict or grievance. Protest songs frequently use melodies of old popular favorites. "Solidarity, Forever" is sung to the tune of "The Battle Hymn of the Republic," while "There Once was a Union Maid" used the tune of "Red Wing." The official song of the civil rights protesters is "We Shall Overcome."

Another form of communication used to solidify the protest group is the slogan. "Black Power," "Brown Power," "Stop Dow Now," "Power to the People," and "Pigs off Campus" are now familiar examples of the use of slogans. Slogans are often used as cheers with a cheerleader in demonstration or rally situations ("Hey, hey, LBJ, how many kids did you kill today?").

Protest groups also use symbols to express their cause and to identify their group. These symbols are sometimes very powerful, sometimes quite artistically designed, and sometimes accompanied by a detailed and complicated mythology. Some of the symbols currently seen are shown in Figure 22.

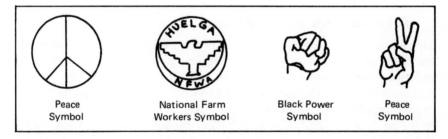

| Peace Symbol | National Farm Workers Symbol | Black Power Symbol | Peace Symbol |

Figure 22 Protest Symbols of the Sixties

The Viet Nam war protesters have used the peace symbol, a symbol utilizing the old religious sign of eternity and unity (the circle), the inverted cross, and the three branches from a single stem. The symbol is simple and easily reproduced for medallions and posters.

The thunderbird symbol is used by the National Farm Workers Association under the leadership of Cesar Chavez. It is a black thunderbird on a red background and it suggests, in a way, ancient Aztec architecture.

The raised fist is used as a symbol by Black Power advocates. The use of this symbolic gesture by two athletes from the United States during the playing of the Star Spangled Banner at an awards ceremony of the Olympic Games in Mexico City in 1968 represented a climactic point in the use of this symbol.

Some symbols are kinetic (requiring movement)—for example, the rhythmic, arm-in-arm swaying that often accompanies the singing of "We Shall Overcome," and the double handshake of the Muslims. Another symbol, not included in Figure 22 is the black panther selected by Huey Newton and Bobby Seale for their militant Black Panther Party.

A fourth use of communication to solidify protest groups is in-group publications. Colleges and universities have seen a number of underground and in-group newspapers created during the sixties including the *Berkeley Barb* at California, the *Spectator* at Michigan, *Bauls* at Purdue University, the *Pterodactyl* at Grinnell, and countless others. Other protest magazines and newspapers with even wider circulation include *Ramparts*, the *New Left Review, World Revolution, Challenge, Village Voice*, and *Liberation*. The contents of these protest newspapers and magazines stress articles expounding their causes, grievances, symbols, and ideology. They serve a unifying function for the protest group.

Alternatives to Violence

There are no short and easy answers to the problem of violent protest, but there are some principles and practices of which man is aware that constitute guidelines and objectives toward which he should strive. Although events of the sixties suggest that segments of our society have grown impatient with talk and legal forms of protest and have turned to illegal and violent forms as the chief means of gaining their ends, there must be no abandonment of the principle of the indispensability of speech communication to the mutually beneficial integration of men into satisfying and wholesome relationships. Talk is indispensable to the achievement of the minimum consensus required for community among people who have no choice but to live together. There are no satisfactory alternatives to talk, and therefore, all sane men who value freedom for themselves and others must promote speech communication and must learn to make it succeed.

Second, the legal and peaceful means for handling protests must be made viable—men must realize and accept the responsibility of *providing justice* rather than *protecting their power and wealth*. The system of a representative, democratic government, at all levels, will have to be made to work for all people.

Third, the channels of communication between protesters and governing bodies and agencies, as well as the channels of communication among various groups must be kept open. Schulberg (author of *What Makes Sammy Run?*) went to the heart of Watts shortly after the riot there. He later wrote: "Watts is an explosive social condition because, on top of its other troubles, *there are no channels of communication between it and more prosperous communities* [p. 111]."

We can develop planned intergroup experiences to open channels of communication between groups. The Conference of Mexican-American Youth in Los Angeles is one example of involving youth from the ghetto with other youths. There have been several such projects throughout the nation, and reports of the success of these programs are promising. Some of the intergroup programs have involved using youth of various ethnic and cultural backgrounds in clean-up campaigns and other community-improvement work programs. Such programs go beyond preaching brotherhood and understanding as they establish communication lines and an opportunity for an ongoing, intimate experience.

Fourth, we must learn to discriminate between legal protest and illegal protest, between demonstrations and riots or revolutionary acts. Individually and collectively, we must learn to use communication so that demonstrations do not escalate into riots, and individuals who do not believe in violence must acquire the intrapersonal communication ability to resist the manipulation attempts of anarchists and revolutionists. Specifically, we must learn to cope successfully with rumor, misuse of mass media, and inflammatory communication in potential riot situations.

Sixth, we need continued and improved efforts to develop a new confidence and trust in police. Greater attention to police recruitment and training is necessary. As persons at the center of events that trigger riots, policemen need a sympathetic understanding of the ghetto; skills in less offensive ways of dealing with people; an understanding of the strategies and tactics that agitators, radicals, and revolutionists use to create a scene, to invite police violence, and to gain mass media exposure; and skill in intrapersonal communication in highly charged emotional moments as well as in interpersonal and public communication. We should remember, however, that *all of society* has had a hand in creating the injustices that underlie riots. For too long the public has made the police scapegoats for all of us.

Finally, as a society, we need quick improvement in conditions—an honest and concerted societal effort to redress the wrongs too long perpetrated on repressed peoples. We need improvements that are visible and tangible—improvements which testify to the nation's *willingness to redress injustices* and to the nation's *caring*. Sprinklers, swimming pools, playgrounds, low-cost movies, more frequent collection of garbage, the requiring of essential repairs on housing, extermination of rats and roaches, a careful checking of the prices and quality of food offered for sale, greater consumer protection, prompt and courteous response by police when ghetto people call, and countless other efforts that could be implemented with reasonably fast and tangible results are necessary. It is important that the goals selected from those identified by protesters be goals that can be reached. Too many promises have gone unfulfilled, and too many utopian panaceas have failed. Results of this kind of happening produce despair, frustration, and anger.

Riots are, in a way, an act of hope—hope that America may at last listen. Unfortunately, too many Americans have not attempted to understand protest. It is difficult for some Americans to believe in speech communication—to believe that attempting to *understand* the roots of rioting is desirable. Too many people equate trying to understand riots with condoning rioting and violence. No society can tolerate massive violence, any more than an organism can tolerate massive disease. Looting, burning, and killing cannot be condoned; but in addition to curbing violence, attention must be given to understanding those who protest, to discovering the causes of protest, and to taking action to provide justice and opportunity to all. Communication can play a vital role in this effort. The skills and factors involved in intrapersonal communication (perception, using language, and thinking), interpersonal communication (attraction, hostility, defensiveness, contrary goals, roles, etc.), and public communication (credibility, organization, logical validity, psychological validity, values and needs of receivers, physical environment, etc.) are operative in protest communication. Singularly, as well as in innumerable combinations, factors from all levels are involved in protest communication. The challenge to us as individuals and, collectively, to us as a nation, is to learn to apply to our behavior what we already know about communication, and to continue to seek a more complete and accurate understanding of the phenomenon of human communication.

For Further Reading

1. Allen, Rodney F., and Adair, Charles H. *Violence and Riots in Urban America.* Worthington, Ohio: Charles A. Jones Publishing Co. 1969.
2. Bernstein, Saul. *Alternatives to Violence.* New York: Association Press, 1967.
3. Fischer, Louis. *Gandhi: His Life and Message for the World.* New York: Mentor Books, 1954.
4. Grant, Joanne, *Black Protest.* Greenwich, Conn.: Fawcett Publications, Inc., 1968.
5. Kerner, Otto (chairman of the National Advisory Commission on Civil Disorders). *Supplemental Studies for the National Advisory Commission on Civil Disorders.* Washington, D.C.: Government Printing Office, 1968. 1968.
6. Lomas, Charles W. *The Agitator in American Society.* Englewood Cliffs, N.J.: Prentice-Hall, Inc., 1968.
7. Masotti, Louis H., and Bowen, Don R., eds. *Riots and Rebellion.* Beverly Hills, Calif.: Sage Publications, Inc., 1968.
8. Walker, Daniel (director of the Chicago Study Team). *Rights in Conflict (A Report Submitted to the National Commission on the Causes and Prevention of Violence).* New York: Bantam Books, 1968.
9. Waskow, Arthur I. *From Race Riot to Sit-In, 1919 and the 1960's.* Garden City, N.Y.: Doubleday & Company., Inc., 1966.

Index

301